The Farm Bloc

The Farm Bloc

BY WESLEY McCUNE

GREENWOOD PRESS, PUBLISHERS
NEW YORK   1968

Preface

Bloc, like "spit," has come to be a horrid word, but no accepted substitutes have evolved. Farmers and others who do not like the term probably should blame newspapers for its promiscuous use, as the two short words, "farm bloc," are an editor's dream for fitting many connotations into a punchy headline.

The way was paved for a farm bloc when, in 1789, it was decided at the Constitutional Convention to have a House of Representatives based on population and a Senate of two members from each state. By banding together it technically became possible for senators from rural states to control the fate of legislation against the desire of a numerical majority of the people as a whole.

From that mathematical root grew a plant which may not be indigenous to the United States but has often become a unique centerpiece in the American political panorama. As such, the farm bloc has been hit by more than a usual number of brickbats. If I throw any of them it is not because I want to kick farmers around. No one wants to do that; nor does anyone want to buy food at prices unfair to the farmers who work long hours to grow it.

Neither am I worried about the existence of a farm bloc.

In the American scheme of things pressure groups are more to be encouraged than damned. It is certainly not proposed that they should be eliminated; in fact there are not enough. The premise underlying this book is that all blocs should live in glass houses. That can be said equally for the labor bloc, the silver bloc, the business bloc, and all other blocs.

I am told, on one hand, that the farm bloc is a group of grasping clamorers indulging in the worst of hog-trough politics—that its arm is in the public treasury up to its shoulder. On the other hand, I am assured that it is the product of a fortunate twist which the founding fathers gave farmers to help them hold their own against the more powerful metropolitan population. This book purports to be only a reporter's account of the issues involved, an analysis of policies held by the organizations who shape the issues, and a critical look at the leaders who keep the issues alive.

W. Mc.

Washington, D.C.
April, 1943

Contents

The Farm Bloc

I

Chips Off the Bloc

A VISITOR to Washington, D.C., will never see the farm bloc, yet he will brush against it many times.

Its center of operations is Congress, first on the list for sight-seers in the beautiful and once quiet capital city. Since its formation in 1921 the farm bloc has functioned through committee meetings, cloakroom intrigue, telephones in each congressman's office, buttonholing in the cold stone lobbies of the Capitol, logrolling in the House of Representatives and Senate, and—occasionally—an old-fashioned oration before the microphone of either House.

Anyone who visits his congressman in the spacious Senate, Old House or New House Office buildings is doing the same thing that representatives of farm organizations and every other pressure group do every day. Few are the states, if any, whose citizenry does not include growers of some kind of farm commodity, whether it be common wheat and corn or fancy citrus fruits, nuts, turkeys, or avocados. The notion that the farm bloc is a group of willful Western and Southern congressmen is a fallacy. When a legislative crisis impends it is the votes of congressmen from Eastern and Northern states, who also have rural constituents, that put the farm bloc over to its accustomed victory.

Seekers of the farm-bloc shrine will not overlook the Agriculture Committee rooms of the Senate and House Office buildings, for it is there that the formal farm program is readied for congressional passage. But a twenty-four-hour wait in either of the elaborately furnished, high-ceilinged rooms would reveal little of what really goes on. Farm congressmen who have packed both committees by the rule of seniority learn quickly that one phone call or an abbreviated caucus is often more effective than a dozen official hearings. Nevertheless, the full-dress part of the bloc, the parade of farm-organization big shots, eventually passes through the two rooms.

Looking westward from the Capitol building, through the front door which—like that of farmhouses—is rarely used as an entrance or exit, one faces the remainder of the bloc's physical plant. A long green mall disappears in the Potomac River just behind the breath-taking white monument to the martyrdom of an Illinois farmer named Abraham Lincoln. To the left, along Independence Avenue and near the 555-foot shaft to a master Virginia farmer of his day, George Washington, are the Department of Agriculture's central buildings.

There for ten years an army of agronomists, economists, administrators, entomologists, horticulturists, statisticians, home economists, messengers, file clerks, and janitors has been running the vigorous farm program of the Franklin D. Roosevelt Administration. Through the miles of corridors of these buildings has passed a new high in volume of businessmen, farmers, officials of other government agencies, and congressmen in the great quest for information, rulings, special favors, and someone to hear new ideas. For as the New Deal farm program has grown vigorous, affirmative, and far-reaching it has gathered around it a bumper crop of lobbyists, both pro and con. All have special interests to protect. Some seek sanctuary in the motherly department; others call to damn it.

Across the width of the mall and on down Washington's 14th Street to the downtown office section one can be in a minute at the Washington office of any of the big national farm organizations: the American Farm Bureau Federation, the National Grange, the National Farmers Union, and the National Council of Farmer Cooperatives. Each is staffed by a handful of men versed in the policy of their organization and in the art of impressing the rest of Washington with that policy. Also these are the headquarters for the influx of organization presidents when debate grows hot in the Capitol. A score of offices of regional and specialized commodity lobbies punctuates near-by buildings.

At 1600 Pennsylvania Avenue, N.W., is another landmark of the farm bloc, the White House. For more than twenty-five years President Roosevelt has been a member of the National Grange; for the past eleven he has been signing bills into law in behalf of agriculture. As a native of Hyde Park, New York, he was an estate farmer, even growing Christmas trees. As President of the United States he still would rather hear "Home on the Range" than any other song.

Across West Executive Avenue, in the old-fashioned building which houses the State Department, Bureau of the Budget, and a select group of White House advisers, is a Special Executive Assistant to the President by the name of Eugene Casey. Both the function and machinations of young Maryland-dairy-farmer Casey are a mystery. He is supposed to be a liaison between the White House and the Department of Agriculture, a job which sounds very much like that of the Secretary of Agriculture. He whips around the rural empire on unannounced chores for the President, almost never makes a speech, and attends practically no committee meetings.

One of Casey's main missions in life is checking on the loyalty to his chief of the thousands of Agriculture Department workers all over the country. He could be described as a trouble-shooter were it not for the fact that for every tangle untied he develops at least one new problem. Farm men who have not been told who Casey is have no idea how to react to his visits, and those in the department who disagree with his personal opinions marvel that he keeps his unique job. One Casey function is to contact Capitol Hill on farm affairs, which puts him in the position of keeping the farm bloc powerful, but not more powerful than the Administration. In his office large autographed portraits of top Democratic-party chieftains indicate the importance he places on the latter condition.

Who are these farmers whom so many people represent, speak for, and talk about? The impression that they sit around potbellied stoves and cracker barrels in country stores, talking about the weather, is a romantic one which farmers might wish were true; but it is not. Nor are all farmers named either Si or Zeke. Describing the nation's farmers is not that easy. There are gentlemen-farmers, sharecroppers, homesteaders, cattlemen, sheepherders, truck gardeners, orchardists, plantation owners, dairymen, and others.

Farmers vary by climate, region, type of agriculture pursued, politics, religion, color, and income level. For the purpose of fitting them into the farm-bloc jigsaw pattern the latter is as pertinent as any. In 1935 and 1936 the National Resources Planning Board, with the aid of the Bureau of

Labor Statistics and the Bureau of Home Economics, scoured the country for a statistical picture of the income and expenditure habits of the rural and urban population. In part, these are their generalizations about the farmers:

Roughly one fourth of the nation's farm families were receiving direct relief or had net annual incomes of less than $500. Slightly fewer than one fourth had incomes of $1,500 or more. About three fourths of the income of rural inhabitants not on relief was cash paid for their crops or labor; only a fourth of the rural income came directly to the farm on a "non-money" basis—that is, in the form of home-produced food, fuel, ice, etc., and having a house provided.

What was the income and what was bought with the income of the group which fell midway between the poverty-stricken and the rural elite? The median income of all farmers in 1933–36 was estimated at $965. That means that approximately one half of them were above that figure and one half below. Expenditures of the group with incomes from $1,000 to $1,249 a year were summarized as follows (figures include the estimated value of "non-money" income):

Food	$ 537
Housing	128
Household operation	97
Clothing	104
Automobile	88
Medical care	50
Recreation	21
Formal education and reading	18
Personal care	17
Gifts, welfare, and income and poll taxes	24
Other expenditures	53
TOTAL value of family living	$1,137

What those of the moderate-income group had in their homes was even more graphically explained. Only 16 per cent had running water, half of whom had hot and cold water in kitchens and baths. Ten per cent had indoor toilets; one eighth had central heating systems. Less than one third had telephones, but 71 per cent had cars. A few over half had radios; 39 per cent owned refrigerators, of which only 4 per cent were mechanical.

Ninety-five per cent of the housewives had canned food, averaging 200 quarts a year; 85 per cent made expenditures for newspapers, 51 per cent for motion pictures. Families in this moderate-income group visited the doctor five times a year. Forty-four out of each hundred lived on rented farms.

Individual variations were many. From the dust bowl of the Midwest and the squalor of the Southern sharecropper to the solid homes of the corn belt and citrus plantations of the Far West and Florida is a long distance. Within the four corners of the United States there are hundreds of types of farms, each having its ups and downs with the weather, the insects, and the luck of other farmers as reflected in market prices.

The contrast is sharp between the 8.9 per cent of farm families who were receiving public relief and the 4.1 per cent who received from $3,000 to $10,000 a year. In the long shadows of dairy barns which are kept cleaner than many farm and city dwellings Carolina Negro sharecropper families lived on $221 worth of food.

Another way to classify farmers is by the type of life they and their families lead from day to day. In *Grapes of Wrath* author John Steinbeck portrayed the migrant tiller of Western dust so vividly that a whole nation became "Okie" conscious overnight. A special House Committee was appointed to study the problem of migratory labor. Erskine Caldwell's record-breaking play, *Tobacco Road*, did somewhat the same thing earlier for the "po' white trash" of the South who were so physically and mentally subdued that they were not even able to migrate.

While the downtrodden became the characters in best sellers, the mythical average farmers led lives characterized by neither travel nor front-porch sitting. The average farmer works from early morning to late evening. If the weather is also average, his crops will yield enough for a payment on the mortgage and a down payment on new farm machinery. His family will get a few new clothes right after the summer harvest—or buy material to make their own. There will be no vacation for the average farmer unless he slips away for a day of fishing near by. But Saturday night in town, to market a little produce or just to go to town, is an institution for his family.

There will be very few movies and very few books for the long winter evenings. Probably none of the children will be graduated from college, but several will have a year or two at a business school, agricultural or teachers' college. Meanwhile the family will be a pillar of the community, may never hear of such things as juvenile delinquency, and will be happy by itself. It probably will hold a family membership in one of the farm organizations and will follow at least one farm journal. In philosophy average farmers will be easygoing, in economics they will favor co-operative buying and selling, and in politics they may be anything.

There is also an upper crust among farmers. Some of the crustiest are actually not farmers at all, because they operate the enterprise by remote control. Constant expansion of acreage and the number of hired men working for a wage transform some farmers into counterparts of the squires of old, but instead of being called squire they may be given certificates of leadership and master farming by rural magazines.

Their buildings always glisten with paint, and some of their huge barns display some prosaic name like Goodacres, Meadowland, or Cherrydale. Like many of the middle group, their barns are comparatively finer than their dwellings. These farmers are not only pillars of their rural community, but they extend interests into the nearest small town, usually in the form of being a director in the local bank. They are used with great regularity on miscellaneous agricultural committees and travel often to the state capital or major market center for conventions and sundry meetings. They probably belong to the Farm Bureau Federation, the Grange, or both, as well as to a fraternal order and a marketing co-operative in the nearest town. They not only know market outlooks from one year to the next but are looked to by their neighbors for advice and example in achieving agricultural success.

Nor are all constituents of the farm-bloc farmers. There is a powerful voice of business—both big and little. Partly through mutual dislike for organized labor, and partly because of inherent conservatism, the alliance of agriculture and business grows stronger.

The United States Chamber of Commerce, which maintains a templelike structure across Lafayette Square from the White House, has had an agricultural division for years, during the past fifteen of which it has employed Delos James to conduct studies, keep the chamber informed, write pamphlets, and spread good will among farm groups in Washington. That he has done. James's portly figure and Western-style hat are familiar around the capital; in fact,

James was with the Department of Agriculture before joining the Chamber of Commerce.

The chamber's Agriculture Committee, which oversees James, is composed of big farm operators and heads of companies that process farm commodities. It has been quick to criticize Federal programs which encroach on the established channels of trade without leaving a profit with the businessman, but defends crop restriction as the essence of a studied market, the same technique which industry uses to keep from producing a "surplus."

A second point at which industry and the farm bloc converge, though in a minor way, is the National Highway Users Conference, "a fact-finding, information-giving, and co-ordinating agency, acting in behalf of the development of highway transportation in the public interest." Chairman and guiding spirit of the Highway Users since its foundation in 1932 is Alfred P. Sloan, Jr., top power in the General Motors Corporation. Sloan also represents the Automobile Manufacturers Association, which is the largest single contributor to the $100,000 or $150,000 annual budget derived from a miscellany of member organizations.

Representatives of the general farm organizations are sprinkled through the governing committees of the conference, and L. J. Taber, past master of the National Grange, is secretary-treasurer. The conference's paid director, who heads a large staff in Washington, is Chester H. Gray, lobbyist until five years ago for the American Farm Bureau Federation and still of some importance in the Grange.

A third item of significance in the effort of industry to hold the moral support of agriculture, sometimes making it a silent partner in farm-bloc proceedings, is the program of the National Industrial Information Committee. Sponsored by the National Association of Manufacturers and composed of the cream of New Deal enemies, the committee functions under the following officers: national chairman, J. Howard Pew, president of the Sun Oil Company; vice-chairman, Ernest T. Weir, chairman of the board of National Steel Corporation, and the other vice-chairman, C. M. Chester, chairman of the board of General Foods Corporation.

The purposes of the committee have been explained by Chairman Pew as helping to return to the nation, when hostilities have ceased, "one of the essential freedoms for which we are fighting and producing—the freedom of initiative."

On the back of each donation blank are listed nine media of public information being used by the committee, including church and women's groups and radio programs such as Fulton Lewis, Jr.'s, Production for Victory weekly broadcast. An enclosed brochure pictured under the heading of Mass Appeals an obviously rural meeting of some sort, captioned: "Conferences between businessmen and farm leaders, clarifying problems and points of view and defining methods of closer co-operation with one of America's most influential minorities."

Another illustration of the fact that not all who sport the farm label are in overalls is the backing of the potent *Farm Journal and Farmer's Wife*, self-acclaimed to be the most influential farm periodical. Editor of the *Journal* since 1921 has been Arthur H. Jenkins, who is also treasurer of the corporation. His brother, Charles F. Jenkins, part owner, is a director in the Provident Trust Company and in the Provident Title Insurance Company, as well as treasurer of the Deemer Steel Casting Company.

Four owners of the *Journal*, who act through an agent,

are four members of Pennsylvania's archconservative Pew family. J. Howard Pew, mentioned earlier, is also a director of the Philadelphia National Bank, the Sun Shipbuilding and Dry Dock Company, and the American Petroleum Institute. J. N. Pew, Jr., has been with the Sun Oil Company since 1908 and is vice-president of Sun Shipbuilding and Dry Dock. The other two members are women: Mary Ethel Pew and Mabel Pew Myrin.

It is indeed a conglomerate crew which sails under the flag of agriculture. A map of the United States showing in color each type of crop and animal produced is kaleidoscopic proof of the multiplicity and overlapping. Every state has at least one special-interest group.

As a rule these segments stick together, but occasionally they stray apart; for example, the feeders of hogs might decide that the corn farmers were getting too much for the feed. More often, however, anticipation of such situations leads to a cozy logrolling arrangement, in which the two agree to seek higher prices for both products. Logrolling is made easier by the fact that few congressmen represent only one crop.

Trading votes need not always be on a formal, commodity basis. Personal friendships among veterans of the Washington farm game are enough to push the lighter skirmishes through to victory for the bloc in general. Competing rural leaders meet around many capital committee tables. With very few exceptions the representatives have been around town a long time and have put aside the cutthroat variety of competition.

A luncheon club, conducted with informality, may be as productive in lining up support for a unified program as are twice as many hours in congressional office buildings.

One such group, called the Farm Hands, meets weekly at the Harrington Hotel to compare notes on the past seven days' grist of announcements and gossip. The forty or more farm representatives, food-trade spokesmen, congressmen, publicity men, journalists, and department officials who keep the club going are one vehicle of the farm bloc. It is they who carry much of the ammunition up front for all-out assaults.

II

Agricultural ABCs

By THIS TIME everyone is familiar with some of the catch-words, slogans, and nicknames of the numerous New Deal farm programs: *parity, plow under every third row, AAA, resettlement, rehabilitation, surplus removal, corn-hog program, soil conservation, the ever-normal granary, and food-stamp plan.*

But although these terms ring familiar to most people, they are really understood by few. Consumers, particularly, have never learned that they have a daily stake in most of the alphabetical innovations. Of equal importance is tracing the origin of the major programs in order to see where pressure groups entered the scrambled scene. Standing behind most of the labels are special interests, though not all of them came with the New Deal.

Cornerstone of the farm program, laid in place before 1932, is this thing called parity. So solidly entrenched is parity that many agriculture partisans fear it is more a fetish and ritual than a sound basis on which to build a structure of as many tiers as the farm program.

An official explanation of it runs like this: "Parity price means a price for the farmer's product which will give it an exchange value, for things the farmer needs to buy, equivalent to that in a specified base period. The base period mostly used as 'par' has been the five prewar years, 1909–14." Those years were chosen because they represented a high point in agriculture.

A clause in the Agricultural Adjustment Act declared parity to be the national policy and defined it in about the same number of words. The only way to understand its application, however, is to follow an illustration of how parity is calculated, for—like the protective tariff—it tends to become so complicated that only those who have a financial interest in it know how to use the formula.

First, a base price for the period 1909–14 is determined. This is done by averaging the prices reported by farmers to the Department of Agriculture during those years. For example, the average price of cotton was 12.4 cents a pound; wheat averaged 88.4 cents a bushel, and corn was 64.2 cents a bushel.

Second, an index is calculated of prices paid by farmers for items of living, such as food, clothing, and furniture, as well as items used in production, like plows and tractors. Taxes on real estate and interest charges are added. In the month of January 1942, for example, this procedure gave an index of 146, meaning that farm-commodity prices then would have needed to be 146 per cent of the 1909–14 base prices to have had the same purchasing power as in the base period.

The third step is to adjust the base-period prices by the index of prices paid by the farmer. Following the examples already given, the base-period prices are multiplied by 1.46. Thus the *parity* price for cotton in January last year was 1.46 times 12.4 cents—18.1 cents a pound. The parity price for wheat was 1.46 times 88.4, or 129 cents a bushel. For corn it was 93.7 cents a bushel.

What is frequently forgotten is the fact that parity is a changing, rather than a fixed, price concept. That is, the index of prices which the farmer has to pay other people constantly shifts. A new list of parity prices is published each month from information gathered by huge staffs of the Bureau of Agricultural Economics and the Bureau of Labor Statistics.

All this is another way of saying that if a farmer got $100 for 100 bushels of wheat, for example, in 1909–14, and could buy a new stove and a new suit with that $100, then his returns today should enable him to buy the same goods for 100 bushels of wheat. With this in mind, see where six widely consumed farm commodities stood at Pearl Harbor time in relation to parity:

Cotton	91	per cent of parity			
Potatoes	82	"	"	"	"
Apples	79	"	"	"	"
Eggs	89	"	"	"	"
Hogs	98	"	"	"	"
Wool	141	"	"	"	"

Against this statistical sketch, a glimpse of the history of establishing parity as a national policy is significant.

Just after the World War, farm prices plunged downward in a scare that resulted, at least partly, in the organization of a farm bloc in Congress and the American Farm Bureau Federation. Heated protests led President Warren G. Harding to direct his Secretary of Agriculture, Henry C. Wallace (father of the Vice-President), to call a national conference on the farm problem. It was the first such meeting in history; 336 delegates arrived in Washington in January of 1922 to spend four days in discussion. Twenty farm organizations were represented, as were agricultural colleges, state agricultural agencies, the rural press, and business institutions allied with agriculture.

The kernel of this meeting was described twelve years later by Roosevelt's Secretary of Agriculture, Henry A. Wallace, as follows: "Out of this 1922 conference came thirty-seven legislative recommendations. . . . One of the recommendations looked a long way ahead, for it directed Congress and the President to 'take steps immediately to re-establish a fair exchange value for all farm products with that of other commodities.' "

Thus, although the word "parity" had not yet appeared in farm demands, the word "equality" had been decided upon as a plank in successive platforms. Crystallization of this policy into a statistical index was carried on under the leadership of two men who were not farmers but who were interested in farm income by virtue of their association with a farm-machinery firm, the Moline Plow Company. They were George N. Peek, who became the first administrator of AAA, and Hugh S. Johnson, first administrator of the abortive National Recovery Administration several years later. For several years it was the pamphleteering of these two machinery officials which took the lead in bringing the Department of Agriculture and farm-organization officers to agreement on not only parity but also on surplus control, the seed from which AAA grew a decade later. The guiding hand of these two men illustrates one of the chapters of farm-bloc history which is the most intangible: the extent to which industries allied to the farm have formed a part of the bloc without donning blue denim overalls.

To realize that the production and marketing restrictions of the AAA were not merely ideas of the Roosevelt Brain Trust which functioned with so much controversy in the early days of the New Deal, it is necessary to glance at the McNary-Haugen bill and the Federal Farm Board of Republican days.

First, another excerpt from the 1922 National Agricultural Conference report, this time on the subject of adjusting farm production to demand: "The manufacturer has in the past quickly adjusted his production to price recessions while the farmer has not. When farm production is so large that the product cannot be sold for prices that will maintain a reasonable standard of living on the farms, the supply is too large." Farm organizations were then advised to look to world supply-and-demand factors and make plans so that they could advise their members and "propose measures for proper limitation of acreage in particular crops."

While this policy was being endorsed Peek and Johnson were meeting with highly placed officials and economists to work out mechanics of a plan for getting agricultural equality by having the so-called "surplus" production taken off the home market. Briefly outlined, the plan was this: Compute each year the fair exchange value of each principal crop on the domestic (American) market. Protect this value with a tariff high enough to keep foreign commodities from coming into this country. Form a government corporation to maintain this value by buying at that level the part of the crops which exceeds domestic needs, or is surplus, and sell it on the foreign market at whatever price it will bring. Make up losses from these exports by levying a price per bushel at the time farmers sell their products.

The chief departure from orthodox policy in this plan was the central control to be exercised by a government agency, actually buying and selling commodities to force prices up. The chief fallacy lay in its tariff provisions. As explained in the 1940 *Yearbook of Agriculture* by Chester C. Davis, former AAA administrator, who was appointed War Food Administrator in the spring of 1943, proponents of the plan failed to see that a nation cannot expect to sell exports if it does not allow imports. But in their eagerness to match the unsound advantages being reaped during that period by manufacturers of industrial goods through high tariff walls, farm leaders were asking for still more walls, this time on their own products, and were building up to the awful letdown that came with the international turn to self-sufficiency and artificially controlled foreign trade.

Anyway, the plan was embodied in the famous bill sponsored by Senator Charles L. McNary, of Oregon, and former Representative Gilbert N. Haugen, of Iowa. In front of Congress for four years, up to 1928, this bill in some form was passed twice by Congress with farm-bloc backing but was vetoed each time by Calvin Coolidge.

In 1929, by the Agricultural Marketing Act, the Federal Farm Board was created, chiefly to encourage co-operative-marketing associations, for many people believed that there would be no surplus production if the marketing process of the nation were streamlined for efficiency. Hence the Farm Board was given a fund of $500,000,000 to get co-operative markets started. When the greatest depression of all times hit in the fall of that year, however, the board began to throw its weight and funds into stabilizing the avalanching farm prices by buying up and storing huge piles of commodities.

The devastating depression, coming while crops were still large, made the job too much for the Farm Board and it folded up with the admonition that withholding supplies from market would never achieve stable prices unless production could be held in line with domestic and foreign demand. There was the nub of what was to become the AAA—fixing production. One more development was incorporated in official thinking first, however.

While the Farm Board was floundering around, a domestic-allotment plan was proposed, chiefly by Harvard professor John D. Black and M. L. Wilson, who later became Under Secretary of Agriculture and director of the Extension Service. Their main emphasis was on the domestic market, leaving the exportable surplus to its own ways. Although it appeared in several forms, the idea was this: That part of the crop which farmers could sell in the American market was to be limited to demand and called the domestic allotment. To restrict production to that level, cash benefits would be paid farmers, derived from a levy on processors of farm commodities, that is, meat packers, millers, etc.

By the time the ultraconservative Hoover Administration had been swept out of office, those who had been thinking along any of these lines had risen to the top of the heap. If for no other reason, this was caused by the sickening poverty on every hand that dictated putting men forward who would do *something*—and the bolder the better.

In the spring of 1933, Congress passed the Agricultural Adjustment Act, under which millions of farmers contracted to reduce their acreage in specified surplus crops. In return for deliberately not planting as much as they ordinarily would, farmers were awarded cash in the form of "benefit payments" derived from processing taxes on the commodity concerned. There was no compulsion to agree to reduce plantings—only the inducement of benefit payments. In its first stage this program took the form of actually plowing under every third row of cotton and killing little pigs.

The more militant cotton and tobacco interests soon wanted 100 per cent participation, in order to keep non-participants from reaping the benefit of the higher prices. Therefore, by separate legislation for those two crops, another feature was added—marketing quotas. Under these the restriction was put on marketing, rather than production, meaning that a non-participant would have no way to sell crops which he might have grown in excess of the government-determined quota.

Then, on January 6, 1936, the Supreme Court knocked out the AAA in the nation-shaking Hoosac Mills case by a 6-to-3 vote. Some of the shock came as a part of the reaction against the Nine Old Men who were interpreting the Constitution, but also farmers had lost the keystone of the agricultural policy which had been their only hope. This decision threw out not only the AAA idea, on the grounds that regulating agricultural production belongs to the states instead of the Federal government, but it also nullified the processing tax, as a part of the scheme. Justice Harlan Fiske Stone, now Chief Justice, wrote a vigorous dissent in which he was joined by the late Justices Louis Brandeis and Benjamin Cardozo. It was their opinion that the power of Congress to tax "for the general welfare" adequately covered the act in view of the fact that the "depressed state of agriculture is nationwide in its extent and effects."

Regardless of the legal niceties, Congress and farmers knew that Stone's cautious statement of the facts was true, and within the year about the same thing was being accomplished under the Soil Conservation and Domestic Allotment Act of 1936. Constitutionality was acquired by substituting direct Federal appropriations for processing taxes and making cash payments to farmers only when they fulfilled certain scientific requirements for conserving their soil by proper plowing, contouring, and rotating crops from year to year.

This legislation represented a great change in farm techniques for increasing production, but—by the same token— was ineffective in restricting production. Bumper cotton and wheat crops attested the fact. Therefore farm leaders got together with a vengeance to revamp their own legislation in the form of the Agricultural Adjustment Act of 1938, which is still the foundation of the Administration's farm program. Its new features, plus its rearrangement of the old ones, fit into five rough sections.

First, soil conservation, balanced output, and good farm management. Farmers receive payments not only for stopping soil erosion and planting "cover crops" which will keep the topsoil from blowing away when dry, but also for planning rotation of crops in such a way that those which deplete soil will be followed periodically by those which build it up again. Agricultural educators have long advocated this type of good management, but great strides were not made until it was written into law. The Soil Conservation Act of 1935 had accomplished just that, even though it had been on a co-operative, demonstration basis.

Second, loans, marketing quotas, and parity payments. Producers of basic commodities—corn, wheat, cotton, tobacco, and rice—may obtain loans. Although this mechanism does allow farmers to hold their crops off the market until needed, the term "loan" is somewhat of a misnomer. Actually many farmers have no intention of paying back the advance from the department. The reason is apparent: By directing the department to give loans at, say, 85 per cent of the parity price, Congress has built what frankly is a floor under prices of the five commodities. If market prices fail to rise to the "loan" level of 85 per cent, all the farmer has to do is let the loan lapse and notify the department to take his stored crop. What the process amounts to is the most polite form imaginable of foreclosure. In nine years of operations the Commodity Credit Corporation, which finances the program and holds the commodities, made $2,700,000,000 in loans. Nearly every fiscal year the farm bloc makes an effort, to put it mildly, to raise the figure which here was stated hypothetically at 85 per cent. If it goes high enough, of course, the system becomes price fixing in the guise of lending.

The system of marketing quotas is imposed democratically. If the Secretary of Agriculture finds that supplies are to be excessively high the coming year he may put before the nation's farmers for a vote the question of having marketing quotas that year. If two thirds want them, a quota is set for each farm, based on average records for that farm, and a stiff penalty is imposed on each bushel or pound marketed above that quota.

Parity payments, in cash, are provided by the act whenever the combination of loans and marketing quotas fails to bring farm prices up to parity levels. At this point the principle of parity for farmers reaches the peak of cold mathematical formula—a rigidity of calculation which has led most department officials to raise serious questions as to the validity of running a farm program by formula. Mostly because these soft-spoken critics seldom, if ever, come forth with an alternative, parity calculations continue to occupy the time of hundreds of economists and statisticians.

Third, marketing agreements are provided for in the Agricultural Adjustment Act of 1938, based on previous experience—chiefly that since passage of the Agricultural

Marketing Agreement Act of 1937. Under this innocuous title, organization of processors, distributors, producers, and co-operatives is fostered for the purpose of eliminating unfair trade practices and keeping supply in line with demand. Exemption from the antitrust laws is also provided, a fact which causes increased shaking of heads as these legalized combinations gather more power unto themselves in much the same way that industries operated under the NRA.

Fourth, diversion of surplus production into foreign and domestic channels, and the development of new uses for agricultural products. Under this mandate the department has launched widespread programs for distributing surplus commodities among persons receiving relief of various types. At first such commodities were bought directly in the field and dispersed through depots in crude ways, but in the past few years the Food Stamp Plan, with its distribution through normal (retail, wholesale, etc.) channels of trade, has been added to the direct technique. Also the School Lunch Program comes under this authority.

On the side of developing new uses, the department built four regional research laboratories for that express purpose. On the foreign side, encouragement of exports is carried on by the device of subsidies. Officials admit quite freely that this program is economically unsound—that it is a naked concession to lobbyists and logrollers. At a cost of about $50,000,000 during fiscal '40, the following commodities were subsidized for export: cotton and cotton products, wheat, flour, corn, butter, pears, walnuts, and a number of others which were shipped out for the Red Cross. The ostensible reason for the program is to help farmers capture "their fair share" of the foreign market which other nations now hold because of economic advantages in producing and/or shipping the commodities.

Fifth and last, crop insurance. The Federal Crop Insurance Corporation, within the department, was created with a capital of $100,000,000 and the power to write insurance against loss of crops. Approximately one fourth of all wheat farmers in 1942 took advantage of this great stabilizing program.

This core of the New Deal program has not only raised prices to the entire population—for everyone, even a farmer, is a consumer—but has drained the public treasury astronomically. The gigantic picture was painted recently by the Department of Agriculture in a report to Congress covering the eleven years ending July 1, 1942. The total, $10,108,-000,000, makes a mythical average of about $2,500,000 a day. About $639,200,000 went for parity payments, $2,666,900,000 was expended under the Soil Conservation Act, $1,520,800,000 was for payments under the 1933 Agricultural Adjustment Act, and the remainder went for surplus removal, special cotton programs, crop insurance, and sundry programs.

Republicans read the figures with bitterness against New Deal social objectives; New Dealers cite them as proof that the farmer is getting his due from a friendly Administration; the farm bloc looks at them with no regrets, but declares its opposition to the subsidy system; a few stragglers who have no ax to grind read them with a question: Won't it take something more fundamental than cash subsidies for restricting production to pull the farmer out of his mire?

May 16, 1939, marks the beginning of a potential revolution in agricultural policy. On that day, with press agents and full dress, the Department of Agriculture opened the amazing Food Stamp Plan in its first experimental area, Rochester, New York. Until that day the chief function

of the department's Federal Surplus Commodities Corporation had been to dispose of the so-called "surplus commodities"—those which AAA had not killed before being
born. Part of the revolution lay in the fact that a bold new
system for distributing this food was to be tried out; another
part lay in the fact that the center of gravity of the department was about to shift to the FSCC, under the spiritual
and dynamic leadership of its president, Milo Randolph
Perkins.

In a nutshell, the philosophy of Perkins was that there
could be no surplus of food so long as people were hungry.
In another nutshell, the FSCC Food Stamp Plan sought to
get the surplus to the needy in this way:

Persons certified as being eligible for public assistance
(commonly called relief clients) purchased from special
offices a number of orange-colored stamps at the rate of
from $1.00 up to $1.50 per week per person in the family.
For each dollar's worth of orange stamps the client was
given free a half dollar's worth of blue ones. Both were
turned in at any corner grocery, but the two colors were
exchanged for different kinds of food. The orange stamps
were good, dollar for dollar, for any food item in the store;
whereas the free blue ones were good for only certain foods
listed monthly by the Department of Agriculture.

Originally this list was composed of "surplus commodities," but as the war brought shortages the list was drawn
up quite frankly for the purpose of making available an
approximately balanced diet for persons who could not buy
one. The grocer, as often as he liked, took the accumulated
stamps to redeem them for cash at the nearest office of the
Agricultural Marketing Administration, successor to FSCC.

As explained officially, there were four premises underlying the plan: (1) Most relief families spend only 5 to 7

cents per person per meal for food—roughly $1.00 to $1.50 per person per week; (2) this is not an adequate diet; (3) the national welfare could be served by enabling these families to increase their food consumption, and (4) if this were done, the market for farm products would simultaneously be improved.

The purpose of requiring clients to purchase a minimum of orange stamps was to make sure that their cash purchases of food were not reduced under the plan; for, if the blue-stamp subsidy were merely substituted for normal purchases, there would be no more food moved from farms than without the plan. In its efforts to adjust the minimum purchase requirements to actual purchasing habits and financial resources of the clients, AMA met with only moderate success, however.

In one of the experimental areas, Pottawatomie County, Oklahoma, a variation was tried. Benefits of the plan were extended to low-income families—defined as those receiving less than $20 a week—in addition to relief clients. Failure of this category to participate enthusiastically, and the ramifications in extending such a system to the nation's entire low-income population, led the Agricultural Marketing Administration to bury the Pottawatomie idea long before it announced on the last day of 1942 that the entire plan would be junked on March 31, 1943, because of war conditions.

Before any food-stamp experiments the major surplus-removal program of this agency, which was called the Surplus Marketing Administration for a year or so prior to becoming the AMA, was its "direct purchase and distribution program." This was initiated as a means of buying up huge piles of crops which would otherwise have rotted and sending them around the country to hungry people. Distribution was handled through a depot system, where clients could come to carry away the food in sacks or boxes. It was this that the Food Stamp Plan shoved aside.

Many advantages were claimed for Perkins' stamp baby. It stimulated business by giving processors, wholesalers, and retailers a profit on the food all along the line. By virtue of the same fact, it removed the stigma often attached to visiting a relief depot down by the tracks, as well as removing the burden of toting the load. Under the Stamp Plan, clients had the same selection from grocery-store shelves as the wealthiest customer, so far as packaging, quality, and brand were concerned.

Whereas in the direct-distribution system there was no guarantee that the free food would be used *in addition to* cash purchases, meager as they might be, under the Stamp Plan most of the food obtained free represented a net increase in food consumed. Moreover, business was stimulated to some degree in such ways as by advertising surplus foods to non-stamp customers and by employing more men to handle the increased business.

One of the economic advantages claimed by backers of the plan is especially controversial. They say that prices will be increased to the farmer because of the stamp customers' new purchasing power which bids part of the food supply away from other customers. This means that, as stamp clients benefit, upper-income classes and those on low (but not relief) incomes will suffer from the higher prices. It is a sore point with those agricultural officials who do not like to draw a line down the middle of the low-income population, giving some of them more food at the expense of boosting prices to borderline families.

The advantages to those eligible for stamps are not disputed, however; at least not by those who have seen aged relief clients cry over having butter on the table after years of eating dry bread and those who know that hundreds of thousands of clients have to struggle to collect even enough cash to buy orange stamps.

Arguments against the Food Stamp Plan are these: Government subsidization, even for adequate diets, is questionable. Admittedly the cost of distributing directly is lower than through trade channels, although the use of WPA labor in depots contributed to that fact. It is also admitted that about one fourth of the blue-stamp subsidy is lost to the farmers because of substitution of blue-stamp purchases for normal, pre-plan purchases, in spite of administrative controls. Also, to give clients a good selection of surplus foods, the list was usually so long that effects of the plan were so diluted among the items as to lose real effectiveness for any one commodity. Finally, the plan is administratively not simple, and the stamps suggest "funny money"—or script.

Achievements of the plan, in concrete terms, have been great, regardless of how much greater some other system might have been for the $245,000,000 expenditure from July of 1939 through November of 1942. During that period a monthly peak of 4,000,000 persons received help via stamps; more than 4,000,000,000 pounds of food were made available, with cereals, eggs, pork, and fruits and vegetables high on the list.

One of the symbols of the depressions which cyclically sweep through the vast farm lands is the spectacle of sheriffs foreclosing mortgages on their neighbors' farms. The department estimates that 2,100,000 forced sales have taken place since the World War among the 6,000,000 American farms.

One of Roosevelt's first acts was creation of the Farm Credit Administration, which is now within the department and operates through twelve regional offices to give farmers various kinds of cheap and ready credit which the bankers had not. With the aid of Federal appropriations, FCA's results from May 1933 through 1941 are assuring to the rural populace. Almost 1,000,000 farm-mortgage loans—long-term credit to help a farmer buy or hold his home and land—were made, with a total value of more than $2,500,-000,000. Short-term credit, in the form of quick loans for getting next year's crops in, harvesting them, etc., numbered about 4,250,000 for a total of over $6,750,000,000.

In addition, FCA extends credit to co-operative associations for building plants, storing commodities, and many other purposes. These numbered over 10,000 for over $1,000,000,000 in the first nine years of FCA.

Stated in its most simple way, the Farm Credit system is on a self-liquidating basis, paying its own way, except that the government has furnished much of the capital stock for its beginning and each year since 1933 Congress has voted to chip in a subsidy of one half of one per cent on most of the long-term-type loans. This contribution makes it possible to furnish credit more cheaply than would otherwise be possible and has taken $30,000,000 annually from the U. S. Treasury since 1933.

The political football of the department is its Farm Security Administration, which inherited work begun by the old Resettlement Administration. FSA works among the half of the nation's farmers who were shown by the latest census to have a gross earned farm income of less than $600 a year. Efforts to bring this huge reservoir of productivity into the wartime feeding program, with a little credit and a few materials placed in broken-down farmers' hands, helped stem the political revolt that was led by conservative congressmen and the American Farm Bureau. But, under the guise of "economy," guerrilla warfare continued.

Farm Security has furnished some type of help to 1,600,000 families since 1935. Under its rehabilitation loan program 980,000 families have been put on or kept on their feet, with the aid of trained county supervisors to advise them. Part of the money spent for this purpose is supposed to be lost, as only about 80 per cent of the families are expected to repay their loans. In addition, FSA helps to influence its clients' creditors to adjust debts in such a way as to let the down-and-outers get a fresh and hopeful start.

As part of their physical rehabilitation, FSA organizes medical care from local doctors who were accustomed to getting only a small part of the medical bills paid by the near-starving clients. Over a half million persons have received medical care under this arrangement.

Nearly another half million are participating in the 19,700 co-operatives which the FSA organized and watches over on a self-liquidating basis. By getting together with his neighbors, Si Brown is able in this way to have his stock sired by purebreds, to use expensive farm machinery, and to buy supplies reasonably.

Under a long-term credit program, FSA has enabled about 23,500 tenants to buy their farms. It is also closing out gradually the resettlement homestead projects which it inherited and on which some 14,000 families are seeking a living. Losses are frequently taken on the values of these projects, but FSA cannot sell until it thinks the residents are capable of paying off.

As guardian of the Okies, FSA has erected over 100 migrant labor camps, housing 20,000 families. Though these camps were once the scourge of all adjacent chambers of commerce, they are now the object of favor as sources of labor in America's war boom. The shoe is on the other foot.

Political trouble has followed Farm Security for two general reasons: First, such a helping hand involves considerable bureaucratic supervision, which has often been carried on by young college graduates rather than horny-handed farmers. Second, maintaining family-type farming on reasonably small acreages, with the aid of government credit to those down-and-out, is ideologically communistic and repulsive in practice to the agrarian blue bloods who can afford to talk "economy." Negroes and "po' white trash" are supposed to be as untouchable to the government as to those who live across the tracks from them.

The major programs, involving credit, inducement payments, cash subsidies, and control of production, have been described at some length because of their impact on the farm bloc and vice versa. Those who think of the farm bloc as feeding at a huge trough will find in that trough all these government programs. There are other less dramatic parts of the department's work, however, which deserve brief note because of their important, though more routine, effect as a leavening agent for keeping farmers vocal. Every government agency has its share of educational, promotional, and statistical functions, but those of agriculture are more seasoned than others.

Most important of these, in terms of being far-reaching and influential at the grass-roots level, is the Extension Service. The 9,000 extension agents, who are expected to be versed in nearly everything being done by the department, are paid half by the department and half by local co-operating agencies, such as state agricultural colleges, counties, and farm organizations. In addition, the Extension Service boasts that its "greatest strength" is in its 702,000 voluntary local leaders who, over the years, have become trained and experienced in community leadership of extension projects.

Since creation of the Extension Service in 1914 its county agents have been called on for help on millions of miscellaneous problems, for they are supposed to be the means through which the department's policies, discoveries, and household hints are carried out in the field. Subject matter of their work runs something like this: wartime food goals, diets, cold storage of home-grown food, tuberculosis tests, weed control, grasshopper poisoning, seed improvement, housing, making mattresses, getting electricity, teaching crafts, marketing outlook, public forums, farm management, forestry, and credit. Whether in their offices or out on the farms, the extension agents are the extremities of the department.

Another branch of the department is the Soil Conservation Service, the agency charged with advising farmers scientifically on how to rotate crops so as to build up the soil instead of deplete it, on how to keep their land from washing away, and on how to avoid another disastrous dust bowl with rich topsoil blowing madly around the Midwest.

Quite naturally much of this work is highly technical. Use of new farm machinery and practices such as contouring (taking into account the hills and valleys on an acreage), terracing (like a city lawn that slopes too much to be planted in one steep hill), and strip cropping (planting a strip of beans between strips of corn, for example) have been taught millions of farmers.

But in addition to the technical perfection achieved there is a strange paradox in the soil-conservation program—a paradox that has never been conquered by New Deal planners, that goes to the root of abundant economy versus an economy of scarcity. It is the strange twist of events which put the AAA to restricting production sharply while ordering soil-conservation artists to teach farmers to produce more and more and more from the same acreage of land.

A quotation from a recent departmental publication on conservation will illustrate: "Contouring alone has increased corn production twofold on test farms and in test areas. Also it has required 7 per cent less time and 10 per cent less fuel in the preparation of land and seeding of small grains than non-contouring farming."

Although this factual approach to the paradox is freely admitted, even boasted, the paradox itself is a touchy subject around the department. Now that the war has made it imperative to grab any device for increasing production of most crops, however, the department is beginning—unwittingly, perhaps—to fall into the general admission. For example, the same pamphlet quoted above states this: "Conservation farming is the most effective way to boost output *now*, this year, and also to make possible even more production next year and the year after that, as long as the war lasts and then some." The methods are not new; the frankness is.

Aside from its philosophy of inducing curtailment, AAA has in its favor, however, the fact that the day war was declared machinery existed to *adjust* production to fit food goals. For example, the planting of wheat had to be actively discouraged in order to release wheat land, labor, and equipment for production of soybeans, peanuts, milk, corn, and other crops. Whether those responsible for AAA turned the various faucets off and on quickly enough, or whether they should ever have turned them off, is in the realm of opinion; but the adjustment machinery did exist.

Six days after Pearl Harbor, Secretary Wickard streamlined his department by grouping nineteen agencies under eight administrators, who with three other officials comprise an agricultural "war cabinet" covering all activities. The AAA, Soil Conservation Service, Federal Crop Insurance Corporation, and Sugar Agency were brought together under M. Clifford Townsend, former governor of Indiana, who was named administrator of the new Agricultural Conservation and Adjustment Administration.

The Sugar Agency, just named, executes the Sugar Act of 1937—the sugar industry's special Triple A. Under that law the United States sugar market is divided among the various domestic and foreign areas which supply our sugar. On the foreign side, there is a tariff as high as can be obtained without completely alienating our neighbors in Puerto Rico, Cuba, Hawaii, and similar areas. On the domestic side, payments are made to cane- and beet-sugar farmers who comply with child-labor and minimum-wage standards, promote soil conservation, and plant within restrictive quotas.

It is in sugar, perhaps, that the greatest recent criticism of restricted production has fallen, because of the fact that sugar was the first food item to be rationed while cash payments were still being made to farmers. A pointed example comes from a Colorado housewife. Returning one day from her grocery, unhappy and sugarless, she found in the mailbox a check for cutting sugar-beet production on her own farm. This peculiar sort of situation was remedied when quotas were discarded for the 1943 crop.

By organizing hundreds of local War Boards, on which AAA men are chairmen, the ACAA—as Townsend's overall agency is called—has been the center of organizing food production throughout the country. The ACAA makes much of the fact that its local committees (the regular AAA committees, not the County War Boards) are elected by farmers themselves. In discussing the value of having so democratic a system, ACAA points to the fact that the farmer committeemen, over a year ago, carried out a person-to-person canvass of nearly all the farmers in America in a little more than one month to map the production program of each farm for 1942. ACAA insists that all this is only a part of its regular program of *adjusting* supply to demand, but in other quarters it is spoken of as throwing the old AAA into reverse. The war ended an era of American agriculture.

III

Prairie Justice

THERE IS A REASON for sometimes calling the United States Senate the Upper Chamber or the Upper House. It not only has certain constitutional functions not given the House of Representatives, such as ratification of treaties and confirmation of presidential appointments, but usually has the upper hand. Because of the fact that each state has two votes in the Senate, regardless of population, a group of senators from sparsely inhabited farm states are able to hold the power of life or death over a bill. For example, roughly the same number of people voted in the 1940 senatorial election in the state of New York (6,400,000) as voted in the ten farm states of Idaho, Minnesota, Montana, Nebraska, Nevada, New Mexico, Texas, Utah, Wyoming, and Washington.

When such an alignment occurs the bloc becomes the modern counterpart of the bold, bad farmers of old who felt compelled to take the law in their own hands and hang cattle rustlers to the nearest tree. After embroidery in Hollywood that long-past practice became known as "prairie justice." Today the Senate farm bloc is the nearest thing to prairie justice.

Titular head, but not really the leader, of the farm bloc

is Ellison DuRant Smith, senator from South Carolina, dean of the Senate (thirty-four years of service), chairman of the Committee on Agriculture and Forestry, and ranking majority member of the Interstate Commerce Committee. Known for years as "Cotton Ed," because of his announced intention, when he entered the Senate in 1909, to get the price of cotton to 15 cents a pound and keep it there, Smith is also a champion of states' rights. The aged and grizzled solon is the epitome of that twist of history which has left Democratic President Roosevelt with senior key congressmen out of tune with his policies.

Just six years after his graduation from Wofford College, in Spartanburg, S.C., Smith was one of the principal figures in the organization of the Southern Cotton Association at New Orleans in January 1905. For the next three and one half years he served as field agent and general organizer of the new movement, until nominated for the Senate in 1908

Rare is the man who catches "Cotton Ed" Smith smiling. His white-mustached, heavily lined face belies the grumpiness which usually reaches such extreme proportions that he keeps colleagues laughing in spite of his own failure to break down. His picturesque and normally profane speech has earned him a reputation as a leading quipper, but it has been worn so thin that capital reporters have become calloused against using much of it in their daily stories.

Wartime exigencies have given Smith many occasions to snort. "Congress has become a clearinghouse, the Supreme Court has vanished, and the entire government has gone to hell," he once said. Of Leon Henderson, Donald Nelson, and Harold Ickes, he snapped: "We ought to take back every bit of power Congress delegated to those rascals." Other Smith witticisms include: "Patriotism these days is spelled 'paytriotism,'" and "You can't win a war by rationing away state and individual rights. And who the hell expects to win one by taking ruffles off ladies' lingerie?"

Although the rough-and-tumble warrior quotes with ease from the Book of Job, Shakespeare, Burns, and the Constitution, his Phi Beta Kappa key is honorary. He did study Greek, however, just to teach himself "plain damned logic." Being the son of a preacher, brother of two preachers, and brother-in-law of two more, Smith might be expected to hold at least an abstract concern for the black-skinned people who, in large part, pick the fields of cotton which he watches so religiously; but when a Negro minister invoked the blessing at the Democratic National Convention in 1936, he ostentatiously stalked off the platform.

A leader of the area which President Roosevelt has characterized as the "nation's number-one economic problem," Senator Smith insists that the South won the Revolutionary War and that "God bless my soul, my forebears lived on parched corn and sweet potatoes to give me a crown of individual rights, and I'm going to wear my crown if it kills me."

Today, although Smith is not taken too seriously, except for the one vote out of the Senate's ninety-six which he controls, he can always be counted on to convene his Committee on Agriculture and Forestry for any purpose—even to hold hearings on bills assigned to other committees. In convening the committee at the drop of a lobbyist's suggestion, Smith is likely to bark to the clerk: "Call up those butt-heads and tell 'em we're going to have a meeting tomorrow."

Such meetings were called in the fall of 1942 for two unusual sessions: fighting with the Army and WPB Rubber Czar William Jeffers over the use of rayon instead of cotton in heavy-duty truck tires, and calling on the carpet three of Washington's busiest executives, Director of Stabilization James F. Byrnes, Price Administrator Leon Henderson, and Secretary of Agriculture Wickard. No matter what degree of merit or scope of interest a given subject may have, Senator Smith can be relied upon to give it the touch of respectability which comes with having a hearing before a Senate committee. The South Carolinian leads other congressmen in the number of relatives on the pay roll and has the most unique ring for the elevator—dots and dashes until the car arrives and the door opens. A typical Smith trip to the Senate floor ends with a chuck of tobacco in the brass goboon beside his desk.

The tower of strength on the Senate side of the bloc is Alabama's veteran, John H. Bankhead, though other members complain that when cotton has been taken care of Bankhead is likely to withdraw to the side lines. Some of Bankhead's effectiveness lies in his domineering approach, much of which he can exercise with dignity because of his seniority—twelve years of service.

Bankhead steers a fairly independent course, so far as the Democratic program is concerned, and talks with reporters most freely only when to do so is in his own interest. A large-framed man, with beetle brows and a bald head, the senior senator from Alabama is an imposing figure in Congress, though when the argument is running against him he can screw up an equally distinctive pout as anger gathers.

The principal cotton legislation, by which acreage and marketing is under strict quotas, bears his name, and he was a staunch bloc leader in the 1942 price-control fight. Though he is generally credited with helping to write the famous 110-per-cent-of-parity clause, and did, it is also known that he privately put himself on record as being willing to go along with only 100 per cent. His subsequent shift to 110 caught the Administration short, but leaders kept their secret about his change.

Another Southerner, Richard B. Russell, of Georgia, is one of the senators who must be consulted on anything involving control of the farm bloc. Russell was the baby of the Upper Chamber when he entered it in 1933, but now holds the important post of chairman of the Agriculture Subcommittee of the Senate Appropriations Committee. In this capacity he is floor leader for the gigantic farm appropriations.

Though Russell never overlooks a parliamentary tactic to aid his side, he plays his cards close to his chest and speaks only when moved. One of those occasions was to help pass the time in the Southern filibuster against the bill to remove poll taxes as conditions for voting in seven Southern states. A former governor of Georgia, Russell is well liked by all and regarded as a reasonable, polite politician.

Another elder statesman of the bloc is Elmer Thomas, of Oklahoma—not to be confused with two other Senator Thomases. Gallery spectators invariably find their eyes straying to the lean and lanky, white-haired Thomas, as his bearing and conduct coincide with the popular picture of a senator.

Thomas' forte is statistics, chiefly on monetary policy and cotton. As the Senate's chief exponent of pet theories on money, particularly silver money, Thomas furnishes the main link between the silver and farm blocs. His chairmanship of the Senate Special Silver Committee, on which only senators from silver-producing states are represented, marks him as spearhead of the inflationary forces which crop out periodically in Congress even in peacetime. The senator denies that he is an inflationist, however, asserting that he only wants to get the dollar up to its full value and leave it there.

One who asks Elmer Thomas the price of cotton at a given moment is likely to be told something like this: "I don't know right now, but at eleven-thirty it was 13.8 cents a pound." Frequently, however, the Oklahoman outdoes himself with figures. On several occasions he has monopolized entire legislative days by explaining statistics to a handful of hangers-on. One such unwinding, on the subject of cotton prices and illustrated with ten huge charts, was stopped only after Majority Leader Barkley whispered in the high Thomas ear that an air raid had been sounded at near-by Baltimore.

Thomas, next to Smith, is the master of convening some sort of committee meeting to serve as a sounding board for specialized views of his own or of influential constituents. He will preside with ease at any caucus called by the Southern Commissioners of Agriculture—or will call one himself. So intense is his interest in getting his new and doubled parity written into law that he will swallow his conservative pride to sit in the same room with John L. Lewis' dairy farmers, but he has only seldom been able to sustain the attention of representatives from the Grange and Farm Bureau.

Oddly enough, Thomas is not a farmer; he is a lawyer who was elected to the Oklahoma Senate upon the territory's having become a state back in 1907. In addition, he is an Elk, a Mason, and a Shriner.

The glamour of the farm bloc is provided by Guy Gillette, of Iowa, the Senate's best-dressed. A popular congressman, the silver-haired Gillette is likely to be seen around Washington carrying his boy's paper route, playing the piano or washing dishes at the Stage Door Canteen.

Though he was once prosecuting attorney for Cherokee County, he has also been a farmer. He has told the Senate that he came to Washington from between the handles of a plow, but he is not one of the die-hard members of the bloc.

The well-known investigation of the synthetic-rubber program, which he headed throughout 1942, was started not as a publicity gag but as a means of finding out how more wheat and corn could be used in making the product —and why Europeans used grain while the United States stuck to petroleum as a base. The now-famous Baruch Rubber Report largely vindicated the belligerence of the Gillette investigation, and officials as high as Donald Nelson have been forced to tell the committee that if the rubber program were being started over it would utilize much more grain.

There is a story behind the Gillette committee story, however, which deserves being told to illustrate the logrolling which often fits in with the farm battle. As counsel to his subcommittee Gillette chose a capable, energetic Washington lawyer named Paul Hadlick, secretary of the National Oil Marketers Association.

Why would an oil lawyer be trying to substitute corn and wheat for oil as the raw material in synthetic rubber? One answer, once given by Hadlick, is that petroleum dealers naturally want more than anything else to get the nation's cars back to full mileage. Getting rubber tires is the quickest way to do that. The other, and not conflicting, explanation is that the Oil Marketers Association has been fighting the big oil operators for years and saw a new chance to put them over a barrel. Substantiation for the latter reason is found in the facts that Gillette has on his office wall an award of service from the association, he has sponsored legislation to divorce the big refiners from distribution of their oil through filling stations, and he wrote a bill to bar from government jobs all oil-company officials who were indicted in the big Madison antitrust suits, which were upheld by the Supreme Court. Thus, though the able, dapper Iowan's subcommittee was referred to as "farm-bloc interests," it was as often speaking for the smaller independent oil companies.

Number-two man on the Senate Agriculture Committee is Montana's scrapper since 1923, Burton K. Wheeler. The bitterly isolationist position of Wheeler before Pearl Harbor and his split with the Administration before that on the Supreme Court fight destroyed much of Wheeler's effectiveness as a farm-bloc leader, but he continues to be active at committee meetings and on the floor in behalf of the agricultural West.

One of the cagiest of the farm-bloc senators is Joseph C. O'Mahoney, of Wyoming, former lawyer and newspaperman and most celebrated as chairman of the rambling Temporary National Economic Committee (TNEC) which delved into hundreds of angles of concentration of economic power. More often than not O'Mahoney stands with the President, but his pointed breakovers make it difficult to predict him and necessary to "sweeten him up" now and then if his vote is to be had by the Administration.

Wool, cattle, and sugar beets are special concerns of O'Mahoney and his junior colleague who was just defeated for re-election, Harry Schwartz. Generally pompous in appearance, a wearer of pince-nez on a black ribbon, O'Mahoney sometimes irritates his fellow senators by delivering them solemn lectures on what he regards as mistakes made by the august body.

A source of curiosity about the Wyoming senator's views

is the fact that the mass of far-reaching TNEC studies which solidly damned several industries contained nowhere a description of the way in which sheepmen of the West have pulled the wool over American consumers' eyes for so many years by use of the tariff and other lobbying devices.

Those are the Democratic leaders of the Senate farm bloc; there are many more in the party who will work for the bloc but who seldom originate major issues or rise often to wage public battle. It should be noted in passing that the presiding officer of the Senate, Vice-President Wallace, was Secretary of Agriculture when the concrete was poured for the foundations which the bloc today stands upon. Though Wallace does not actively support the farmers in terms of buttonholing for votes, etc., in the corridors, his presence on the rostrum cannot fail to be reassuring.

One of the most important features of the bloc, however, is its present independence of the Democratic party. Today it is the point at which the powerful coalition of Republicans and conservative Democrats converge most often. One reason for this is the fact that Charles L. McNary is minority leader of the Senate.

It was during the World War that McNary was appointed to a vacancy, making him now number-four senator in point of service. Having been dean of Willamette College of Law and associate justice of the Oregon Supreme Court, McNary is a lawyer by profession, but he maintains a beautiful farm in Oregon and considers himself *the* farm senator. The McNary-Haugen bill, which he saw vetoed twice, was, even in failure, one of the landmarks of agricultural history. Since the 1932 landslide which set McNary on the minority side of the aisle he has of course been unimportant as a sponsor of legislation, but no one has lined up the farm bloc without seeing him. As one of the best-informed of the bloc, McNary sometimes steps in to knock out a specific provision of some compromise or program, but for the most part he stands by without questioning farm measures.

When the sixty-eight-year-old, solemn-faced, trim-figured Oregonian stands at the minority leader's desk he directly faces Wallace, putting the two 1940 vice-presidential candidates together as living proof that farm leadership in Congress is no mere geographical fluke.

Right behind McNary in seniority is Republican Arthur Capper, who ended his second term as governor of Kansas to enter the Senate in 1919. Many people other than Kansans have heard of the now frail senator with the unruly shock of white hair through one of his many publications, *Capper's Weekly*. Born in 1865 in the tiny town of Garnett, Kansas, where he received his entire schooling, Capper entered the publishing business as a typesetter, moving up rapidly in his home state before going to New York and Washington, in 1892, as a reporter. Returning to Kansas, Capper started buying up enterprises, until he now holds the Topeka *Daily Capital, Household* magazine, *Capper's Weekly, Kansas Farmer, Pennsylvania Farmer*, Kansas City *Kansan, Capper's Farmer, Missouri Ruralist, Ohio Farmer, Michigan Farmer*, an engraving company, and radio stations.

The potency of Capper's publication network can hardly be said to be the sole reason for his success in returning to Washington every six years, but it has probably been the main one. Day in and day out Capper constituents read the praises of their senior senator, dished up by his own editors, obviating the necessity for an expensive campaign.

One of the springboards on which Capper rose to political heights was a unique system which he devised to lend a few dollars to any farm youth who wanted to buy a pig for feeding and marketing. As creditor, Capper not only received interest on his investments but was head of the pig clubs which borrowers formed. Success of such ventures was attested by his three years as president of the Board of Regents at Kansas State Agricultural College. Marrying a former governor's daughter helped also.

As a congressman Capper worries more about shifts in the home sands than attempting to lead people. Into his shy nature is molded a middle-of-the-road stand on really important issues other than those affecting agriculture. Next to running his lucrative news enterprises and voting with the bloc, Capper likes to attend miscellaneous affairs in Washington and can nearly always be counted on to put in an appearance for a hostess and shake hands dotingly with a few guests. His peak of strength as a strategist has been passed, but he can be relied upon to sit frequently at hearings of any committee he happens to be on—though he has dozed off in front of some important witnesses.

In the waning months of the past session of Congress three Republicans ascended to seats of the mighty in farm-bloc counsel: Clyde M. Reed, from Kansas; George D. Aiken, from Vermont, and Hugh A. Butler, from Nebraska. These comparative youngsters joined "the most exclusive club in the world" in 1939, 1941, and 1941 respectively, and represent the crest of the tide of conservatism which was loosed at the November 1942 polls. They were at work a year or two ahead of the swell.

Senator Reed looks as much the part of a farmer as any colleague—but, like many others, he is not a farmer. After a common-school education and twenty-eight years in the postal service, Reed went to the Parsons, Kansas, *Sun*, of which he is now editor and publisher. In 1919 he was secretary to a governor; in 1920 he was appointed a member of the Kansas Court of Industrial Relations; in 1921 he was made chairman of the Public Utilities Commission, and from 1929 to 1931 he was governor of the state.

Reed is one of the bloc's frankest members. While many of them resent being labeled with that appellation, the junior senator from Kansas will stand erect, shake his snowy-white hair, and declare before God and the galleries that he is proud to be a member of the farm bloc.

In debate and committee hearings he is equally candid. When Henderson, Byrnes, and Wickard were on the Agriculture Committee's carpet Wickard cited an opinion of Attorney General Biddle which upheld his inclusion of benefit payments to farmers in calculating parity prices. Reed shouted that Biddle has no legal integrity "and will give any opinion the President wants." When Senator Allen J. Ellender, of Louisiana, who was presiding, rebuked the Kansan for testifying while he was not a witness and for disrupting the order of the hearing, Reed retorted that Ellender would not be as disinterested if the subject were sugar instead of wheat and flour. Reed even sniped at Byrnes, the former senator and Supreme Court justice, for evading questions!

Continual carping at Henderson brought prompt rejoinders from the swarthy price czar who was soon thereafter to resign, but Reed countered with, "You haven't heard the last of this matter," and "We will meet again, Mr. Henderson."

Flour and wheat are the two main concerns of Reed, as might be guessed from the economy of his state, but general farm legislation also arouses him. A sort of side line with Reed is curbing organized labor, even after the voters of Kansas rejected his 1942 effort to return as their governor on that platform.

Because George Aiken comes from New England he is not ordinarily thought of as part of the farm bloc, which illustrates the geographical fallacy that has become attached to the subject in popular thinking. On some occasions Aiken has been the spearhead for agricultural benefits, in spite of the fact that his farm background consists of having nurtured a nursery farm into a large enterprise in Putney, Vermont.

Aiken is described as looking "Vermontish." In politics he followed the traditional route from town representative to speaker of the State House of Representatives, lieutenant governor, and governor. He is regarded as being on the rise in the Senate and a good fellow, but he was perhaps the only senator who refused to concede in favor of the defeated Prentiss Brown that he had done a good job in handling the price-control amendments, regardless of party or merits.

Nebraska's Hugh Butler is a sixty-five-year-old, white-haired, ministerial-looking senator who has done more than the usual share of talking in his first two years. Because he is beginning to be listened to, however, it is significant that his subject is the farm bloc. Though Butler will probably never be a general leader on the Hill, his voice is sharp enough by itself to be effective. It will probably be loud enough to be heard in the House for sugar beets and livestock, since his fellow Nebraskan, Harry Coffee, who once handled those commodities, was defeated for re-election this term.

Educated to be an engineer, and having worked as one for eight years with the C. B. & Q. Railroad, Butler turned in 1908 to the flour-milling and grain business, which he still is in and which explains his quick eye for decisions affecting wheat and flour.

The ranking minority member of the Agriculture Committee, until his defeat last year, was the much-honored veteran from Nebraska, George W. Norris, last of the Independents in Congress. Norris was one of the very few who was as liberal about everything as he was about farm matters. His loyalty to the farm bloc went far, but he ended it where the public interest began. His partisanship for farmers was tempered by consideration for other groups in America—for other blocs, it might be said. Similarly, his thinking was not rutted on farm matters; his greatness sprang as well from opinions and actions in the field of the judiciary, labor, public power, civil liberties, and foreign affairs. Whatever disfavor the farm bloc has fallen into is probably attributable to the fact that few other members have shown a similar broad attitude.

There are at least two other outstanding senators who are for the farmers without being obsessed with farm legislation. During the battle over rural-manpower and national-service legislation, last fall, Senator Robert La Follette, of Wisconsin, chairman of the Education and Labor Subcommittee which had been studying violations of civil liberties among farm labor for many months, rose to introduce five bills for himself and the other subcommittee member, *Elbert* Thomas, of Utah.

Neither the senator's twenty-one-page speech nor the contents of his five bills were widely noted, but taken together they were among the few really fundamental proposals during that period of groping for a national policy. Though duller, the subcommittee report is a sharp change from the table-pounding tactics of commodity protagonists.

"As old as civilization and as fresh as this morning's newspaper" is what La Follette called the problem of farm labor. "The coming of war marked the end of active public concern with the Joads, the Jeeter Lesters, and their real-life counterparts," the Wisconsin Progressive noted. "Now, however, the economic cycle has turned from an era of labor surplus to one of labor scarcity."

Of the eleven million agricultural workers of the nation, La Follette found that about three million are wage laborers, rather comparable to industrial wage laborers. "Their plight," he said, "was an unanswered reproach to national conscience in years of peace. Deprived of the protection of labor legislation, employee organization, or even dependable employment, these agricultural wage workers have suffered for years under a serious national discrimination."

Further emphasizing the fact that wartime conditions of farm labor are mostly accentuations of peacetime circumstances, La Follette declared that "no solution to this farm-labor problem that does not apply the principles of the Atlantic Charter to men on our fields and farms will be effective." The five bills, he explained, would not only further the Four Freedoms at home, but would lay the foundation for a successful solution of the problem of farm labor after the war.

In addition to the bills the senator introduced a resolution asking for a joint Senate and House committee to investigate the problem of the small "family farmer" group. Among other things, this committee would provide a "consistent pattern for the operation of such curative agencies as the Farm Security Administration.

"The entire program of that most vital public organization has been placed in jeopardy," La Follette said, "because of disagreements in Congress. There is a general lack of understanding of the relationship of its work to the war and postwar problems of agriculture."

La Follette next summarized his subcommittee's conclusions after studying intensively the industrialized agriculture of California, much of which has been referred to as "factories in the field" by Carey McWilliams, Commissioner of Migration for that state.

"Our conclusion," said La Follette, "was that the outbreak of violence and strife in California's agriculture was only the most recent 'storm signal' of a profound and long-standing maladjustment in the lives of millions of hired farm workers and small farmers throughout the nation. We recommended that a series of specific new public policies for agricultural labor be adopted."

Further setting the stage for the legislative proposals, La Follette stated: "Poverty, insecurity, low hourly and annual wages, inferior housing and living standards, child labor, the absence of adequate health and educational services, underemployment, unemployment, undirected and unnecessary migrancy, and a lack of any substantial opportunity to exercise the civil rights of labor—these were revealed as the lot of the great portion of the nation's agricultural laborers."

Fourteen blocks down historic Pennsylvania Avenue the American Farm Bureau Federation was mobilizing to fight any move to insert a wage-stabilization clause in a War Manpower Commission directive aimed at keeping essential dairy, livestock, and poultry workers on their farms; but the Wisconsin veteran put his bills in the hopper anyway.

The first bill would stabilize the farm-labor market through public employment exchanges, accompanied by old-age and survivors' insurance and a specially adapted form of unemployment insurance. The second would establish a system of agricultural wage boards to determine "fair wages as distinct from minimum wages" for labor in "industrialized agriculture." The third called for extension of the Wage-Hour Act to the same employees, setting minimum wages and maximum hours.

The fourth would regulate the operations of private employment agencies, labor contractors, and other forms of private recruiting for industrialized agriculture. The fifth bill, described as ultimately being "the keystone arch of any enlightened national policy in this field," would simply extend Wagner Act benefits—the right to bargain collectively in unions of their own choosing—to the same type of workers.

Altruism can buck sectionalism only so long, however. On January 7, 1943, Progressive La Follette wrote Secretary Wickard in protest against sending butter to the Allies. His request that butter be saved for American housewives, he wrote, was "on behalf of the farmers of the country who need . . . help if their domestic market for dairy products is to be preserved and protected from the competitive raids of cheap substitutes while their backs are turned and their efforts are devoted to producing for foreign nations that can use the substitutes just as well as Americans can."

The dairy-state senator declared that "the use of substitutes for butter has been consistently discouraged as a matter of public policy" and that "butter is the backbone of the dairy industry." What he did not need to mention was the fact that five weeks earlier a similar letter had gone to Wickard from the president of the Farm Bureau from the La Follette state of Wisconsin.

In the House of Representatives the man who has worked himself up steadily and solidly to become one of the two or three biggest guns of the farm bloc is Clarence Cannon, chairman of the all-powerful Appropriations Committee, chairman of the Democratic steering committee of the House, and famous parliamentarian.

Born in 1879 in Missouri, Cannon taught history, practiced law, and was elected to the House in 1923. Before the World War he was parliamentarian of the House; he has since edited or authored all of the tomes on that subject, and no congressman who is not up on *Cannon's Procedure* can expect to put anything over on the farm bloc. Especially has this been true since farm legislation became so much a matter of appropriations. Besides being chairman of that group, Cannon is on its Agricultural Subcommittee.

His qualification for this job is not entirely congressional experience for eleven sessions; he also owns a thousand-acre farm in Missouri, where he raises cattle and hogs and enjoys an orchard. Incidentally, Cannon is one of the very few congressmen to list his farm-organization membership, which is Farm Bureau.

It was Cannon who led the bloc's fight in 1942 against allowing the Commodity Credit Corporation to release below parity some of its Ever-Normal Granary wheat and corn to feed cattle, hogs, and poultry for wartime needs. The necessity for such steps was so apparent that the bloc itself was split, but enough logrolling among livestock interests was effected to rout the Department of Agriculture on the issue.

Cannon summarized his adamancy with the defiant statement from the floor that "the only issue is the maintenance of the principle of parity, repeatedly assured agriculture by legislative enactment and which will give the farmers half of the price they received during the last war." Meanwhile the department was worrying about getting feed for poultry, meat animals, and dairy cows. It knew that none would flow into those channels at 100 per cent of parity.

The chairman of the House Agriculture Committee, Hampton Pitts Fulmer, is distinguished by having been elected to the House from South Carolina twelve consecutive times and for having one of the longest and most trivial autobiographical sketches in the *Congressional Directory*. The sheer force of his seniority put Fulmer in the top farm position of the Lower Chamber in spite of the trace of humor with which colleagues meet most of the proposals of the sixty-seven-year-old farmer. Like senior Senator Smith from his state, Fulmer can be relied upon to convene the Agriculture Committee and issue statements often, but he is no leader.

His chief claims to fame are authorship of the Agricultural Adjustment Act and the Standard Cotton Grading Act. During the farm-manpower debate, early in 1943, he proposed that all soldiers with farming experience be mustered out of the armed services, that no more be inducted, and that the Army help harvest crops as the season rolls around.

Fulmer was one of the first to warn from Capitol Hill of a food shortage unless farmers were kept on the farms. On August 19, before the battle royal over amending price control, Fulmer complained that farm hands were being taken away by the draft and lured away by high wages. His proposed boosting of prices differed from that of fellow farm-bloc congressmen in that he not only wanted higher prices at the farm level but asserted that consumers would be spared from paying them because they would be absorbed by "a costly and unnecessary marketing and distribution system which well could be done away with." For good measure he expressed the opinion that the OPA was "hell-bent and determined to destroy agriculture and the small independent business concerns and their employees."

Two months later his committee issued a written report along the same lines as his shortage forecast. Shortly after the new Congress convened Fulmer introduced a resolution to have his group investigate the entire food industry with a view to eliminating waste in distribution. Ordinarily food lobbyists, of which there are many in Washington, would jump on their horses and storm Capitol Hill to head off such a move, but Fulmer's fulminations seldom worry them any more.

Three lawyers, placed strategically in the Democratic majority, are of constant though not specialized help to the bloc: Stephen Pace, of Georgia, author of the outstanding bill to include all farm-labor costs in parity; Judge Malcolm C. Tarver, also of Georgia, who is chairman of the potent Appropriations Subcommittee on Agriculture, and Henry B. Steagall, of Alabama, who came to the House in 1915 and today is chairman of its Banking and Currency Committee, which handles all price-control legislation.

A Republican lawyer of importance is Everett M. Dirksen, of Illinois, member of the Appropriations Subcommittee and frequent reflector of Farm Bureau views through the fact that its vice-president, Earl Smith, is also president of the Illinois Farm Bureau affiliate. Another Republican lawyer, Clifford Hope, of Kansas, whose accumulated seniority since 1927 has made him ranking minority member of the Agriculture Committee, is a standby in farm legislation, though he is not as vociferous as his Democratic brethren in the same group.

A present power in livestock representation is Richard

Kleberg, Texas grandson of the founder of the 1,250,000-acre King ranch which he managed actively until 1924. Democrat Kleberg, who is also a lawyer, came to Congress in 1931. Before and since that time he acquired as long a string of association tie-ups as any legislator, besides being a bank director. At various times he has been on the Executive Committee and president of the Texas and Southwestern Cattle Raisers Association, a director of the National Livestock Association, organizer and president of the Texas Federated Agricultural Association, board member of the Better Beef Association, and president of the board of the Texas College of Arts and Industries. As chairman of the board of King ranch, Kleberg speaks for the largest cattle acreage owned by one family in the United States.

Except perhaps for those congressmen who have financial interests in special commodities, farm-bloc members do not think up farm legislation by themselves. They are urged. One instance of prodding occurred in December of last year when Democratic-party leaders from ten Midwestern states, meeting in Omaha, formed a permanent organization without consulting their national party chieftains. Its purpose was described as the establishment of "a common and united front to assist our great Commander-in-Chief in winning this war and also to strengthen and better serve the Middle Western agriculture states." Coming on the heels of a bitter battle in which the Administration had amended the Emergency Price Control Act to allow lower ceilings on food prices, the action could only be construed as a geographical threat to legislation in the national interest.

Only two senators and nineteen representatives listed themselves in the 1941–42 session as having agricultural occupations. One of the senators added insurance, banking, and manufacturing. Several of the representatives have not depended on farming for years for anything except being re-elected. Re-election, of course, is the key to the farm bloc's power. In November 1942, at ballot boxes all over the country, that was proved—if it needed proof.

IV

Faith, Hope, and Parity

MONDAY, SEPTEMBER 7, 1942, was one of history's strangest Labor Days. Customarily labor's turn to take a day off and hear its leaders and public officials laud the past year's gains or point to new ones, this one turned out to be a day of bad news. While agriculture is not formally included in these annual national pauses, even though farmers are manual laborers, farmers shared attention this time.

Congress gathered, as usual, that day at noon. Like farmers, laborers, and everyone else, congressmen had learned in the press that the Commander-in-Chief would deliver a message on inflation. They had heard that it would contain strong language on the level of wages and food. The usually small attendance had been swelled by all except those who were being challenged that week in primary elections back home.

A reading clerk intoned the words of the President's written text on the dull subject of inflation without benefit of the Roosevelt oral charm, recounting for the absent Executive an April message in which seven points of inflation control had been set forth. Five of these, according to the President, were being tackled by executive order and other administrative action; but on two of the seven fronts the necessary legislation had not been given him. The first sore spot was taxes, the subject by that time of nearly nine months of study in committee. Second, no law had been passed permitting price ceilings on farm products at parity prices.

This much the assembled congressmen had been ready for. What they did not expect was a short paragraph near the end of the long statement applying to the second point: "I ask the Congress to take this action by the first of October. Inaction on your part by that date will leave me with an inescapable responsibility to the people of this country to see to it that the war effort is no longer imperiled by threat of economic chaos. In the event that the Congress should fail to act, and act adequately, I shall accept the responsibility, and I will act."

The lengthy address was sharpened up in that afternoon's headlines:

ROOSEVELT TELLS CONGRESS
TO ACT BY OCT. 1, OR HE WILL

Newsmen furiously buttonholed rebuffed congressmen for quotations as they milled through the ornate old cloakroom on their way back to office buildings.

As the sting of being dictated to died down, congressmen turned to wrangling over details of the step which they knew would have to be taken. Two general alternatives emerged before a series of huddles among Administration leaders in Congress crystallized the strategy. Speaker of the House Sam Rayburn proposed the simplest solution; namely, that a one-sentence bill could be drafted to give the President complete authority for choosing his own method of controlling wages and food prices. Congress was smarting too much for that, however, and its decision to try a detailed formula within which the President and Leon Henderson would have to stay touched off the battle of the century with the farm bloc.

While Congress was thus occupied the statistics of the President's message were soaking in around the country. That very night he had taken to the air to put his radio personality behind his plea to the nation to accept controls on wages and prices. On the agricultural side, Roosevelt maintained basically that wages could not be stabilized so long as the cost of living, food being a major factor therein, kept rising.

Drawing from previously announced figures, the President proceeded to summarize the situation in food. "The cost of all food used by wage earners—controlled and un-controlled—has been going up at the rate of one and one fourth per cent per month since the price ceilings were set in May 1942," he said, adding that "if this rise should be permitted to continue, the increased cost of food to wage earners next May would be more than 15 per cent over the level which existed when the ceilings were set." Moreover, the cost of food items which were exempted by the Price Control Act had been rising at an average of three and one fourth per cent per month since May first of 1942. Within two months after the price regulation of some food items the uncontrolled ones advanced seven and three tenths per cent.

Then, frankly directing his argument to the housewife's pocketbook, Roosevelt listed some of those uncontrolled items: dry beans, sweet potatoes, apples, sheep for lamb and mutton, butter fat, wholesale milk, chickens, eggs, and oranges.

Turning to the situation of farmers, the President who gave them their first real relief program declared that prices received by farmers for their products had shot up 85 per cent since the outbreak of the war in September 1939—and were still rising. Cash farm income, he reported, including government payments, increased from $8,700,000,000 in 1939 to substantially more than $15,000,000,000 in 1942—an increase of about 75 per cent.

The Commander-in-Chief then told the nation that, although the agricultural clause in the Price Control Act is usually referred to as the 110-per-cent-of-parity limitation, it is much worse than that. According to his figures, application of the three other alternatives in the act, based on various dates, would run the average price up to 116 per cent before a lid could be clamped on. Moreover, in making that average, some commodities could go as high as 150 per cent.

These facts were quick to penetrate the homes which had been paying unheard-of prices for food for several months, but what the President promised the farmers in return for lower limitations was overlooked for about a week. After reaffirming his desire to attain parity for the farmer and routinely stating that parity should continue to be calculated by the Department of Agriculture so as to include cash benefit payments, Roosevelt slipped in a guarantee: "As a part of our general program on farm prices, I recommend that Congress in due time give consideration to the advisability of legislation which would place a floor under prices of farm products in order to maintain stability in the farm market for a reasonable future time." That period should be "one year, or even two years—or whatever period is necessary after the end of the war," he thought. The proviso was to be one of two big rallying points for the farm bloc, but its significance was missed for days.

By the time the history-making part of the farm battle was ready to burst loose several lines had been formed. Confusion was caused by the fact that some overlapped. Immediately after two White House conferences, attended by the regular handful of congressional Democratic leaders, the Administration line was written into a bill by Democratic Senators Prentiss M. Brown, able Michigan member of the Banking and Currency Committee, and Robert F. Wagner, New York chairman of that committee. Selection of the Banking and Currency, instead of the Agriculture Committee, was dictated by the fact that the original Price Control Act had been committed there before farm issues were raised. Brown was designated as Senate "floor handler," the man who steers a bill through parliamentary maneuvers, defends its merits during debate, and allots speaking time among supporters.

The Brown-Wagner Bill provided that ceilings could not be fixed on farm prices below parity (instead of 110 per cent of parity) or the highest market price of any commodity between January 1 and September 15, 1942—whichever might be higher. According to its author, this formula would maintain prices at the average then existing. Also the President was to adjust farm prices found to be below the highest levels reached in the nine-month period "to the extent that he finds necessary to correct gross inequities."

In general, the Senate bill drew praise from congressmen, though some of it was limited. When Elmer Thomas, who was to become leader of the opposition bloc, said he was "satisfied" with the measure a comparatively peaceful course through the legislature seemed assured. That was early afternoon exactly one week after Labor Day.

That evening, however, at the opposite end of the corridor which runs through the Capitol, a bill was introduced in the House that bore little resemblance to the Senate counterpart. The House had recessed much earlier, but not before giving Chairman Steagall, of the House Banking and Currency Committee, special permission to introduce a bill during the recess.

Headlines the next morning confirmed the suspicion that the farm bloc would tamper with provisions for calculating parity before allowing any amendment to pass. The Steagall Bill contained two jokers: First, it guaranteed crop loans of 100 per cent of parity instead of the 85-per-cent level then in force; second, it proposed to revise the parity formula so as to embrace all costs of production, including the cost of all hired and family labor. In addition, the Steagall Bill would allow no price ceiling at less than parity or below the highest price prevailing in 1942.

The amazing thing about the Steagall Bill was that, instead of allowing control of farm prices, even at levels then existing, a rigid floor of 112½ per cent of parity would be under them, for the new definition of parity would have raised it 12½ per cent above the level at that time. Aside from the merits of the controversy, it presented a grotesque picture of legislating during an emergency at the request of the Commander-in-Chief.

Meanwhile Leon Henderson had written Speaker Rayburn of the "grave urgency" of the problem, warning that if food prices were allowed to rise to levels permitted under the Price Control Act (averaging 116 per cent of parity), it would add $2,036,000,000 to the nation's cost of food marketing in 1942. That was under the old law. It is difficult to imagine the height of the levels favored by Steagall, but about that time some capital wit changed the three Biblical virtues to read "Faith, Hope, and Parity—and the greatest of these is Parity."

A series of shrewd maneuvers temporarily upset Steagall's farm-bloc bill, however. The night before hearings were to open before Steagall's committee eleven of its members held a rump session to draft their own ideas into a substitute measure. The result was a bill similar to that of Brown and Wagner. Next day a spokesman for the dissenters laid the bill before Steagall, who realized that his committee was against him and agreed to adopt the upstart bill, except that he insisted on writing into it a compromise guarantee of crop loans at 90 per cent of parity. Deletion of the proposed superparity definition was not swallowed by farm-bloc representatives other than Steagall, however. A few days later, during debate on amendments in the House, the original Steagall definition of parity was bounced back into controversy by Paul Brown, of Georgia.

It was on his amendment that observers learned the farm-bloc claims of majority strength were true. The House passed it by a vote of 205 to 172, even after being warned by those who knew that it would be vetoed. Defeat on the parity amendment turned into a complete rout as the House immediately passed the whole inflationary bill, as amended, 284 to 96. A total of 380 congressmen had shown enough interest to put in an appearance—far more of the 435 members than are usually present—showing the white heat generated by farm issues. Success of the bloc in cutting across party lines was shown by the fact that 99 Republicans joined 105 Democrats to put the Paul Brown amendment across.

A handful of dissenters, protesting that consumers were being gouged, were heckled down; but these figures were not challenged: By inclusion of farm-labor costs in the parity formula, the House would raise the nation's food bill an estimated $3,500,000,000 a year and the cost of living 5 per cent.

Meanwhile the Senate had been delaying its showdown until the House acted, although several major amendments had been offered and behind-the-scenes activity was raging. The Senate Banking and Currency Committee had completed its hearings by September 18, the same day its sister group in the House wound up. Actually the corridors, offices, and reception rooms just outside the two chambers were so regularly visited by farm representatives that hearings were perfunctory at best.

The bill sent to the Senate floor turned tables on President Roosevelt by setting a November-first dead line for his follow-up stabilization order, and established September 15, 1942, as the guidepost stabilization date, instead of the House's August-fifteenth level. Both measures contained the 90-per-cent-of-parity loan floor; they differed only in minor details. The Senate bill was reported out unanimously after rejection, 12 to 6, of Senator Bankhead's effort to revise the parity formula to include farm-labor costs. Senator O'Mahoney's proposal, allowing the President to modify ceilings if necessary to increase production or to avoid "gross inequities," was adopted instead.

By September 21 the Upper Chamber had passed routine provisions of the measure, but Senators Elmer Thomas and Carl Hatch (New Mexico Democrat) had each dropped bills in the hopper to compel inclusion of farm-labor costs in parity. Their efforts were later merged, making one big hurdle for Administration leaders Barkley, Brown, and Wagner.

First of the parliamentary tangles which always accompany the farm bloc on its march came when Barkley stopped Thomas' attempt to refer his amendment to the packed Agriculture Committee instead of to Banking and Currency. Completely undaunted, Thomas announced that the Agriculture Committee would hold a meeting on his proposal the next day anyhow.

Floor-handler Brown assured his alert colleagues that the discretion he wanted lodged in the President would not be used to freeze farm prices and that he expected a rise in the price level to 5 per cent more by December of 1943. Senators Lee ("Pass the Biscuits, Pappy") O'Daniel, Democrat of Texas; Hiram Johnson, Republican of California, and "Cotton Ed" Smith, of South Carolina, felt, however, that Congress should fix definite ceilings rather than leave them to "some bureau" and the President.

On September 26 word spread that the Administration had cooked up a compromise which would direct the President to allow for production costs in fixing farm ceilings. Senator Thomas, after a conference with farm leaders from downtown and the country, announced, however, that there was no intention of abandoning the idea of requiring the President to use the superparity formula. While Barkley claimed enough votes to effect the compromise, Senator Russell, of Georgia, a backer of Thomas, admitted that under a "favorable" Administration the compromise might be more beneficial than the mandatory proposal; then he expressed fear for his colleagues that the plan would be carried out by Leon Henderson, whom he described as essentially a consumer representative.

The next day, as give-and-take continued, Thomas

warned that the compromise was "meaningless" to farmers and that if his measure were defeated the farm bloc would wheel out a series of amendments designed to "guarantee that the farmers will receive a fair and square deal." With only three days remaining before the dead line, it was obvious that the controversy would have to go into a conference committee of House and Senate.

On September 28 few new issues were injected; both sides parried and jockeyed against the inevitable showdown on the compromise. After another meeting with four big farm organizations Thomas stated that two more than a majority of the senators would vote for his bill and that the farm bloc would try to show that the compromise amendment would "drive the country into a food shortage."

A usually militant farm-bloc member, Senator Clyde Reed, Kansas Republican, said there was little difference in the two proposals, however. "The difference," he said, "is that which lies between Tweedledum and Tweedledee. This is a face-saving contest. The farm leaders want to save their face and the Administration leaders want to save the President's face. Frankly, I would like to see both save face."

Victory for the farm bloc came on September 29, two days before the dead line. Putting all cards on the table, with the chips already down, the Thomas-Hatch amendment passed by a vote of 48 to 43. The show of strength came after Barkley, in a long speech, had declared that farmers were receiving $6,500,000,000 more in cash for their goods than in 1939 and were paying out only $500,-000,000 more; but the farm senators' assertions that farmers could not produce their goals without receiving the new kind of parity prevailed. With thirty hours remaining, tempers frayed and nerves frazzled from the long sessions, the bill was yet to be passed in entirety and sent to conference.

The victory was short-lived, however. On the last day of September, Barkley's amendment finally dominated by a vote of 86 to 4. Under it, price ceilings would be lifted wherever they did not reflect labor and other cost increases since January 1, 1941. Also it would require an "adequate wage" to farm labor in computing the costs. No one knew at the time just how much the measure would affect prices, but Barkley explained to the Senate that he was supporting it to "preserve the legislative process." Later government statisticians opined that the bill would permit farm prices to rise an average of 4 to 10 per cent, depending on how many types of farm labor were included. Senator Thomas still claimed a victory and said that the amendment differed from his version only in language.

One day after the October-first dead line the House accepted the Senate bill, 257 to 22, as recommended by a fast-acting conference committee, and the White House received the engraved bill with its ink scarcely dry. Late that same night the President signed it and conferred with fourteen top-notch advisers to speed an implementing executive order. The bloc had won a 90-per-cent-of-parity floor and had kept ceilings from going below parity or the highest level between January first of 1941 and September 15, 1942. The Administration had knocked out the 110-per-cent clause and won limited discretion in considering labor costs in food-price ceilings. Tired senators took time out to pat each other on the back.

Next day the President put Supreme Court Justice James F. Byrnes, former Administration stalwart from South Carolina, on the front pages by announcing his resignation from the Court to become director of the newly created

Office of Economic Stabilization. Price Administrator Henderson clamped tentative price ceilings on nearly all previously exempt grocery items, bringing 90 per cent of the family food budget under control. The *battle* was over, but the *war* was not.

In the next two weeks farm spokesmen downtown and on the Hill realized that Henderson's first ceilings under the new authority had used controversial and allegedly false concepts of parity. The Administration, by including government-subsidy payments in its calculation of parity, had again stirred the hornets' nest. The Senate Agriculture Committee summoned Henderson, Wickard, and Byrnes to stand on its carpet and justify their mathematics.

Henderson denounced an attempt to "gun" him out of his job and to "sabotage" the OPA, and estimated that farm-bloc demands would add $100,000,000 to the price of bread alone. Senator Reed charged flatly that the President's interpretation had repealed congressional determination.

Economic Czar Byrnes, an old hand at Senate maneuvers, cited in his defense the interpretation given by floor-handler Brown when explaining to the Senate the meaning of the conference-committee report which was accepted. At this, Senator George Aiken, Vermont Republican, charged that Brown's explanation had been a deliberately false one, inserted surreptitiously in the records. An intracommittee squabble followed on what Brown had said during the heat of debate, regardless of what changes he might have made in the *Congressional Record*.

When, in early January, the defeated Senator Brown was named Price Administrator to succeed the ailing and/or junked Henderson, the controversy was far from settled.

Though none of the amiable Michigan lawyer's enemies tried to block his Senate confirmation, they watched with jaundiced eye his first days in OPA, hoping to find true the undenied rumor that he had been put there to smooth political bumps.

For nearly two months, during which the November elections netted Republicans a gain of 44 seats in the House and 9 in the Senate, all was quiet on the legislative front of the anti-inflation war. But things were stirring down Pennsylvania Avenue. Lines were forming for an attack on the Administration's parity victory that was to be reminiscent of the bombing of Pearl Harbor a year before.

Newspaper readers on the morning of December 4 suddenly learned that the House had passed *without a dissenting vote* a bill to include all farm-labor costs in the calculation of parity—the measure it had passed once before to precipitate a farm-bloc battle. Without a day's warning Representative Stephen Pace, of Georgia, after getting approval of the House Agriculture Committee, ran the bill through with a short blast at price controllers and without one word from nonplused Democratic leaders.

As part of his whipping action Pace read a statement from Paul V. McNutt in which the Manpower Czar had informed him that a program was being drafted which "calls for adjustment of farm wages to bring the income of farm workers more nearly in line with those of industrial workers."

This, Pace said, "threw consternation into the ranks of all members of Congress, and also into the farmers. If they have to pay industrial wages, it will be impossible to produce a crop."

Immediately after the pile-driving House action Senator Thomas announced that the Senate Agriculture Committee would receive the bill at once, and predicted the group would report it out without amendment. His prediction was true. Within two days the Senate Committee had passed the Pace Bill unanimously.

What had happened? There were no indications that the Administration line on parity had changed. How had the coup occurred, coming so soon after defeat on the same issue? The answer lies in two movements.

First, a few days before passage of the Pace Bill the Senate Agriculture Committee had acted as a sounding board for its own and interested farmer protests of price ceilings. On November 30 the committee, augmented by other farm-state senators, unanimously approved a resolution authorizing a "full and complete investigation" of:

1. Maximum prices for agricultural commodities.

2. Subsidies, "direct or indirect."

3. The Commodity Credit Corporation, "particularly with reference to losses sustained because of such operations in agricultural commodities for the purpose of maintaining maximum prices or otherwise."

Raising another issue, Senator Burton K. Wheeler, who presided at the session, told newsmen: "I think that . . . it is the unanimous opinion of farm-state senators that the administrators of (the price-control law) have been erroneously including payments to farmers in fixing of price ceilings."

Second, but more important, a group of state secretaries, commissioners, and directors of agriculture arrived in Washington and went to Capitol Hill. Two days before passage of the Pace measure a group of these all-powerful officials let off steam to the Senate Agriculture Committee.

Tom Linder, of Georgia, most militant of the state officials' lobby, asserted that a food famine was inevitable unless agriculture is designated a war industry, farm workers exempted from the draft on that basis, and agricultural controls relaxed. R. A. Trovatten, commissioner from Minnesota, presented the official organization views to the committee, after which Senator Elmer Thomas promised to try to arrange a conference with WPB Chairman Donald Nelson. Trovatten firmly added that "farmers are almost put in a strait jacket by some of the rules made by these bureaus in Washington."

Top agriculture officials from South Dakota, Ohio, Nevada, and Wisconsin described conditions as they saw them among their respective farmers. Herman Ihde, acting director from Wisconsin, proposed that the 40-hour week in industry be abolished, putting all on a 54-hour basis.

After a week-end intermission farm senators returned to the Hill to find themselves with an ally in the form of a parliamentary knot in which four rather important bills were caught. So many solons were out of town that small filibusters started at the drop of a hat. Senator Bennett C. Clark, Democrat from Missouri, stalled for two days to amend a Mexican claims bill, and Senator Patrick McCarran, Democrat from Nevada, started talking to death a bill to release non-monetary Treasury silver for war use. Behind these two was trapped a bill to increase by $5,000,000,000 the borrowing authority of the Reconstruction Finance Corporation to continue its huge war program. About this same time both Houses were wrangling over an Administration settlement of several issues with Panama, Congress insisting that the arrangement was a treaty and should be ratified by the Senate.

Seizing upon the general befuddlement, the farm bloc's Senator Thomas tacked onto the RFC measure, essential to the Administration, a rider making parity include the cost of farm labor. The bloc was riding in on the use of all congressional devices mentioned in civics books: filibusters, riders, quorum calls, logrolling, and—in the opinion of many—pork barreling.

Congressmen were so eager to return home for a few weeks before beginning the new 78th session that measures like those of Pace and Thomas were left on base by adjournment; but they did not die. The new Congress returned to its three office buildings loaded for bear. Pace revived his bill and Thomas renewed his drive for a super-parity formula. The defeat of Senator Brown was hailed as a symbol of popular feeling on farm affairs and his appearance at OPA was eyed skeptically, even though he is personally friendly with all who know him. Superparity advocates claimed that the people who re-elected them had given a mandate to take things into their own hands. Their battle flag was hoisted again.

V

First Partakers

AFTER THE SMOKE OF DEBATE had cleared from the Lend-Lease Act more and more people started noticing that about one billion dollars of it was to be spent on food. But it was months before the agrarian isolationism that had helped fight the Lend-Lease Bill was harnessed for the production of that food. True, farmers were enjoying the biggest crops in years and were increasing their operations according to their best-known formula—official predictions of next year's market price.

The increase, however, was small stuff beside the mounting requirements for our allies and our own appetites. Even in the days of national defense, with housewives spending more of their husbands' fatter pay checks at the corner grocery store, officials proclaimed that the Arsenal of Democracy would also be the Larder of Democracy.

A more glamorous version of the same thought gained currency on Department of Agriculture posters: *Food will win the war and write the peace!*

The beginning goals for lend-lease aid and our own military use were large, but their size did not begin to penetrate until official estimates for the marketing year beginning in mid-September of 1942 were drawn up. Expressed in terms

o,f the proportion of our total supply which would be taken
for these purposes, they are:

	Per Cent
Eggs	20 to 25
Dry edible beans	25
Canned salmon	60
Canned pilchards (sardines)	60 to 70
Beef, pork, veal, and lamb	25
Lard	33
American cheese	60
Dry skim milk	45
Evaporated milk	29
Butter	10
Dry whole milk	60
Canned fruit and juices	25
12 canned vegetables	35
Dried apples, apricots, peaches, pears	95 to 100
Raisins and prunes	50

The size of the farmers' job is evident. That some of these
same items will be rationed is not necessarily an indication
of farmers' failure; the job of becoming the Larder of
Democracy is a tremendous one.

It was on April 3, 1941, that Secretary Wickard announced his basic proposal for getting food and livestock
enough for a global war. The technique chosen was not
new. It was financial inducement. The Surplus Marketing
Administration of the department, he revealed, would thereafter buy huge stocks of pork, butter, and eggs frequently
enough to maintain prices of those commodities at levels
which would bring "reasonable returns" to the farmers and
insure an "adequate supply" for British needs. Without in-
quiring into the merits of guaranteeing prices to farmers

in view of what was being done for labor, industry, or any other economic bloc, it can be stated that Wickard was inducing his farmers to throw their thinking into reverse and release the productive power which years of AAA training had put on the shelf.

It was often but erroneously observed in that transitional period that, luckily, the United States' traditional surplus of crops would be rushed into the fight. The fallacy in that offhand opinion is that the real surpluses, in the old-fashioned sense of the word, did not happen to correspond to the needs of the Allies. Aside from some highly seasonal surpluses, such as apples and citrus fruits which can be packed in some concentrated form for shipping abroad, the surpluses of recent years have been in bulky cotton, wheat, corn, and the minor cereal crops. The Allies needed mainly pork, dairy, and poultry products, like lard, pork cuts, canned milk, cheese, and eggs. This competition for a select list of foods cast a lengthening shadow over the rural landscape.

As might be expected, it was at this point—when high prices might be written off as part of the war—that the farm bloc started riding high. An examination of the alternatives which lay before Wickard on how to get new levels of production lays bare the roots of the bloc's strength. Within this category the story of pork is most illustrative, because, first, it has been subject to control from both the pig-production end and the corn-for-feed end, and, second, it was one of the early items to get beyond the reach of housewives.

According to a department report issued early in 1941 it was certain that the number of hogs marketed in the first quarter of 1941–42 marketing year would be smaller than in 1940. Regardless of who was to blame, pork supplies

were decreasing just when they were needed most. The
Secretary was forced to take action. Being a veteran corn-
hog farmer himself, he is presumed to have known what
was coming. The choice, in general, lay between two
courses: He could release huge stocks of government-held
corn for hog feed at an economical level, or he could jack
up the price of hogs artificially, making their production
profitable either way. What the latter course lacked in
economic soundness it made up for in political appeal.
Subsequent battles with the Farm Bureau Federation over
release of even spoiled grain for feeding were to prove that.

The relationship of corn to pork is one of the many
complicated chapters in agricultural lore which have kept
the curtain drawn so long between consumer and farmer.
In its mathematical form it is called the corn-hog ratio and
has carried the strength of scripture among farmers ever
since it was worked out by an Iowa farmer named Henry
Wallace. The idea is this: It normally requires 11.6 bushels
of corn to equal in value 100 pounds of hog. When the
ratio is higher than 11.6, corn is too expensive to be fed to
hogs. Before Wickard's April-third program the ratio had
been as low as 9, and hog production had been unprofitable.
With hogs at the artificially supported price of $9 per
hundredweight, however, the ratio became favorable for
more production.

The reason for high corn prices is clearly traceable to the
fact that the farm bloc wrote into the Agricultural Adjustment Act of 1938 a mandatory, strait-jacket provision for
the determination of corn prices in the form of high corn-
loan rates. There was little point in going to the trouble of
feeding hogs when the stored-up corn could be turned over
to Uncle Sam for payment of the loan. Quite naturally the
shortage developed.

But as hog production was declining, corn stocks were shooting upward. Government stocks from foreclosed loans grew from only a few million bushels in 1938 to around 475,000,000 bushels in 1940. The department estimated that by the fall of 1941 stocks would have reached about 600,000,000 bushels if the new floor under hog prices had not interceded, making it profitable to feed the grain.

Up to that point, however, everything had worked out in conformity with another program, the Ever-Normal Granary. Ample supplies existed against any foreseeable emergency. One of those emergencies had arrived, and the corncribs of the land were bulging. The process of turning the corn into pork awaited only the signal from Washington to open the granaries—the philosophy of the Ever-Normal Granary had momentarily been justified. But Wickard refused to unlock the bins. Of course he knew that Congress would challenge him if he did, but he refused to stick out his neck.

Instead the Secretary cautiously released a trial balloon in the form of pointing out the desirability of greater hog production. There were two reactions to his feeler. On the one hand, the Nebraska *Farmer*, well-known rural journal, commented: "If the government wants to stimulate the greatest use of corn and clear its decks of burdensome storage supplies, it might better lower the loan levels to a point consistent with profitable use."

On the other hand, the majority of the farm bloc spread alarm at the idea of cheap corn. One lobbyist expressed the fear that farmers might "go crazy and shove pig production up 10 to 15 per cent."

Everything about pork but its production climbed. By February of 1941 the price of pork at the average butcher shop was 24 per cent higher than in the same month of the previous year. By April first the country-wide average for pork chops was over 30 cents a pound. Each month new highs were reached.

It was about this time that the British demands for pork and other products became a hard reality. As the battle of the Atlantic became tighter, cries for help grew louder. The need for speed, plus demands of the farm bloc, turned Wickard's decision to stimulation of production by forced high prices.

Everyone had a finger in the pie except consumers. What had happened to them? Was there not a Consumer Division in the National Defense Advisory Commission? Had there not been for years a Consumers Counsel in the Department of Agriculture? Henderson was supposed to be known for his mistrust of high prices and attacks on special-interest groups. Why was there no protest against Wickard's decision to induce production at the expense, literally, of consumers?

The pathetic story of consumer agencies in the government is a confused one, but a thumbnail sketch of one chapter in it explains much of the farm bloc's success. The department's Consumers Counsel, though an able official, has always been in the impossible position of being assigned to protect consumer interests while being paid by the Department of Agriculture. The better he does his job, the more apt he is to be fired.

The Defense Commission's Consumer Division, on the other hand, owed no allegiance to anyone but the public; it was established on a par with William Knudsen's Production Division, Edward Stettinius' Priorities Division, etc. But its head, Harriet Elliott, was not the heavyweight necessary to keep up with the rough-and-tumble fighting that marked the early days of the defense program. As dean of women at North Carolina University she was able and efficient, but the intricacies of Washington and pressure politics were not for Miss Elliott, whose quiet persuasion technique was no substitute for table pounding.

About the time her staff had built up pertinent data and was in a position to function effectively Miss Elliott was reduced in rank to assistant administrator of the newly created Office of Price Administration and Civilian Supply under Henderson. This move need not have buried her, as Henderson's history is one of consumer interest. In fact, he was once a consumer representative on the NRA. Moreover, it seemed that Miss Elliott would be nearer to the source of price orders, so that she could swing the ax from closer range. She was completely outmaneuvered, however, until one day it was learned by accident that she had returned to North Carolina.

Unfortunately for her reputation with consumers, she did not leave until after signing a historical statement for which she will ever be criticized. It was her joint endorsement, with Henderson, of Wickard's decision to jack up prices. Tacked inconspicuously at the end of the Wickard press release of April 3 was this simple declaration which went almost unnoticed by the press: "This program contemplates moderate price increases for certain commodities over the two-year period which will cover the costs of additional production required during the coming year. At the same time, it should forestall more extreme price advances later on by insuring consumers of adequate supplies."

Miss Elliott, it is known, had been advised of the wisdom of releasing corn rather than boosting prices on pork, but she went along with the crowd. Henderson had just previously "stabilized" lumber, steel, and scrap-metal prices at or below the market level, but he departed completely from that formula for food. When asked about that very fact at his first press conference after appointment to OPACS, Henderson stated that "he didn't know as much as he should" about the principle of parity, but could be expected to follow the "Administration line" on agricultural matters. Actually he knows a great deal about parity. For example, during his time on the Securities and Exchange Commission he was tutored in parity by Edward C. Eicher, former high-parity congressman from Iowa and SEC chairman.

What Miss Elliott did not do was to call attention to facts like the official estimate that the price of pork chops would jump from 25 cents to 35 or 40 cents a pound because of this program alone. The pattern of thinking which pushed the Consumer Division into oblivion (it was finally merged with OPA's information setup) is an old one in Washington. It was inscribed years ago, with two other quotations, above the front entrance of the Department of Agriculture:

> *The husbandman that laboreth*
> *must be first partaker*
> *of the fruits.* SAINT PAUL

The general tug of war over basic feed prices, of which the pork situation is only one part, comes each year at appropriation time on Capitol Hill. The farm bloc's annual field day comes when the Department of Agriculture's budget is up for justification and debate. Not only do the farm leaders get to come to town at those times to testify in behalf of their respective payers of expense accounts, but the Secretary of Agriculture and his advisers are summoned for a review of the past year's programs. It is the ideal time to put the department over a barrel—maybe even a pork barrel—and exact promises of good behavior for the ensuing year. The experience of two war-year appropriation struggles demonstrates the farm-bloc variations on the theme of "Food will win the war and write the peace."

Early in 1941 the Farm Bureau, as the strongest group in the bloc, announced its intention of getting commodity-loan legislation boosted to a level of 75 per cent of parity. By the middle of May both sides of Congress had gone the Farm Bureau ten points better; they had fixed loans at 85 per cent of parity on five basic commodities: cotton, wheat, corn, tobacco, and rice. The latter two, which are "basic" only to those who grow them, were then up to that level; but it was estimated officially at the time of debate that raising the level to 85 per cent on all five would inflate the cost of living about 10 per cent. The Farm Bureau insisted that it would be only 5 per cent.

President Roosevelt signed the bill, technically a clause in the Commodity Credit Corporation appropriation, with the statement that farm leaders in Congress had promised him that prices would not go above parity. Assuming that the President was speaking truthfully, it was just one year later that the pledge to him was broken, when the same farm leaders wrote the famous 110-per-cent-of-parity floor into the Emergency Price Control Act. They apparently had a short wrestle with their consciences before doing so, for the mimeographed drafts of the act which were first flashed to waiting reporters showed the figure "110" was written in ink over a crossed-out "100."

Another farm move of that period was not so successful. The Senate Agriculture Committee, which always puts its hand in appropriation matters as well, recommended for parity and other cash benefits the staggering total of $1,333,000,000. This time the Administration balked. The President's Budget Bureau, in consultation, of course, with Secretary Wickard, tried to knock $450,000,000 off the sum to divert it to mounting defense expenditures. Henry Morgenthau, Jr., Secretary of the Treasury, lashed out on at least two major occasions in support of the Budget Bureau and told a press conference that the difference between the Budget request and the Agriculture Committee demands was an amount equal to 6 per cent on annual normal corporation taxes.

The reason for using Morgenthau, instead of Wickard, to oppose pressure for more farm money was never made clear. It was generally assumed that Wickard asked someone else to turn the heat on farm leaders with whom he had to remain popular. Certainly Morgenthau could not be classified as anti-farm, however. He was chairman of the governor's Agricultural Advisory Commission of New York under Franklin D. Roosevelt and governor of the Farm Credit Administration early in the New Deal. As part of a concession for getting the 85-per-cent loan level, the bloc allowed the $450,000,000 margin between Morgenthau and the Senate Committee to be whittled down to $212,-000,000.

About the same time another pressure bloc, the dairy congressmen, was putting pressure in a different way on the department and Henderson's price controllers. At an unpublicized and overlooked meeting about forty congressmen got together Monday night, April 21, 1941, to see what could be done about getting higher prices in defiance of the statutory mechanism then being established for regulating farm prices. In a letter to each of the 435 members of the House the confab was called by Representative Joshua L.

Johns, of Wisconsin, who signed it as chairman of the Republican Congressional Delegation from the state which calls itself America's Dairyland on license plates. Johns's occupation is listed as lawyer, farmer, and businessman; he was president of Kiwanis International in 1933.

After outlining Wickard's April program for supporting prices on several commodities including butter, Johns wrote this summons to his colleagues: "This is such an important matter to all farmers of the United States that the Wisconsin delegation feels that there should be a meeting of all congressmen and other interested groups held to discuss and take some action requesting, and if necessary, insisting on the Department of Agriculture fixing a price sufficient on all farm products to receive the same treatment as others are receiving in the National Defense program."

The caucus was held in the House Agriculture Committee hearing room and was visited by Chairman Fulmer, of that committee, long enough for him to announce his intention of introducing legislation which would force higher payments to farmers.

Besides the House members present, there were two or three senators and two officials from the Agriculture Department who appeared in behalf of Wickard at the request of Johns. They were Carl C. Farrington, vice-president of the Commodity Credit Corporation, and Oris V. Wells, economist in charge of the Division of Program Development and Co-ordination in the Bureau of Agricultural Economics. Henderson was invited, but wrote the group afterward that he had been out of town.

The two agriculture officials no doubt wished later that they had been as fortunate as the price administrator, for they were subjected to a nerve-racking third degree from the dairy representatives. Mainly they were asked why their boss had not set his price goal much higher—particularly on dairy products, but also on pork and poultry items. Then it was mentioned that under the Secretary's program he held authority to sell back on the market quantities of the very foods he was buying up for lend-lease. The power had been written in as a safety valve to keep him from getting stuck with an unusable stock of commodities or with runaway prices that could be deflated by throwing the commodities on the commercial market.

At this point it was indignantly suggested to the guests from the department that their agency was becoming more and more of a consumer agency. Specifically, Wells and Farrington were quizzed about the fact that the department even had a Consumers Counsel on its pay roll.

The congressmen had put their collective finger, unwittingly perhaps, on a contradiction which becomes more obvious daily: that a so-called "fair" price to the farmer can never be also a "fair" price to the consumer. One of the two definitions must be changed before both groups can be permanently happy. This is a pill which of course could not be swallowed by a group such as was meeting that night, but it was not the subject for which they had congregated. Of more importance in stirring up their feud with consumers was the background fact that the Consumers Counsel had once suggested that some people might want to try a substitute for butter. There is no place on Wisconsin license plates for substitutes for butter.

Parity, as has just been shown in the dairy field, is by no means the only goal of the farm bloc. Once parity is attained, or abandoned as impossible, the strategy becomes one of jockeying side issues around to the advantage of an interested group. This usually involves a restrictive formula

—some way to stifle competition. In the cases of beef and wool that restriction takes the form of building tariff walls or something equivalent and settling down to enjoy the fruits of protection.

The cozy situation of the wool industry was attained largely while the director of purchasing for the Office of Production Management was Donald M. Nelson, present chairman of the War Production Board and holder of a great reputation as a shrewd buyer and executive head of Sears, Roebuck and Company. In the spring of 1941, while Congress was considering extension of its old law to exclude foreign products from acquisition by the government, unless three conditions made it almost impossible to get domestic goods, the wool lobby called on Nelson. F. R. Marshall, secretary-treasurer of the National Wool Growers Association; C. J. Fawcett, general manager of the National Wool Marketing Corporation, and J. B. Wilson, secretary of the Wyoming Wool Growers Association, told the procurement chief that woolmen were not getting the benefit they should from the defense program. Nelson apparently did not try to convince them that the program was for the benefit of no particular group, for he offered them concessions by which future bids for wool were to be let at a time and in a manner favorable to the growers.

According to a letter from Nelson to Senator O'Mahoney, inserted in the *Congressional Record* on April first of that year, the lobbyists "were in full accord and seemed to be tremendously pleased" with the agreement reached. This impression was confirmed by a public statement from Nelson's office which explained that the move had been taken to "enable the woolgrowers to benefit more directly from the defense program."

Even though the bulk of foreign-grown wool comes from one of the United Nations, Australia, the armed services have an arrangement whereby premium prices are paid for domestic wool. The quartermaster of the Army submits bids for woolens of three types—all American, part American, and all foreign—paying more for the first two.

The industry once tried to justify its deal by citing figures to the effect that about one half of the 1941 production of shorn wool had not gone into consumption by September 27 of that same year, thereby supposedly proving that there was an abundance on hand which should be used before importing lower-priced foreign wool. Early in the next month, however, the War Department issued a release stating that the domestic wool supply was too low for comfort. An anonymous government official confided that one reason for the shortage feared by the War Department was that wool associations had advised members to hold back their wool in order to cash in on a rising market.

Against the industry's assertion that there has been no need to let down trade barriers to Australian wool stand cuffless trousers and the fact that the WPB limitation order on wool allowed civilians only 22½ per cent of a base, normal consumption for three months ending in January of 1943 and 40 per cent from then until July 31 of this year.

In appraising the wool bloc it is not immaterial to note that the head of WPB's wool section is Kenneth Marriner, who came to Washington from the wool industry, and that the largely uneconomic wool industry of the country has been protected by tariffs for years on the sale of about 600,000,000 pounds a year to American consumers. "Business as usual" can be applied to agriculture as well as to other industries.

The congressional farm bloc is quick to scent the most remote threat to its supremacy. Late in November of 1942, President Roosevelt asked for a third War Powers Bill to lift bans on importation of certain information, aliens, and strategic material. After administration leaders explained its necessity there was no opposition expressed on Capitol Hill to letting the President do what he said would be done under the enlarged power, even though most of the explaining was done in closed committee meetings for military reasons.

But many congressmen, including those from agricultural districts, read into the bill all sorts of dire, unmentioned potentialities. Some only feared the President would tear down immigration restrictions, but the farm bloc imagined itself in danger of having great stocks of farm products brought into the country to compete with theirs. At that very time meat rationing had been announced for the near future, butter rationing was probable, milk was short in many cities, and canned foods had been limited at the wholesale level; yet the bloc yelled as if it faced obliteration.

Testimony of War Shipping Administrator Emory S. Land that no ships would be available to bring in large quantities of food failed to salve the congressmen. Republican gains in that month's elections fired the suspicion and revolt against the Administration in the direction of clipping executive wings.

The lobby marched up Pennsylvania Avenue and beat on the door of the Ways and Means Committee. Charles Holman, for milk; J. G. Montague, attorney for the Texas and Southwestern Cattle Raisers Association, and J. H. Connaughton, for the Hot House Vegetable Growers, stood pat against letting any agricultural products into the country. In addition, Holman and Connaughton served notice that their organizations would fight renewal of the reciprocal-trade-agreements program, authority for which expires automatically on June 12, 1943, unless renewed by Congress.

Representative Frank Carlson, Kansas Republican, assured the protesters that if the War Powers Bill reached the House floor he would try to amend it to guarantee that the "quarantine" on beef would not be tampered with. More than any other foreign-trade issue the beef bloc worries about competition from Argentine and Chilean beef. One reason is an instinctive defense against a product which could undersell theirs; another is the fact that the dread foot-and-mouth disease can be carried from infected areas of those countries into healthy countries to sweep through its herds.

Ostensibly for the latter reason, Congress empowered the Secretary of Agriculture to quarantine trouble spots. Those clamped down on, however, say that only parts of each country are infected, leaving no reason for banning meat from disease-free parts. Each time reciprocal trade with Argentina or Chile is mentioned, beef becomes the block. Domestic producers will not budge from their position that the two Good Neighbors are unclean. The department, recognizing the political hot spot it is on, sent out a scientific mission to re-examine the sanitation problem, but its report has not been released.

Meanwhile Chile and Argentina are allowed to sell canned meat (canning kills the disease), but only where the cattle bloc has not cut them out by special legislation in the name of something other than sanitation. If the strategy seems like that used by the dairy industry against margarine, there is a reason—beef and dairy cattlemen work together in the anti-competition corner.

No consumer wants to pay food prices so low as to take advantage of or exploit the farmer who raised the food. No consumer wants sweatshops on the farm. He will gladly pay enough to be fair, but drawing the line between fair and unfair prices is difficult, perhaps impossible. Even the proponents of parity admit that their formula is not the ultimate answer, but only one measure. Therefore consumers and farmers will be at loggerheads over prices for a long time to come.

But what consumers resent and will continue to feel is an unjust burden on them are the restrictive measures by which uneconomic segments of the farm bloc perpetuate themselves. Of course the story of artificial marketing laws, sanitary restrictions, and tariffs is not peculiar to agriculture; but it does involve agriculture heavily. Even though farmers may be building up to a house of cards which will tumble overnight, the consumer dislikes being gouged while the paper structure goes up. In many instances the first partaker has become the only partaker.

VI

The Milk Lobby

HALFWAY UP THE BLOCK FROM 17th on Washington's I Street, also written "Eye Street," is the fountainhead of pressure from the most firmly established of all farm organizations. Distinguished from the other miscellaneous buildings along there by an American flag over the door, the three-story structure also attracts attention by a polished brass name plate beside the entrance:

AGRICULTURAL
CO-OPERATIVE
HEADQUARTERS

AMERICAN INSTITUTE
OF CO-OPERATION

NATIONAL COUNCIL OF
FARMER COOPERATIVES

NATIONAL CO-OPERATIVE
MILK PRODUCERS'
FEDERATION

WASHINGTON MILK
MARKETING ORDER

NOTARY PUBLIC

Proprietor of this unique establishment is Charles W. Holman, secretary since 1921 of the organization which owns the property, the National Co-operative Milk Producers' Federation. The federation, though only one of many members of the institute and the council, acquired its big red stone house eleven years ago and rents space to the others. Also the veteran Holman's personality runs through, and sometimes dominates, other activities at 1731 Eye. It should. He accurately claims to be the oldest living Washington representative of agriculture, having started in 1917 by working for passage of the Capper-Volstead Act —the Magna Carta, yea, the Bill of Rights of co-operation to this day.

Until passage of that famous statute, farmers who organized to bargain for prices and marketing conditions were liable to prosecution under the antitrust laws. Their co-operation to eliminate middlemen in the distributive process and to eliminate cutthroat competition among themselves was unlawful. Now there is no such barrier, and farmers have honeycombed their markets with two kinds of co-operatives: producers and purchasing. The Department of Agriculture has estimated that during the 1940–41 season there were in existence 10,600 co-operative associations of both kinds, having a membership of 3,400,000 and an annual volume of business of nearly $3,000,000,000.

The farm bloc has roots in each of these, especially the one directed by Charlie Holman. Not only does the Milk Producers' Federation speak for a majority of milk farmers, measured by volume, but milk farmers, in turn, contribute the largest single chunk to the total farm income in America. Also the federation is the most aggressive of the co-ops on the legislative front; it is the only division of the National Co-op Council which supports a Washington office. Because it so often stands on its hind legs, the federation is usually thought of as a separate organization. On a par with its parent, the Co-op Council, and with the National Grange and Farm Bureau, the Milk Producers are one of the "Big Four."

Holman has been secretary of the Milk Producers for all five of the association's presidents. First was Milo D. Campbell, who retired to become the first dirt farmer on the Federal Reserve Board of Governors. He was succeeded by Judge John D. Miller, who was later elected president of the National Council of Farmer Cooperatives, in which capacity he served about nine years.

Next came Harry Hartke, described by Holman as a prominent businessman who got mad because farmers in his community weren't getting a square deal. He had a dairy farm himself and formed an organization which went on strike for forty-one days when the dairy distributors of the market area refused to recognize it. After winning the strike the outraged farmers bought out the largest dairy— or, rather, are still buying it year by year—and went into the distribution end of the business for themselves.

Nathan P. Hull was the next head of the Milk Producers. Hull not only served twenty-one years as president and was interested in the Co-operative Institute, but once was master of the Michigan State Grange and manager of its insurance company. He is now operating the dairy farm on which he was born.

The incumbent head of the organization is John Brandt, of Minnesota, who founded and is now president of the powerful, militant, and gigantic Land O' Lakes Creameries. Brandt had served on the Milk Producers' Board of Directors for years, as is the usual line of succession, and has been a leading conservative figure in the Northern dairy lands for years.

Charles Holman is a big man—both in size and around town. His dark-clothed frame is a familiar one in Washington, though he wastes little time in advertising his wares except where fertile soil lies. Gray and balding, Holman can transform himself, by clamping a pair of pince-nez on a sturdy nose, from a tough-looking ex-dairy farmer, which he is not, to a rugged-looking businessman, which he is.

From his office, a former front parlor, the milk lobbyist operates by long-distance telephone, local telephone, and taxi. Anyone stopping at the big red building will probably walk by Holman's open door before passing on back to the large quarters of his staff and the converted dining room which encloses high-strategy meetings too large for his slightly musty but efficient office.

His vigorous, twenty-two-year fight for dairymen has made for Holman more enemies than some lobbyists have, partly because not all on whom he must exert his pressure go in for the temper-tantrum type of influence. Others admire his frankness, tap his great fund of knowledge, and remain on intimate terms with him. Of course there are many in town who see eye to eye with the boss of 1731 Eye Street. But few remain who remember Holman's early association with the long-defunct Industrial Workers of the World.

An expert judge of congressional sentiment, Holman can predict results of a close vote, though he maintains that he never tells a member of Congress how to vote. That part of the game he leaves to others, while he stirs up the communities involved.

Contrary to the system used by many association secretaries in writing annual reports, that used by Holman is comparatively frank. An examination of his 1941 report to the federation annual convention, plus the association's resolutions, reveals the cards which Holman plays in Washington.

First he recalled the two Chicago Emergency Defense Meetings which were called by the federation in May and August of 1941. The farm leaders who convened there, the report stated, "demanded agricultural equality with industry and labor. They opposed rigid price fixing on farm commodities by the government. They called for a cessation of labor disturbances which were proving inimical to the national defense. They insisted on prices to farmers which would compensate them for current production as well as for increased capital outlay, particularly in the light of the government's request for increased production —just as industry receives a cost-plus guarantee for its defense production."

The second of those meetings was more concerned with parity and a need for its redefinition upward. "They indicated their belief that the prevailing legislative conception of parity was antiquated and unfitted to meet the present needs of farmers—a concept which tied farmers to an income level equivalent to that which they received as long ago as 1909 to 1914."

Continuing with his own annual report, Holman opined that the parity determination "tends to freeze the farmer's standard of living at the base period, while the real income or purchasing power of industrial workers continues to rise with increasing wage rates and shorter hours resulting from improvements in industrial technique."

Therefore he advocated an entirely new parity concept, a movement in which he is still a leader. Not only would he change the base years to the period of 1920 to 1929 inclusive, but he would have the Bureau of Agricultural Economics use a radically different method in computing parity. Instead of counting commodities purchased for family living as about half of the technical index, Holman would not count them. But, whereas BAE does not now consider the wage rates of city workers, Holman would use them for one half of his proposed index—a maneuver which would hoist food prices many notches.

The anti-labor position of the federation has never been concealed. It takes two forms: resisting unionization of dairy operations specifically, and falling in with general anti-union political activity. On the former, a 1941 resolution of the convention is clear in stating that "not only are the war industries besieged with strikes, but the pressure tactics of many in the labor field are gradually finding their way into agriculture, particularly the co-operatives." Opposition was summoned to "this unwarranted interference of whatever character with the marketing of farm products." No effort was made to explain why, for example, wage workers in pasteurizing plants should not be allowed to join a union as much as are any other workers.

The federation's second anti-labor line is evident from its demand for amendments to the National Labor Relations (Wagner) Act and the Fair Labor Standards Act (wages and hours). In its simplest sense, this takes the form of asking "adequate exemption and protection for agriculture," but that request has screened a reprehensible chapter in labor-relations history.

A combination of pretenders and bona fide farmers has fought for years to keep farm hands from coming under social legislation on the grounds that their peculiar conditions make it both impossible and undesirable to regulate them. The impossibility of aiding a great many agricultural workers by legislation alone is admitted, but efforts to exempt men who pack fruit, shell nuts, pick vegetables, and work in processing plants are mostly phony evasions of responsibility. They parallel closely the original fight to exempt newspaper employees from the Wagner and Wage-Hour acts on the grounds that to include them would destroy freedom of the press. While there was room for arguing both points, the advocates were not sincere in doing so.

On the affirmative side of the legislative front, Holman reported fair progress. A bill introduced by Representative Herman P. Kopplemann, of Connecticut, was designed to "prohibit milk dealers from participating in any manner in the affairs of bona fide milk producers' co-operative associations or bargaining agencies." This bill, "which the federation assisted Mr. Kopplemann in drafting," was showing only little progress, however.

Of a brighter nature, Holman told his convention, was a sanitary import bill, on which the federation "collaborated" with Representative August H. Andresen, of Minnesota. This measure was "designed to tighten the protective features of such laws as the Lenroot-Taber Milk and Cream Inspection Act, the foot-and-mouth embargo provisos of the 1930 Tariff Act, and other health measures which are on the statute books." Most of these Holman will take credit for having fostered, and most of them are camouflage for keeping foreign competition from the milk and beef farmers of the United States.

Holman's chief legislative worry at that time was a bill by Representative Robert L. Doughton, chairman of the powerful Ways and Means Committee, to remove import duties, excise taxes, or other restrictions on articles certified by the government to be defense articles. In practical application, Holman moaned, it could mean the duty-free importation of dairy and meat products without regard to sanitary restrictions now imposed by the same Lenroot-Taber Act and the foot-and-mouth embargo provisions of the 1930 Tariff Act. After noting that the federation opposed the measure in "communications directed to many congressional leaders," Holman sighed that "Committee hearings on the bill, for the time being at least, have been abandoned."

The foreign-trade picture looked bad for the Milk Producers. Although farmers have traditionally been the butt of high protective tariffs, because prices paid by them for industrial goods have been jacked up by high tariffs, the reciprocal-tariff program of the Administration has failed to mollify Holman. By reciprocation, Secretary of State Cordell Hull has sought to reduce tariff barriers gradually with a score of nations. Quite naturally patrons of each commodity would rather see some commodity other than theirs make concessions to competing imports in the name of international good will and prosperity. Milk producers are like that, only more so.

The core of Hull's administration of the Trade Agreement Act has been Latin-American relations, and the success of his policy in that field has been pointedly demonstrated by the invaluable allegiance of Good Neighbors during this war. Perhaps the most delicate of these relations were with big Argentina, whose politics were not clearly anti-Axis and whose economy happens to correspond to that of our agricultural West. When it came time, therefore, to draft an agreement with Argentina, the State Department had to reduce import tariffs on *something*, if Argentina were to have any reason to enter into the arrangement for exporting goods to the United States. Among the products chosen were cheese, casein (the protein of milk), canned beef, oleo oil (beef fat), cattle hides and skins—all items of selfish interest to the Milk Producers' Federation and essential in keeping Argentina one of the Good Neighbors.

In view of the trouble that came later in holding Argentina in line—or at least away from Hitler's side—the comments of Holman on the Argentina problem are significant: "In 1940 . . . we imported from Argentina about 81 million dollars' worth of goods, of which 72 million dollars were represented by agricultural products. Out of these agricultural products, at least 57 million dollars, or 79 per cent, were for products that are directly competitive with American farm products. In the face of these facts it is inevitable that the United States farmer must pay the bill for any trade agreement with a country like Argentina." American milkmen will never make Good Neighbors.

Needless to say, the Milk Producers filed a brief against agreements with Argentina, as well as those with Cuba and Uruguay. The absurdity to which they have carried their personal ideas of foreign policy is illustrated by this concluding excerpt from Holman's report on foreign-trade matters: "Every effort to protect this country from the spread of disease infection by means of sanitary restrictions has been fought in late years by the Federal authorities."

The Co-operative Milk Producers depend on manipulating price levers as the way to increase their just share of income. When, in August of 1942, there was growing talk of giving Leon Henderson, as price czar, power to subsidize producers whose goods ought to be under low price ceilings for the sake of holding down the cost of living, the Executive Committee loosed a terrific blast of steam in the direction of the Department of Agriculture on the whole subject of subsidies. Flowery-worded excerpts are self-explanatory:

Opposition to class or group governmental subsidies has been a historic policy of the National Co-operative Milk Producers' Federation. Only under particular circumstances of grave extremity can such a subsidy be even condoned. Under conditions of non-necessity a subsidy becomes a cancer on the body of our economic life. At best it is but a poor patchwork to cover an injustice or to atone for an inequality. . . .

Before and after Pearl Harbor, persons in high official places have been spreading the subsidy snare before the feet of both the willing and the credulous. With respect to commodity prices, this snare has been laid in the paths of both the processors and the farmers. . . .

Great publicity usually accompanies such price payments to farmers. The general public is led to believe that they are special wards of the government marked out for privileged treatment. . . . We regret that the present Federal policy appears to be one of continuing to fight any normal advances in the prices of agricultural products. . . . We urge the nation to remember that dairy farmers of the nation have been particularly involved in the present war effort.

Washington officials who had seen the Milk Producers join with others to form early Administration policy favorable to subsidies and to get artificial legislative restrictions even more effective than subsidies were not impressed by the change of heart. Nor would they be surprised, in time of a dairy-products shortage, to read from the same release a vigorous protest—delivered *after* Pearl Harbor—against existence of stockpiles of dairy products which might conceivably be used to depress prices.

Over eight years ago Holman conveniently listed for his membership twenty-four separate achievements up to that time, mostly before the New Deal, on the congressional front. Some are very technical, but a short list of the others tells as well as anything what the federation went after and got. Sole credit for the accomplishments was not claimed, but in all cases the hand of Holman and his well-oiled machine was boastfully heavy.

As Holman explained it, "Since 1921 the federation . . . has worked with an increasing number of agricultural groups on the general principle of 'one for all and all for one.' Arrayed against powerful industrial lobbies, any other program would have been futile." The more significant accomplishments follow:

The Capper-Volstead Co-operative Act, already explained.

Packers and Stockyards' Act, which brought the wily packing houses and livestock markets under government regulation.

Passage of a bill to stop the "pernicious traffic" (interstate) in filled milk, a combination of coconut or cottonseed oil and evaporated skim milk.

Lenroot-Taber Act, which set sanitary standards high enough to bar milk from Canada.

Emergency Tariff Act of 1921, initiating, among other things, a tariff on butter of 6 cents a pound. (The Tariff Act of 1922 boosted this rate to 8 cents, and when butter continued to come into the United States over that wall, the federation succeeded in obtaining by presidential proclamation an increase to 12 cents. The Tariff Act of 1930, copied from the federation's brief, ran the figure up to 14 cents. There it stuck.)

Legislation creating the Bureau of Dairy Industry and a Co-operative Marketing Division in the Department of Agriculture.

The Brigham Bill, establishing a color test for margarine so as to subject it to heavy tax on the theory that it was being palmed off as butter.

Inclusion in the Agricultural Adjustment Act of twenty-two amendments having to do with making milk a basic commodity and establishing the marketing-agreements system.

The various accomplishments remaining were mixed in with this statement of interest: "The federation has been keenly interested in securing immediate independence for the Philippine Islands, favoring a short transitionary period and low trade quotas"—that is, low competition for members of the federation by kicking the Philippines out of their legal position as an American state in matters of trade.

Activities of the federation are divided between representing milk producers, as against other parts of the milk industry, and helping to represent the entire industry. An example of the former is Holman's leadership in redefining parity prices. An example of his function as only one of several blocs within a big bloc is his position as chairman of National Dairy Month, once a year, an industry-wide promotional stunt.

There are many other dairy associations. Evaporated milk, dried milk, butter, ice cream, and cheese each have their own trade groups. Also there is a Dairy Industry Committee and a Milk Industry Foundation, each of which has a Washington office.

On either score—as a farm lobbyist or as a promoter and protector of one commodity—Holman has earned a reputation as one of Washington's most effective operators.

The American Institute of Co-operation, of which Holman is also secretary and guiding hand, is primarily educational rather than operational. Nevertheless its background and organization throw some light on how part of the farm bloc operates and who its leaders are. According to Holman's own history of the movement, presented at its 1940 meeting, the institute grew out of sessions of the World's Dairy Conference at Syracuse, New York, in 1923, when Holman suggested the revival of what were known as Conferences on Marketing and Farm Credits or similar names. Holman had organized and served as secretary to four of those conferences before the World War caused their discontinuance.

Purposes of the institute, which was organized soon after the Syracuse meeting, included "keeping alight the torch of self-help through utilization of the co-operative method," widening the horizon of seasoned workers in the co-operative movement, and acquainting younger people with the principles of the movement. By January of 1925 the institute had been incorporated under the laws of the District of Columbia as a college.

From that year it has met annually on a different and prominent university campus, hearing lectures on the co-operative principle, until the present war caused it to be suspended. That is not to say, however, that the only influence of the institute has been academic; the overlapping of officers between it and other groups is important.

For example, it was at the first institute meeting that several co-operators decided to integrate their scattered groups into a national organization for action. At the 1928 meeting, on the University of California campus, Holman was authorized to study formation of such an association. The result was the National Council of Farmer Cooperatives. Holman served without pay as secretary of the council for two lean years; he is now one of its directors. When the institute was shelved for the duration its chairman, vice-chairman, and one director either had been or were to be a president of the Co-op Council. Also, Louis J. Taber, while still master of the National Grange, was a director of the institute.

Thirty-two trustees, from about as many farm groups, govern the affairs of the loosely knit alliance. The thirty-five "Participating Organizations" of the institute—those which elect its trustees—include the big general farm organizations as well as commodity associations in cotton, fruit, poultry, wool, potatoes, pecans, livestock, eggs, raisins, and even insurance.

Although the institute did no lobbying, it bulwarked the entire pressure game and of course had headquarters at 1731 Eye Street.

VII

Blocked Margarine

Say, we tried some of that oleomargarine the other day—couldn't get any butter—and y'know it's not bad."

While that line is being repeated from coast to coast as a result of the war-born butter shortage, the dairy lobby works overtime to keep first users of the mysterious butter substitute from forgetting to return after the war to their first love, butter. In fact, it is so engaged in postwar planning that it refuses to drop its tradition of gouging consumers. The great American ignorance of margarine, pronounced either "mar-gar-in" or "mar-jar-in," has been no oversight. It has been planned.

All states except Arizona have enacted some type of law regulating margarine. Two thirds of them flatly prohibit the sale of yellow margarine, which explains the tired arm of the housewife who wants hers yellow and has to mix the little packet of powdered coloring that comes with each pound. The original reason for drawing the color line in table fats was to prevent fraudulent imitation of butter, but under modern labeling laws the purchaser has only to read the word "oleomargarine" on a package. Idaho and Utah not only prohibit the sale of yellow margarine but also tax it 10 cents per pound.

Twenty states ban margarine from use in state institutions, although a few of these allow their convicts to eat it. Twenty-three states have excise taxes ranging from 5 cents on uncolored to 15 cents on colored margarine. Sixteen states require licenses either to manufacture, sell, or serve the maligned product, with fees ranging from $1 to $1,000. Wisconsin goes so far as to hunt down consumers who buy margarine from out of the state and taxes them $1 a year. Several states lift the usual ban enough to allow margarine to be made from raw materials grown in their borders—a measure taken in blunt retaliation to the butter interests that authored most of the restrictions.

When lobbyist Holman wrote, in November of 1941, that "no single issue in these troublesome times has so challenged the dairy industry as has the problem of oleomargarine," it was no fault of his that trouble has been caused. He would ban the competitor forever. As it stands, the controversial substitute for butter has been well hidden from rich and poor alike by almost every device known to lobbyists and pressure groups. It is the only food product discriminated against by Federal tax and one of the few kicked around by states.

In early years dairy producers could base their death struggle with the substitute on the use of foreign oils as opposed to domestic oils, but that was stopped by the war. Since hostilities American oils have made up an increasingly large proportion of the raw materials going into margarine.

Also, in the old days margarine was literally a substitute, an inferior product. By adding vitamin A, however, the industry has fortified its child for the battle and offers consumers a table fat of caloric content and nutritive value equal to butter. The vitamin-A content of butter varies from 1,400 to 27,000 units, depending on the cow's living habits, but neither butter nor margarine should be depended upon as the best or most inexpensive source of this vitamin.

But the encouragement of health authorities to fortify the once lowly margarine has given Holman's group ammunition for trying to discredit the competing food. For example, the federation's 1941 resolution on butter advertising urged that "the American Dairy Association . . . concentrate on butter advertising, and in such advertising bring home to the people of America the facts concerning the nutritional value of this natural product which needs no injection of vitamins or other synthetic properties to make it appear better than it is."

Though war casualties to shipping solved one problem for the dairy interests, the insult of insults came in June of 1941 to infuriate them. The Food and Drug Administration, part of Paul V. McNutt's Federal Security Agency, issued a Federal standard for oleomargarine which permitted the use of milk solids (which give butter its characteristic flavor) in margarine! It was not required—only permitted.

"Nothing that has emanated from governmental departments has so outraged dairy farmers," Holman wrote. For perhaps the first time it had become a crime to allow—not compel, but allow—a product to be improved in taste and quality.

Soon after McNutt's order, which he issued in the interests of fortifying the entire American diet, the dairy lobby fumed over another act of governmental impertinence. On July 5, over a nationwide radio hookup, the Consumers Counsel of the Department of Agriculture worked into a radio skit some forthright advice on margarine. A consumer audience was told that margarine can be used as a butter substitute and may even be cheaper in spite of the taxes on it.

To Holman it was an "enraging episode," a "coup," and a "telling blow." This language was paraphrased by Representative A. H. Andresen, Minnesota lawyer, in a letter to Secretary Wickard and on the floor of Congress; but it failed to dislodge the scientific backing which margarine has compelled, for a long list of scientists has endorsed use of vitamin-enforced margarine.

That was a hard year for butter-protagonist Holman, for with his pet going sky-high in price and working people needing more fats than ever, the restrictions on margarine stuck out like a sore thumb in all their phoniness. Both products contain 80 per cent fat by Federal regulation. At a conference on these and other state barriers to the war effort, chiefly those in transportation, margarine taxes were condemned by M. L. Wilson, McNutt's nutrition chief, director of the Department of Agriculture's Extension Service and formerly Under Secretary of Agriculture. Wilson could hardly be called an oleo stooge, but he was immediately called many other names.

The special Federal-State Conference on War Restrictions, held in May of 1942 under the auspices of the Department of Commerce, was programmed by A. H. Martin, Jr., director of the Marketing Laws Survey. This agency, which began as a WPA research project, had finished studies on state antitrust, price, dairy, and liquor laws, and had gathered exhaustive material on interstate trade barriers. The dairy study alone ran six hundred pages, including all laws passed by pressure groups and a few in the public interest.

Representatives from all forty-eight states were called to Washington to sit around a big table for the purpose of knocking out as many as possible of the barriers to truck transportation and food flow and other stumbling blocks to war mobilization which had been ignored in peacetime. The most fiery speech of the session was delivered by Lieutenant General Brehon Somervell, chief of the Army's Services of Supply, the two-fisted man who has to pour material into hungry Army camps; but many other government officials spoke in behalf of free trade between states in time of emergency. Wilson was one of these. He started his address with an introduction to the particular problem with which he was concerned and thought all state officials should be concerned: An estimated 40,000,000 of our 130,000,000 people —roughly 30 per cent—are not getting a "good diet."

Punctuating his statement with language familiar to farmers, he added: "Some folks say that America has taken better care of its livestock than of its human beings."

Next Wilson quoted from recommendations made by the National Nutrition Conference which had met in Washington the previous year:

Special-interest groups, through private combinations and pressure on public authority, have erected interstate or regional barriers which reduce the opportunity for efficient distribution of foods into consumer's hands, such as discriminatory administration of milk ordinances. We recommend elimination of such restraints.

We oppose the following state or Federal legislation: (a) laws which discriminate against wholesome nutritive foods, such as taxes on colored and uncolored margarine; (b) laws or regulations which favor food products according to the locality in which they are produced, such as laws which permit eggs to be labeled as fresh only if they are produced within a certain area; (c) special taxes to place special kinds of retailers at a disadvantage with others; (d) excise, sales, and processing taxes on foods; (e) price maintenance and unfair sales laws which permit and encourage private price fixing without public control; (f) state marketing or prorate acts which tend

to increase monopoly control and raise prices of foods to consumers.

Supplying the true significance of his indictment, Wilson
then added that "few people who are intimately acquainted
with the functioning state and federal government will con-
tend that many of these state laws and regulations are anything but protective tariffs for commodities produced
within the states."

Those were strong words for all blocs, farm included;
but Wilson then went into what he labeled the "extreme"
example of oleomargarine. Explaining that everyone is interested in avoiding fraud and misrepresentation in food,
Wilson presented the statistical picture of tax discrimination, then gave his version of the impartial judgment of
science: "Margarine fortified with vitamin A becomes a
suitable spread, nutritionally, where butter is out of reach
of the family's pocketbook." Actually many authorities
omit the last qualifying clause. Finally Wilson asked the
assembled state representatives to accept the word of
science.

Officials leaving the august Department of Commerce
auditorium were impressed with the straightforward presentation of this and other challenges. They had not heard
yet from the dairy bloc. The next day butter-champion
Holman had issued a two-page press release that sounded
as if it had been written in a fit of rage. It probably had.

"In his attempt, apparently with some higher official
approval, to turn the support of the Federal government
over to the oleomargarine interests," Holman stormed, "the
speech of M. L. Wilson . . . was sublime only because it
reached the heights of the ridiculous.

"In utter disregard," Holman continued, "of the fact that

more than fifty years ago the Congress found it necessary to safeguard the public health by preventing unethical and fraudulent practices of what was then the oleomargarine industry with respect to production of the product in imitation of butter and sale of the product as butter, Mr. Wilson offered the product to the public as being a new means of improving the diet of the nation in time of war."

Next Holman complained that Wilson disregarded the "congressional policy of requiring the oleomargarine industry and the handlers of the product to pay a slight tax in order to defray the administrative expenses of inspection."

His proposal would also permit the industry "to absorb this tax into their own profits and the public would never know the difference," Holman noted.

But the butter lobbyist was just getting started: "In making this announcement, he had for a background the action of the President's nutrition conference about which the oleomargarine lobbyists and their governmental allies swarmed so thickly that the situation was notorious."

After explaining that other background consisted of Mc-Nutt's action in establishing Federal standards for margarine ingredients, which he said "legalized practically all of the past practices of oleomargarine makers," Holman came to that bitterest pill of all—McNutt had "permitted the use of butter flavoring to make the product taste like butter, and of benzoate of soda to prevent it from going rancid on the grocery shelves." (He didn't mention the fact that in some states, because of the dairy lobby's effectiveness, margarine cannot be kept on grocery shelves, but must be ordered specially by any customer who wants it.)

"We are prepared to take our case to the Congress and as a final resort to take it into this year's congressional elections," he barked.

Last came the peroration: "It is a tragic situation when a government official attempts to use the people's devotion to the war effort as a means of enlarging an already profitable industry at the expense of the dairy farmers, who are now suffering from an economic disparity with other agricultural groups, who are faced with rising production costs, and who, under the recent blanket cutback price-freezing order of the price administrator, in many instances must have their own pittance prices reduced. Such a policy, in the face of continuous wage-rate increases allowed and often abetted by Federal agencies, is bound to create a feeling of despair among our people. This despair will be followed by widespread resistance."

One year after the conference the Federal law was unchanged and only one state had relaxed its gag.

But sewing up most state markets for butter is not enough. For years Holman has been the watchdog of a proviso in several appropriations bills which dictates that no part of the funds shall be used for the purchase of oleomargarine, with trivial exceptions. These frank restrictions apply to the Veterans' Administration (hospitals and homes), St. Elizabeth's Hospital in the District of Columbia (for the mentally ill), and the War and Navy departments.

The bloc goes whole hog against letting the armed services feed their men whatever is best. When Senator David I. Walsh, of Massachusetts, chairman of the Naval Affairs Committeee, merely sought to amend the proviso so as to allow the inclusion of oleomargarine in the official Navy ration wherever climatic or other conditions render the use of butter impracticable, Holman reported to his members that "the federation immediately went into action in opposition to the measure." As matters stood after at least one and one half years of war, the Navy was barred from using margarine for anything but cooking purposes. The Army could use it only when climatic or other conditions made the use of butter impracticable—or when soldiers specifically requested it.

However, margarine does have friends in the farm bloc, though most of them work quietly. The loose alliance of backers of the raw materials which go into the product —soybean oil, cottonseed oil, and beef products in particular —stand behind unshackling margarine. Most of them stand so far behind, however, that margarine is to date little more than their stepchild.

As the two raw-material blocs charge into a head-on collision, the picture is roughly this: Milk for butter is produced in the New England, north-central, northwestern, and a few other states; whereas the material for margarine comes largely from the South and increasingly from the Midwest. Obviously Holman's apprehension was justified in 1941 when two Southern representatives introduced bills to repeal the Federal taxes on retailers of margarine.

Of particular significance is the fact that one of them, Hampton P. Fulmer, from vegetable-oil-producing South Carolina, is chairman of the House Committee on Agriculture. On the effort to remove the $6 tax on retailers of uncolored oleomargarine and the $48 tax on those of colored margarine, Holman lamented: "Historically, the former tax has been on the statutes since 1902 and the latter since 1886. They are a part of the pattern of legislation which organized dairy farmers fought for and secured in the early days marking the advent of oleo as a butter substitute."

The other bill was written by an Alabaman, Representative Sam Hobbs, and was in retaliation to the Gillette-

Andresen bills which sought to ban, among other things, margarine flavored with milk. Hobbs's measure, oddly enough, would prohibit the interstate shipment of *butter* containing artificial color or flavor.

By way of a prophetic admission, Holman wrote that "the dairy industry must gird itself for the most important fight it has had as yet in the battle of oleo versus butter. It should realize that it must fortify itself with the needed additional nutritional data of which at present it is woefully lacking, if it is to be heard by those in authority."

Meanwhile those in authority were interested in facts like these, left by butter-man Holman with his Milk Producers: "The current level of oleomargarine consumption is close to 400 million pounds on an annual basis. Before the war started the (price) spread between butter and oleo was about 16 cents per pound. Last year this spread averaged 20 cents, and for the month of September 1941 it averaged 25.5 cents. As may be expected, this widening spread has pushed oleomargarine consumption to a new high level."

Nowhere has the bloc-within-bloc aspect of farm pressure been more clearly laid out than in a five-page, single-spaced letter from National Cotton Council President Oscar Johnston to Representative Clarence Cannon, chairman of the powerful House Appropriations Committee. Writing under date of April 20, 1942, Johnston was protesting the press report of a meeting one month earlier of a special Congressional Dairy Committee representing twenty-four states.

According to the press dispatch, Cannon had told colleagues that they must "drive home" to Southern congressmen that the use of butter substitutes does not increase the price of cotton. The congressmen had met with leaders of the dairy industry "to map strategy against pending legis-

lation to repeal licenses for retailers of oleomargarine."
Johnston further reminded Cannon that the news story had
quoted him as follows:

"Cannon also declared the Department of Agriculture
was 'honeycombed' with men who are getting outside salaries, and Charles Holman, Washington representative of
the National Milk Producers' Federation, declared the 'oleo
people' were 'well entrenched' in the Department of Commerce, the Bureau of Agricultural Economics, the Consumers Counsel division, and the Federal Security Agency."

Conceding that the use of margarine does not increase the
price of cotton, Johnston asserted in his letter to Cannon,
however, that "the use of margarine does . . . substantially and materially contribute to the income of the American cotton farmer" because of the fact that margarine consumed the cottonseed oil produced on 257,478 farms by the
same number of families.

"If these figures are correct," Johnston wrote, "even my
good friend, Charles Holman, a leader of the dairy bloc,
will agree that the use of margarine is of vital importance
to the American cotton farmer."

Punching the point home, Johnston added: "In addition
to using the quantity of cottonseed oil above stated, there
were consumed in the manufacture of margarine in the cal-
endar year 1941, 78,628,791 pounds of soybean oil, 67,321,-
911 pounds of domestically produced milk, and 12,627,503
pounds of salt."

Denying that the council represents margarine manufacturers, Johnston asserted that "the function and objective
of the National Cotton Council is to promote and expand
the consumption of cotton, cottonseed, and the products
thereof.

"In efforts to achieve this objective," he stated, "the council . . . has fought, and shall continue to fight, with all its power, all its ability, and all its resources, the effort being made by dairy interests and manufacturers of dairy products to stifle or suppress traffic in margarine where that commodity is manufactured from domestically produced ingredients."

The indignant Southerner then drew a contrast between dairymen's attitude toward margarine and the cotton industry's attitude toward its own competing fiber, rayon. "Rayon," he wrote, "is produced by a very limited number of corporations whose stock is rather closely held and whose resources are almost unlimited. The Cotton Industry has witnessed serious inroads made by rayon. We have sought to fight this by proclaiming and advertising the value and virtue of cotton products. We have not sought to forbid or to penalize the use of rayon by the American public by legislation."

Within the year the Cotton Council was to fight bitterly a move to substitute rayon for cotton fiber in Army truck tires, but while writing Cannon, Johnston was feeling eloquent about his industry's attitude toward competing technological improvements. He next dwelt on the entrance of aralac, a fiber made from milk.

"Just as science has produced a table spread from cottonseed, it has produced a textile fabric from milk," he wrote. "If the Cotton Industry should wage an all-out campaign to secure legislation stifling the use of aralac, we should be no more unreasonable, and no more antagonistic to scientific progress, than the dairy industry is being when it uses the same methods to stifle the use of margarine."

The climax of Johnston's rebuttal to Cannon came when he turned to the subject of labeling margarine so as to prevent its being palmed off as butter. Turning on his best irony, the council president wrote: "To the same extent we feel that butter should not be colored, labeled, or sold under any circumstance which might reasonably deceive the buyer into believing that he was buying a chemically pure margarine product."

Another pressure bloc which at least wants margarine to have an even break is an association known as the Southern Commissioners of Agriculture, whose secretary, C. C. Hanson, has his office in the Raleigh Hotel of Washington, D.C.—just below the Mason-Dixon line. It is this association's opinion, also, that because great quantities of Southern-grown oil, like cottonseed and peanut oil, go into the making of margarine, the dairy industry is not entitled to exclusive consideration on taxes and sales. In activating this idea, "Colonel" Hanson keeps his Southern commissioners supplied with ammunition for overcoming the long lead of butter.

Typical of his activity is the memorandum sent to members on November 12, 1941, by way of bringing up to date figures on the amount of home-grown products flowing into margarine. "This chart provides an excellent answer," the colonel wrote, "to those people who would outlaw margarine by claiming that it is a foreign product. It will be noted that the use in margarine of domestic oils, both vegetable and animal, continues to rise, while the use of foreign oils continues to decrease."

Moreover, a new character, the phenomenal soybean, is rapidly upsetting the established lines of both these blocs by driving a deep wedge roughly through the geographic middle of the farming area. Use of soybean oil in margarine, for example, has grown from 3,000 pounds in 1932 to an all-time high of 92,152,000 pounds in 1942. The margarine interests are not unmindful of their new ally. In states like

Iowa, where the overlapping of soybean and milk pressure plays more every day into their hands, they hold the coats while bean and milk factions do the fighting.

The impetus which the shifting alignment of blocs has given to a scientific, rather than blindly protective, basis for evaluating the relative merits of butter and margarine is dramatically illustrated by an incident which also puts the operating technique of Charlie Holman under a microscope.

Some time before the annual convention of the General Federation of Women's Clubs, in 1942, the clubs of several states had passed resolutions in favor of abolishing the Federal tax on oleomargarine. Being an organization representing some 2,000,000 women from kitchens all over the nation, there was an understandable interest in the subject. The resolutions were approved by the national Board of Directors and placed in the hands of the federation's legislative chairman, Mrs. Harvey Wiley, widow of the author of food-and-drug legislation.

About this time Holman entered the picture by going to Mrs. John L. Whitehurst, of Baltimore, national president of the Women's Clubs. Friends of Mrs. Whitehurst say that she found the butter advocate so unreasonable that thereafter she refused to see him in person and required that further negotiations be in writing. Be that as it may, it is clear that Holman then attempted to have Mrs. Whitehurst removed from membership on the Maryland State Board of Agriculture. His charge was that because her organization was even entertaining an anti-butter resolution she, personally, became an enemy of the farmers who were supposedly represented on the Maryland Board. His efforts in that direction were unsuccessful, but his demand to be heard by the convention, which would pass on the issue, was granted. However, Mrs. Whitehurst thought it only fair to invite also an oleomargarine representative and an impartial nutritionist as third speaker.

"That would be unfair," Holman protested; "it would be two against one!"

Nevertheless the program included appearances from the three men, and Holman set up headquarters in the Texas Hotel in Fort Worth—a suite of rooms in which he could plot with delegates from dairy states for the impending floor battle. Suddenly, however, he informed officials that he had withdrawn his request to appear—and that therefore no one else should appear.

By this time talk of the feud had nearly overshadowed the formal convention theme: "Pan America." Word of Holman's personal difference with the ladies' president had done no good for the cause of butter and, in general, had made leaders determined to thrash the controversy out. One of his delegate spokesmen came from Holman headquarters with a motion that none of the advocates be heard. An amendment was offered to make the motion read that only Dr. Anton J. Carlson, head of the department of physiology of Chicago University, who had by then arrived in Fort Worth, should be heard. By a narrow margin the scientist was allowed to speak, but Holman sulked in his suite near by.

Apparently his lieutenants were active, however, for next morning the convention was caught napping and a motion carried to postpone determination of the fight. The meeting ended without renewal of the issue, and Holman claims that the General Federation *defeated* a promargarine proposal. Neutral observers, however, think that margarine won the war even if it might have lost the battle, for most delegates returned home to their grocery lists with a bad impression of the dairy lobby.

What have the margarine manufacturers themselves done to fight back? Do they not have a big propaganda outfit with slick press agents and suave buttonholers?

The lobby of this wicked, iniquitous, conspiring substitute product was for years one aging man and a stenographer, more recently tucked away on the tenth floor of the Munsey Building with no pipe line to Congress. It was back in 1920 that Dr. J. S. Abbott, former Food and Drug Commissioner of Texas and scientist in the Bureau of Chemistry of the Department of Agriculture, became secretary of the Institute of Margarine Manufacturers. After holding that job for seventeen years Abbott saw the industry split from under him over the issue of a protective tariff on foreign oils for use in margarine. He resigned from the institute, believing that the industry should shift to a domestic raw-material basis, and within a few days had been made secretary and director of research of a new group: the National Association of Margarine Manufacturers. That job he held from 1937 on, but the institute eventually capitulated on principles and he once again became sole paid representative of the industry.

In the span of a long life, which ended in January of this year, Abbott authored about four hundred articles and bulletins on the stunted product, while maintaining membership in several scientific societies. He went to Congress only occasionally, and in general felt it useless to beg Congress for a fair deal for his wares—even though they became practically 100 per cent American. Abbott reflected on many a chapter in the fantastic history of margarine and probably knew more about the subject than anyone else.

But he was not capable of being the lobbyist at which the dairy industry constantly pointed its long finger, even though it was he who represented margarine at the Fort Worth convention.

Although farm friends of margarine are not vociferous, they are rallying yearly. Besides the soybean industry, the Southern Commissioners of Agriculture, and the cotton bloc, margarine is befriended by cattle interests who find profit in selling millions of pounds of beef oils to manufacturers annually. But no congressman braves the wrath of the dairy lobby to stand on his hind legs and ask even an openly competitive chance for margarine.

Yet in 1942 the production of margarine for consumers and Lend-Lease totaled nearly 500,000,000 pounds, while that of 1941 ran 368,256,000—and butter was about to be rationed at the end of 1942. Plants were running at top speed to make a product so improved that customers might stay with it after the war, and there was new peace within the industry.

A few days after Christmas of 1942 the Margarine Manufacturers took an important step. Though the true meaning of the announcement was missed, the association revealed that it had hired as its first paid president Paul T. Truitt. There were two stories behind Truitt's new job.

First, the Washington office of the association was to be doubled overnight, effective January 1, 1943, by the man who had been directing since 1939 the government's efforts to throw down interstate trade barriers. It was Truitt who had arranged the TNEC hearings on barriers to margarine and many other commodities and who had kept a big hand in the special conferences called by the Department of Commerce to study ways of knocking down those restrictions which hampered the war effort.

Second, a few weeks before Truitt's appointment five new member manufacturers had joined the association, bringing it up to a score of 18 out of 21 eligible belonging. Four of these five were the Big Four of the packing industry: Swift, Armour, Wilson, and Cudahy. With money in the coffers and a president with fifteen years of experience in the progressive merchandising of Sears, Roebuck and Company, the margarine industry was ready to fight back.

More internecine warfare had been started in the farm bloc.

VIII

The Co-operative Way

THE National Council of Farmer Cooperatives, contrary to what some might think, is not a stuffy club of zealous people who think that economic co-operation is the great panacea for the world's ills. Nor is it an alliance of the co-op filling stations and grocery stores which dot nearly every community. After years of patient building, the co-operative way, as represented by the council, is big business. In 1942 the Co-op Council, as it is called, listed about 4,500 separate organizations as affiliates. These, it reported, are scattered throughout all the states and nearly every county in the nation. Their members and other customers total over 2,000,000 persons whose business runs about $1,250,-000,000 annually.

To get to the rock bottom of the farm bloc one must look to this network of closely knit business structures, even though the organization is "non-political" in the technical sense of the term. For, according to the Department of Agriculture, more than one half of the country's farmers patronize co-operatives in some phase of their operations. Patronage takes the form of marketing farm products through a local "producers' co-op" or of buying co-operatively farm supplies such as seed, gasoline, tools, and fertilizer, which go into food and fiber production.

Analysis of the Co-op Council's 4,500 affiliates is a book in itself. Few, if any, dinner-table items are untouched somewhere along their route by co-operative hands. The council's thirteen divisions, each of which is autonomous, embrace such widely differing geographical and commodity groups as cranberries, turkeys, calavos, cotton, milk, apples, rice, grain, cattle, wool, potatoes, mushrooms, all kinds of nuts, eggs, raisins, and tobacco.

In spite of this potent coalition of forces from almost every congressional district, the Co-op Council rarely speaks politically. It will take sides on legislation, but it will not take on a party label or endorse candidates. H. E. Babcock, recent president of the council and long-time leader in its activities, stated this position in his dedication of the council's 1942 *Blue Book:*

> The political power of co-operatives in the United States is potentially enormous. Not even the two great trade-union groups can match the membership, the capital, the skilled manpower, and the control of the media of communication which already are in the hands of the assembled farmer co-operatives of the United States. Fortunately, however, the political power of co-operatives is a sleeping giant which has never been aroused. I pray God it never shall be.

The giant opened one eye, however; for the year had not ended before the Co-op Council, under Babcock's own lash at first, had joined hands with the Grange and Farm Bureau to carry on what has been described by several old-timers as the most effective lobbying seen in years.

The time was September 1942; the place, Hotel Washington's roof-top Rose Room; the occasion, a hybrid gathering of the Co-op Council's special Assembly of Delegates and various other farm leaders who were called in to get concerned about amending the Price Control Act. Shortly after President Roosevelt's famous October-first ultimatum to Congress, Ed Babcock, who was then council president, signed the rush call to arms, crying that agriculture was in danger. It was he who presided over the three-day meeting of nearly one hundred agrarians, their lawyers and agents.

In addition to top men from the council's thirteen divisions, the following guests were present: F. V. Heinkle, president of the Missouri Farmers Association (a large general farm organization which works closely with the council through its co-ops); Oscar Heline, president of the National Co-operative Elevator Association; R. P. Juhnichen, representing the Washington Packers; Grange Master Albert S. Goss; Farm Bureau President Edward A. O'Neal, and Eric A. Johnston, president of the United States Chamber of Commerce.

It is officially claimed by the Co-op Council that Goss, O'Neal, and Johnston merely dropped in to extend greetings to the assembly, as other big shots have done annually in the past; but eyewitnesses report a different story. According to them, the flames of rural indignation were fed by O'Neal's stump-speech declaration that "everybody knows that the President is controlled by the CIO" and Johnston's assurance that he would get word out to his local chambers of commerce to help the farmers along.

Next the delegates approved unanimously a proposed amendment to make mandatory the inclusion of farm-labor costs in determining parity prices. Significantly, this action was followed by instructing Babcock to appoint a three-man committee to study the unfair publicity being given farmers on price-control matters.

Shifting to the Hall of Nations, in the basement of the hotel, the delegates appointed a resolutions committee, then recessed until after dinner in order to buttonhole congressmen. A similar recess was taken the third day. Both of them occurred during the most critical hours on Capitol Hill.

The resolutions adopted in the closing hours of the session do not reveal the intense political repercussions of the caucus. Rubber conservation, demand for a food administration to eliminate "widespread conflict, bickering, and confusion" among Federal agencies, and a pat on the back to the Farm Credit Administration's Co-operative Research and Service Division were put on the record, instead of an account of what had really been going on those three days.

The Public Relations Committee reported that unfair and unfavorable publicity in the past six to twelve months "overshadows in importance every effort that may be made by farm organizations to secure fair legislation." Preparation of a defensive statement, for local circulation, was recommended.

Buried at the end of the confab's grist was a formality which deserves more attention than the few lines which it got in the record. It was the action which amounted to severing the weak tie between the Co-op Council and the Farmers Union, and revealed the council's basic conservatism.

One of Babcock's telegraphic invitations had gone to the general manager of the Farmers Union Grain Terminal Association, one M. W. Thatcher. Only eight or nine months earlier the council had reluctantly accepted Thatcher's request for membership. The reluctance, or skepticism, had been caused not only by the fact that

Thatcher stands high in the Farmers Union, but also because he is an unorthodox grain operator.

Immediately after the council's hotel-room blast at the Price Control Act, Thatcher walked out of the meeting and sent its officials the following telegram:

AFTER LISTENING CAREFULLY THIS MORNING TO THE STATE-MENTS AND THE ONE LEGISLATIVE PROPOSAL PRESENTED TO THE MEMBERS OF THE COUNCIL RELATING TO THE ANTI-INFLATION BILL NOW BEFORE CONGRESS I FIND THEM SO UNRELATED TO THE STATEMENTS FURNISHED US AS THE BASIS FOR CONVENING THIS CONFERENCE AND SO OUT OF HARMONY WITH THE POLICIES OF THE NATIONAL FARMERS UNION WHICH SPEAKS FOR US ON NATIONAL LEGISLATION THAT I RESPECTFULLY REQUEST THE MINUTES OF THE CONFERENCE TO RECORD OUR ORGANIZATION AS HAVING HEREWITH WITH-DRAWN FROM FURTHER ATTENDANCE.

Gasping for breath after this long sentence, the delegates unanimously considered the message a "request for discontinuation of membership" in the council and accepted it as such. A few weeks later Thatcher's organization branded the severance as completely arbitrary and asked partial refund of dues. The council waived a proviso of its bylaws in order to make the refund and wind up the whole affair, but its leaders will admit privately that Thatcher was kicked out for personal reasons rather than having resigned. The incident served to drive deeper the wedge between the Farmers Union and other members of the bloc.

When the Price Control Act had been amended—without the labor-cost proviso, but with a 90-per-cent-of-parity floor—few Washington observers had caught the true story of the Washington Hotel strategy. Snatches of it appeared in columns, such as Drew Pearson's Washington Merry-

Go-Round, but in general all eyes were on the ball, upon Capitol Hill. In retrospect, however, the Co-op Council is given credit for emerging as a very real lobby mechanism. The true picture appeared in the October issue of *Co-operative Digest*, a journal published by Roy H. Park, who also does research work for the Grange League Federation Exchange, a major council member.

This show, it may be said, was masterminded by co-operative agriculture [wrote the *Digest* reporter]. This dims not at all the prominent roles played by Albert S. Goss, master of the National Grange, and Edward A. O'Neal, top man of the Farm Bureau. But a quick perusal of the blasts leveled by the nation's press at the farm people who fought the Administration puts dynamic H. Edward Babcock, then president of the National Council, on record as the guiding light of the whole farm cause.

Farmer Babcock, director of the School for Co-operative Administration in Ithaca, N. Y., chairman of the Cornell University board, writer, operator of farming properties in New York and New Mexico, was indeed the No. 1 figure in the first hectic week of the two-week fight in Congress. It was he who called nearly one hundred delegates of National Council members together in Washington to carry the fight into the cloakrooms of Congress and the office of congressmen and senators, friend and foe alike.

It was lobbying in the grand style [the *Digest* continued], but not the kind of lobbying to which Congress is accustomed. . . . Unprofessional in their approach, unschooled in the maze of parliamentary technicality that guides congressional strategy, these co-op men went to their home-state delegations and talked turkey. . . . Ed O'Neal and Albert Goss popped into the meetings from time to time. Charles Holman, whose pipe lines to congressional confidences are many, provided the needed data on developing trends. . . . Never before in its nearly thirteen years has the National Council of Farmer Cooperatives climbed

into the forefront of a legislative fight as it did last month. . . .
What the press and public came to realize last month is that the
National Council speaks for more farmers than any of the other
groups.

Two personal changes were made at the special meeting,
putting two key officials even farther forward. Because of
the press of other duties, Babcock stepped back to vice-
president of the council, moving to the top Charles C.
Teague, California's "dean of co-operators." Since Teague
lives so far from Washington headquarters of the council,
important authority was delegated to energetic Executive
Secretary Ezra T. Benson.

The council has had only four presidents, most of whom
had Holman do their executive work, to put it mildly. The
first was Charles O. Moser, selected from the cotton co-
operatives. Then came the venerated Judge Miller, who
served nine years in the job as well as being onetime president of the Milk Producers' Federation, largest division of
the council. Miller was also foremost in building the entrenched Dairymen's League Co-operative Association,
Inc., of New York, and has been its general counsel since
1917. He is now president emeritus of the council and
remains quite active in its affairs, though past eighty-five
years of age.

Next in line was Babcock, a familiar figure in Northeastern agricultural circles. Besides being chairman of the
governing board of Cornell, Babcock devotes much of his
tireless energy to affairs of the unusual Grange League
Federation Exchange, which he organized. The words in
this marketing-and-purchasing co-operative come, respectively, from the Grange, the Dairymen's League, and the
Farm Bureau Federation. Continued growth of the powerful and successful alliance bespeaks the collaboration which

can be obtained from blocs within the bloc on economic matters and demonstrates capable leadership.

In addition to holding these top jobs and overseeing a sizable amount of his own land, Babcock is copublisher of the *American Agriculturist* with Frank Gannett, who owns a string of anti-Administration newspapers, was once assistant to the chairman of the Republican National Committee, and was the leader in organizing the National Committee to Uphold Constitutional Government, a collection of professional New Deal haters.

A minor Washington mystery was touched off when it was discovered that Babcock, right in the middle of his farm confab, had suddenly packed up and caught a train for Ithaca. Council leaders attempted to explain away the mystery by saying that their venerable chieftain had told them, on being elected president, that he could serve only one year, but other insiders felt that people just do not sign wires for an emergency meeting, then duck the consequences.

Another school of thought goes back several months to a dinner held by Babcock and his Grange League Federation to acquaint farm leaders in the Northeast with a rising Western personality, Farmers Union President James G. Patton. Babcock, those who hold to this school of thought say, is too tolerant of differences of opinion to stand idly by while the Farm Bureau, Grange, Milk Producers, and his Co-op Council banded together against the once friendly Administration and the Farmers Union and dissenting state groups within the Farm Bureau, notably the Ohio contingent led by its secretary, Murray Lincoln. As they see it, a series of good-will feasts had Babcock almost to the point of swinging his large following over to the camp which was not pulling price levers during the war. Everything was running smoothly when Babcock threw his bolt of lightning via telegraph wire. Many months later none of those who had nearly joined hands with him officially had been able to get from Farmer Babcock the smattering of an explanation. Meanwhile the schism had grown.

It is the present council president, Charles C. Teague, whose background explains the council's recent extremes. Because he constantly boasts that over 2,000,000 *farmers* are speaking through the council and him, the biography of spokesman Teague warrants thorough examination. According to *Who's Who,* Teague is a banker and agricultural adviser who was born in Maine in 1873 and received LL.D. degrees from the University of California and the University of Maine. Back in 1893 he settled in Santa Paula, California.

In that locality Teague is president of the Teague, McKevett Company, the California Orchard Company, the Santa Paula Water Works, the Farmers' Irrigation Company, and the Soledad Ranch Company, and has been president of the First National Bank of Santa Paula for fifteen years.

On a broader geographical scale, Teague is vice-president of the Security First National Trust & Savings Bank of Los Angeles, has been president of the Agricultural Council of California since 1910 (the state counterpart of the National Co-op Council), president of the California Fruit Growers Exchange since 1920 (owners of the famous Sunkist brand name), president of the American Institute of Co-operation, and president of the California Walnut Growers Association since 1912. In 1942 he was made honorary president of the latter group for life. Also, Teague was a member of Hoover's Farm Board.

On different fronts, Teague is listed as being a consulting professor on co-operative marketing at Stanford University's Graduate School of Business, a director of the National Advisory Board of the university, a regent of the University of California, a Republican, a Universalist, and a Mason.

What *Who's Who* does not say about Teague is that he heads the Fruit Growers Supply Company, purchasing subsidiary of the Fruit Growers Exchange, and was a big cog in raising money for the infamous Associated Farmers of California, Inc.

Few good things have been said about the Associated Farmers, except by its shifting membership and its non-agricultural financiers. Having shot its wad in the middle and late 1930s, the organization has gone down in national history as California's bid for a native form of Ku Klux Klan and Black Legion, but not without having terrorized unionists, would-be unionists, and persons who looked as if they might someday want to become unionized just a little. Only part of its feudal vigilante activity and strike breaking was formalized by even phony deputy-sheriff badges; most of it was sheer lawlessness.

A lengthy, thoroughly documented account of that disgraceful chapter of Western history was painstakingly gathered by Senators Robert La Follette, of Wisconsin, and Elbert Thomas, of Utah (two farm states), acting as a subcommittee on violations of free speech and rights of labor. The senators' report, issued in 1942, found Associated Farmers' activities to be grouped under three classifications: opposition to unions of fieldworkers, opposition to unions of packing-house and processing-house workers, and opposition to unions in industry.

"From these local activities of the Associated Farmers,"

the report concluded, "arose the most flagrant and violent infringements of civil liberties which the committee studied in California. Espionage and the blacklist were not infrequent. Strikebreaking was a specialized technique of the organization."

The committee also explained the conditions which bred the Associated Farmers. "The economic and social plight of California's agricultural labor is miserable beyond belief," its report stated. "Average annual earnings for agricultural laborers are far below the minimum standard necessary even for the maintenance of an existence on proper levels of health and decency."

As part of the cause for these symptoms, the committee observed that "while more than one half of the farm units are small, that is, under fifty acres, agricultural production is dominated by the large-scale farm or large-scale operation."

Pointing at the custom of keeping a docile labor reservoir on hand to do the bidding of this type of commercial agriculture, the committee stated:

A year-round force of hired hands, employed chiefly in the milk, poultry, and livestock industries, and amounting to some 50,000 throughout the state, must be supplemented by a labor force of at least three to four times that number to perform the necessary hand operations of cultivation or harvesting in various cotton, fruit, and vegetable industries. The labor to meet this demand cannot be found on the farms of California or in the neighboring cities. . . . The roving casual-labor supply which this type of production necessitates has been drawn since the earliest days of California agriculture from successive groups of imported alien labor.

As indicated, those conditions are well known to that area; therefore it cannot be doubted that Charles Teague knew what he was doing when, in 1935, he raised $4,418.30

for the Associated Farmers from the citrus and walnut industries which he headed, in order to maintain by crudest devices the status of farming which his associates have thrived on so long.

As found by La Follette and Thomas, Teague's Walnut Growers and Fruit Growers Exchange did not officially contribute money to the Associated Farmers, but did allow their offices to be used as meeting places and did circularize local affiliates on the advisability of contributing locally. In fact, thirty affiliates of the California Fruit Growers Exchange (which distributes about 75 per cent of all California citrus) chipped in by levying 20 cents on every carload of oranges shipped. The Walnut Growers were solicited by General Manager Carlisle C. Thorpe on a basis of $1 per 400-bag car shipped.

The senators found that the chief backer of the Associated Farmers was the California State Chamber of Commerce, of which Teague was a director from 1932 to 1939 at least. The committee also listed the Teague-McKevett Association as having contributed $26.40 to the Associated Farmers in 1935. Other financial angels of the organization at that time included the Bank of America, Columbia Steel Company, Pacific Gas and Electric Company ($1,850 in two years), and several oil and railroad companies.

Incidentally, it was Teague who kindled Holman's interest in co-operatives while the latter was doing a series of articles on marketing for a Texas farm journal. After a swing through the orange and lemon country of California to study the Fruit Growers Exchange and a conducted trip through Teague's own extensive holdings, Holman put aside journalism and set out to preach the gospel of co-operation.

And it is Teague who introduces himself as only a farmer.

The council's delegation of more authority to Secretary Ezra Benson amounted to a vote of confidence in the interesting man who had been doing its executive chores since April of 1939, when a reorganization called for a new secretary. As an operator, Benson is quiet, methodical, efficient, and tireless. He enjoys good personal relationships around town and has to exercise a wide variety of functions in the field of price regulations, priorities, farm credit, disposal of surplus crops, and promotion of numerous commodities.

Benson has lived close to the co-operative way all his life. He was born in the tiny town of Whitney, Idaho, into the faith of the Church of Jesus Christ of Latter Day Saints (Mormon), a faith built largely on co-operation. After two years at Utah State Agricultural College he put in two and one half years as a Mormon missionary in England and Europe, where he studied British co-operation thoroughly. Soon after returning to the United States he was graduated from Brigham Young University and moved back to his home county to a 160-acre farm to feed lambs and cattle.

As an advanced student, Benson received a master's degree from Iowa State College and had a year's ride on a fellowship at the University of California. Between times he was a county agent in Idaho and headed up the agricultural-economics side of the Extension Service at the University of Idaho from 1930 to 1939. During the last three years of the latter job Benson was an organizer and secretary of the Idaho Co-operative Council, affiliated with the National Council.

Now, just over forty, the bespectacled, executive type of secretary to about 2,000,000 people, occupies the floor above the elderly Holman, where he directs a staff of three secretaries and two male assistants. One of these works full time on a recently formed organization of which Benson is also secretary: the National Committee for Farm Production Supplies. The committee is composed largely of heads of farmer co-operatives, but also embraces the Grange, Farm Bureau, and Farmers Union. Its job is to work on technical matters such as getting priorities on farm equipment.

After business hours much of Benson's time goes into church affairs, as he is president of the Washington stake (diocese) of the Mormon Church. Whatever lobbying Benson does is not likely to be marked by tobacco smoke and liquor, as he uses neither. Besides being a Rotarian, he sometimes finds time for Boy Scout work, gardening, and hiking. Always he is devoted to his two boys and three girls.

Farmers' co-operatives, more than any other farm group, have a tangible economic motive in keeping organized labor under control—or unorganized. The picking, packing, and shipping of citrus fruits, berries, and nuts, the shearing of sheep, and the milking and feeding of cows require considerable wage labor. In many respects those operations are similar to assembly-line jobs indoors; but farmer employers have historically opposed efforts to bring their wage earners under the same protective legislation enjoyed by industrial labor. In addition to fighting off social legislation for its own workers, many successful operators of this type resent advances of organized labor anywhere.

Indicative of this frame of mind are a few sentences from Benson's report on his stewardship during 1941.

Throughout the year [he wrote] the council worked on legislation designed to protect agricultural production, packing, and distribution from labor troubles which threatened to impose serious handicaps on the industry's contribution to the defense program. Taking the leadership, the council developed a bill which was nearly ready for introduction in the fall, when a rash of serious strikes in defense plants prompted the introduction of several labor-control bills.

The farm organizations temporarily halted action on their own bill to review the situation, but late in November resumed their efforts to have remedial legislation introduced which would protect agriculture from the detrimental effects of such labor practices as the secret ballot, force and violence, closed shop, mass picketing, secondary boycott, hot cargo, collection of illegal fees and compensation, and jurisdictional strikes.

Granting that the kind of farmer who belongs to the co-op marketing associations may be subjected to unsavory excesses which have crept into organized labor at times, such as a strike of truck drivers which results in a carload of peaches rotting, still people who want to be friends of both labor and agriculture are embarrassed by the measures to which some farm leaders will sign their names. One of these was introduced shortly before Pearl Harbor by labor's foremost enemy in the House of Representatives, Howard W. Smith, of Virginia. While baiting labor, Smith is sometimes spokesman for the Maryland-Virginia Milk Producers' Association, of which he is a wealthy member and which is affiliated with Holman's federation. Smith is the epitome of a gentleman-farmer or country squire who lives from the work of others as a commercial agriculturist. Besides nearly strangling the Wagner Act, Smith can be counted on to pop up with a new kind of shackle for any new situation, real or imagined. Here are the official comments of Secretary Benson in behalf of colleague Smith:

"On December 3 the drastic Smith labor bill was approved by the House of Representatives, and for the first time definite progress was apparent toward the solution of some of the labor difficulties besetting agriculture. Then, on December 7, America went to war. The entire labor picture underwent a transformation."

Since the beginning of war, Benson explained, the only labor activity by farm organizations was a joint letter sent by them to the President's labor-industry conference which set up the National War Labor Board, asking that the closed-shop issue be outlawed for the duration of the war.

Briefly, some of Benson's other activities were: sitting in on meetings arranged by the U. S. Chamber of Commerce, church groups, land-grant colleges, and others; exerting influence toward Surplus Marketing Administration purchase of surplus commodities grown by council members; obtaining diversion programs satisfactory to producers; gaining for co-operatives contracts for a huge volume of lend-lease food shipments, and maintaining "a splendid unity of opinion and effort" with the Grange and Farm Bureau.

Only a few of that year's Co-op Council resolutions did not duplicate parts of Benson's report already referred to, but those few are noteworthy in view of the political emergence of the potent organization. After plumping for maintenance of free enterprise, which it declared "may be strangled by bureaucracies," the council expressed disappointment at President Roosevelt's veto of the Logan-Walter Bill, which would have wrapped the executive branch of government in such legal red tape and hocus-pocus that its anti-Administration authors could have watched the New Deal strangle—and not so slowly. The council even admitted that a few improvements could be made in the Logan-Walter Bill, then urged early enactment of a law "that will regulate the regulators."

An interesting paradox of that year's resolutions grew

out of declarations on two subjects: labor and marketing agreements. On the first subject, labor, the council asked for "extensive protection against labor practices which result in delay or *limitation of production*." (Italics added.) At the same time the council asked for extension of the marketing-agreements program of the Department of Agriculture to non-basic crops as well as to basic crops. Under that program, of course, production and/or the supply to be marketed in any season can be greatly limited and usually is. And, too, council members have been great beneficiaries under the diversion programs, whereby the government subsidizes growers to get a portion of some crops off the regular market in order to maintain prices artificially. To consumers, the pot was calling the kettle black.

In view of participation in these programs, it is interesting to note what the council had to say that year on another aspect of organized labor: "The right to work is the right to live. The principle of the compulsory closed shop and hiring hall is both monopolistic and a denial of the constitutional right of the individual to seek and obtain work free from coercion, intimidation, or the payment of tribute." Farmers who have tried to sell their milk in some areas controlled by dairymen who belong to the council have made similar charges against the maker of this one. The merits of a closed shop seem to depend on whether one is inside or outside.

Another resolution urged the Department of Justice to continue its investigation and prosecution, if necessary, of any elements of the retail-distribution industry carrying on unfair trade practices. The interesting, if not humorous, aspect of this plank is that the man who shortly thereafter became council president, Teague, is under indictment by the same Department of Justice for violating the same antitrust statutes. On the occasion of Teague's first attendance at Secretary Wickard's monthly meetings with farm leaders, Teague nearly monopolized the session with a vigorous denial of guilt. A few months later he was still trying to get Wickard to intercede in the case.

Policy statements since early 1942 have been issued with increased snap and zest as the council has become more public-relations conscious. Several of the most important have been released jointly with the Grange and Farm Bureau, but never with the Farmers Union, in spite of the union's foundation in co-operatives.

A key example of this collaboration was issued jointly by Benson, Goss, and O'Neal on November 4, 1942, in the midst of an agricultural-manpower dilemma. The Administration, seeking to remove a blight of long standing on our relations with Mexico, decided early in the year to bring in no migrant Mexican laborers without guaranteeing them a decent standard of wages, living conditions, and tenure of employment. In fact, the Mexican government insisted on some such policy. Certain seasonal laborers of American citizenship were given similar guarantees if transported long distances to help with distressed crops. Administration of this program was vested in the Farm Security Administration because of its experience in managing migrant camps in the land of the Okies and elsewhere.

But such standards were a blow to commercial farmers who were accustomed to picking up seasonal labor, including docile Mexicans, for rock-bottom wages. While the War Manpower Commission was working out a program for keeping essential farmers on their jobs, and Arizona cotton planters were balking at meeting the standards of decency imposed by FSA before bringing in men to pick the essential long-staple cotton for parachutes, the farm triumvirate sounded its horn.

"We are greatly concerned," they stated, "over what we consider the misdirected efforts of agencies of government to fasten upon farmers and farm workers far-reaching bureaucratic controls and restrictions. Under the guise of the war effort, a social revolution is being perpetrated upon the American people."

Then the blame was placed on labor. "It is an indisputable fact," they continued, "that the terrific drain of manpower from the farms—well over 1,500,000 in the past twelve months—is due to the refusal of this Administration to deal effectively with industrial wages which have spiraled to unprecedented levels. Surveys show that twice as many farm workers have been lured into industry by fabulous wages as have joined the armed forces under Selective Service."

Turning to the Mexican and seasonal American labor, the three officials declared that "plans to bring needed workers from Mexico were loaded down with so many impractical requirements that so far farmers have obtained but little real help from this source." Plowing under of Arizona cotton for lack of labor was cited as an example, without explaining that planters had been offered the workers in time to do the job.

A release issued five days later by the Co-op Council alone went even further. "Refusal of the present Administration to discard its prewar concept of the use of labor in industry has resulted in disgraceful inefficiency and a wastage of labor that is retarding our war effort," the council's Executive Committee stated.

"While war workers in Russia stay at their jobs an average of 66 hours a week; in Germany, 60 hours; and in

Britain, 56 hours; in this country the average work week is only 43 hours, with thousands working less than 40 hours," it added. "A majority of American farmers, deprived of adequate farm help, are working 43 hours every three days—not every week."

As has been seen, members of the Co-op Council did not suddenly take on their dislike of organized labor the day Japan bombed Pearl Harbor. Their attack on the gains of labor, operating with some of the Co-op Council's own techniques—collective bargaining for a fair return—is longstanding. Most members would not be members unless they lived from the returns of a special commodity which requires a reservoir of labor at seasonal peaks. And, often justifiably, they have seen practiced on their precious ripe crops the ugliest of trade-union practices.

But fair wages is only one subject in organized labor's gains; it has also attained social security, unemployment compensation, workmen's compensation (for injuries), and miscellaneous safeguards which appear in collective contracts. Rather than imitate organized labor in respect to security, the organized marketers of farm commodities have gone after little more than higher and higher prices. Insofar as they have gone farther than price manipulation, they have turned to even more artificial means of support: marketing agreements, diversion programs, restricted production, in some cases, and new parity definitions.

The walnut-diversion program will demonstrate not only the lengths to which one commodity group has gone to ride on an artificial wave of prosperity, but will show why some officials snicker at the pious anti-subsidy pronouncements of Teague, for he was founder and president of the California Walnut Growers Association.

While American consumption of walnuts was dropping after 1929, the industry was gathering more walnuts from newly bearing trees. In 1933 Uncle Sam came to the rescue with a marketing-agreement program whereby one half to two thirds of the annual crop was sold on the American market at an agreed price supposedly fair to the grower. All the walnuts in any year could not be put on the market without wrecking the price to the industry; hence the artificial division. The "surplus" was, by agreement with the government, sold at roughly half price. The mixture of the two prices, of course, netted a higher return to the grower than if nature had taken its ruthless course.

Some of the diverted, half-price walnuts were shelled and sold with the aid of a government subsidy. When this was not enough for the industry a system of subsidizing the export of walnuts was started. During the five years ending in 1940 these benefit payments totaled nearly $6,250,000, even though demand for the product was falling off. Because new trees were still coming into production, the industry was bound to need more cash help each year, taking the program out of the emergency category under which it might have been justifiable at one time. Trouble was being bred.

The walnut is only one of nearly a score of commodities glorified by this system or one of its modifications. In fiscal '40 the Surplus Marketing Administration reported surplus-removal expenditures on commodities such as these: dates, figs, loganberries, pecans, prunes, peanuts, and milk. This kind of bait is so attractive to lobbyists and pressure groups that it has been said of several of the Department of Agriculture's commodity specialists: "They ought to be on the grower's pay roll!"

As for Teague and his walnuts, again it is difficult to accept in good faith his bolts against subsidies or allowing other countries to export their surpluses. It seems more likely that the great co-operator is increasingly interested in co-operating with political enemies of the Administration.

IX

National Grange

DOLLARS IN THE POCKET AND COURAGE IN THE HEART

THE OLDEST FARM ORGANIZATION is also the most conservative, but it has not always been so. Historians of the National Grange, Order of the Patrons of Husbandry, looking back on more than seventy-six years of its life, recall formation by a handful of government clerks, a period of near revolt when the old granger movement fought for and got regulation of railroads and other trusts, and several periods so tranquil that the organization almost fell asleep.

Back in January 1866, O. H. Kelley, a clerk in the Department of Agriculture, was sent through the South by Isaac Newton, who was then Commissioner of Agriculture, to look into the rural aftermath of the devastating Civil War. Just what Kelley reported to the government is not clear, but the National Grange of today is the result of two of his conclusions: That farmers needed an organization and that he became more welcome on his journey after it became known that he was a Mason.

The idea for a secret fraternity, closed to non-farmers, was there born; Kelley's niece added the principle that women should participate equally with their farm husbands, and Kelley started telling a few Washington friends about the idea. When, having adopted a constitution and a secret ritual, he called the first meeting of the Grange, it included the following friends: J. R. Thompson, an official of the Treasury Department; William Saunders, superintendent of the Department of Agriculture garden and grounds; William M. Ireland, chief clerk in the finance division of the Post Office Department (to which agency Kelley had since transferred); Reverend John Trimble, another Treasury official; Reverend A. B. Grosh, an Agriculture Department clerk and high in the Independent Order of Odd Fellows, and F. M. McDowell, a vineyardist of New York State.

These seven men, none then farming, founded the National Grange of the Patrons of Husbandry on December 4, 1867, in a tiny brown building which stood by itself on the corner of Four-and-a-half Street and Missouri Avenue in Washington—Saunders' office. Kelley was made secretary, and Saunders became the first national master.

Resigning his Federal job, Kelley started into the Northwest to organize with no assets but a fraternal "God bless you and your efforts" from his six colleagues.

Things were hard those early years. At the third annual session of the National Grange, Worthy Master Saunders delivered his inaugural in the presence of Secretary Kelley, his only listener. By the end of 1872, however, more than 1,000 granges were scattered over more than half the states. The national office had begun to pump out literature and ritualistic paraphernalia, including a knife for each granger to remind him "never to break a twig or a flower, but always to cut it smoothly with a knife so as not to injure the plant." Thus was the member instructed, a Grange historian writes, "in his intercourse with his fellow beings to correct an error tenderly and with the smooth edge of affection, and never to bruise a wound he wished to heal."

Several trials vexed the Grange in its adolescence. At one time the majority demanded and got a distribution of the $54,825 in the national treasury to local granges, each getting a paltry $2.50. Again, in the confusion of organization, the Grange gates were left wide open and "men whose capital was invested in enterprises inimical to the farmers, and whose farms were perhaps their garden plcts," were received into the Grange. "Everybody," complained an old-timer, "wanted to join the Grange then: lawyers, to get clients; doctors, to get patients; merchants, to get customers; Shylocks, to get their pound of flesh; and sharpers, to catch the babes from the woods." One grange was organized on Broadway among bank presidents, sewing-machine manufacturers, and Wall Street speculators. "These wily men," it was recorded, "sapped the very foundation of the Order, and rendered it almost lifeless in more states than one."

To counteract such depressing chapters as this, the Grange resorted to a fascinating but unsuccessful system for buying members' farm supplies at cut rates. Agreements were made with manufacturers of articles such as plows, engines, and even parlor organs, whereby grangers obtained fat cash discounts by ordering from "confidential" price lists issued only under the Grange seal. Eventual disclosure of the bargains to non-members soon ruined the contracts, however, and the scheme folded up.

The secret and feminine-equality features of the Grange were not always an advantage in organizing new areas. This was true in the South particularly, where a number of secret groups had played on class prejudice after the Civil War and opposed the Grange as another possible troublemaker. Besides attacking the Grange as a woman's-rights movement, thousands of persons asked suspiciously: "What do farmers want with women in a secret society?"

Through seventy-six years the fundamental precepts of the Patrons of Husbandry have not changed. Louis J. Taber, national master from 1923 to 1941, once attributed this to the fact that they "were founded on eternal truth."

Intentionally, the bulwark of the oldest farm organization is its 8,000 local and Pomona granges, scattered throughout thirty-seven states. The term "grange" is a specialized revival of an archaic word for farmhouse and today refers chiefly to community halls where young and old grangers meet at least once a month for spiritual, educational, scientific, or political fellowship—or all four. Many small communities, and by no means are all of them in the West, have only a school, a church, and a Grange hall in the way of public buildings.

The open Bible is a fixture at each meeting. After a prelude of ritualistic and other business the assembled neighbors may hear a lecture from one of their seniors, a debate by visiting students, or some other educational program. Then a bit of entertainment, with light refreshments, is in order.

Above the local or "subordinate" granges in the official pyramid are county or "Pomona" granges, as they are called, from the Latin for fruit. General economic matters, as well as co-operation with county extension agents and higher ritualistic work, are seated in the Pomona.

The state grange, standing above the two subdivisions, is extremely important in the organization. Voting at national conventions is carried out on a state basis, the state master and his wife casting all votes—just as the U. S. Senate is based on geographic representation.

Similarly, only the state masters and their wives are officially members of the National Grange, and all officers are chosen by and from that select group. Others, the rank and file, are members of the Order of Patrons of Husbandry, but convenience of reference has made the entire organization come to be known sweepingly as the National Grange. All members are eligible to attend conventions, and an average of some 7,000 do; but they do not vote.

Between annual sessions the Grange is governed by a hierarchy of officers bearing titles peculiar to fraternal orders: There is a Master, Overseer, Lecturer, Steward, Chaplain, Treasurer, Secretary, Gate Keeper, and Lady Assistant Steward, as well as three women ritualistic officials known as Ceres (grain), Pomona (fruit), and Flora (flower). Each of the latter presides at ceremonies for inducting grangers into Fifth, Sixth, and Seventh degrees respectively. In addition, the inner sanctum of Grange ritualism, the Assembly of Demeter, is presided over by a High Priest, Archon, and Annalist. An Executive Committee of three and a three-man managing board of the *National Grange Monthly* are other parts of the governing pyramid.

At each convention a number of standing committees, on subjects such as foreign relations, home economics, insurance, and good of the order, are chosen to carry on detailed business of the Grange.

Members are constantly reminded that this pattern of organization has put their order where it now stands, and must keep it there. The long presidential address of veteran National Master Taber, delivered just before his retirement at the Diamond Jubilee of 1941, illustrates the seriousness with which grangers take their affairs.

. . . the most important achievements of the Grange have been in the community life of the Republic [he said]. For seventy-five years local granges have been meeting either every week, two weeks, or monthly, as occasion requires. More than 200,000 of these local community gatherings have been held every year throughout our history. This has removed isolation from the farm; it has brought the opportunities of education, development, and self-help within the reach of all. The Grange is not just a farm organization alone. It is the gathering place for the farmer and his family.

Today [Taber continued] some advocate the formation of tenant, sharecropper, and farm-labor organizations. These are not needed, as wisely the Grange did not make wealth or class the test of membership. Those interested in agriculture, with good moral character and a desire to help improve community life, find the Grange door swinging open, admitting them to larger fields of usefulness. It is probable that in every grange in the nation can be found landowners large and small, tenants and hired help on the farm, each taking his place, seeking to enrich rural life. The material, legislative, community, and educational service of the Grange does not tell the full story. The power of fraternity, although a silken cord, binds our members in a common cause, as a band of steel. Without the fraternal and ritualistic side of the Grange, there would be no great celebration today.

Of equal importance [he declared] has been the place of woman and youth in our fraternity. Had the Grange been just a man's organization, and had there not been the finer qualities of woman and the enthusiasm of youth, the tombstone of our fraternity would have been moss-grown and forgotten. The glory of the Grange, however, is its emphasis on patriotic, moral, and spiritual ideals. It has sought to build a better citizenship; also to help create an indestructible America.

Reaching a little more into the future, Taber continued:

In these days of radio, movie, and streamlined progress, there are many who believe that fraternal organizations will lose their impetus and power. The automobile and airplane are eliminating time and space, but they cannot change the human heart. Fraternity, brotherhood, and the finer things of community life cannot be destroyed. The grange that neglects the ritualistic side of its work neglects part of its heart and soul. Education will have a larger place in the Grange programs of tomorrow. Legislation will be brought more clearly to the fireside of the individual Patron. Our economic and insurance programs will be greater factors in the daily life of all. These facts cannot change the need for fraternity that binds together human hearts in times of partisan bitterness, financial distress, economic boom, and storm. Should the ritualistic procedure of our fraternity ever fall into thoughtless or careless hands, disintegration and slow death await us.

On the next page Master Taber sounded the battle cry for a bigger, better-paid staff "to meet the impact of the next quarter of a century." Reminding his brothers and sisters that there are thousands of labor unions which pay business managers more than state grange masters receive, Taber stated that "the Grange's greatest weakness has always been the lack of income of state and national organizations, sufficient to employ the needed help to serve the farmer efficiently." Citing the Washington staffs of the American Federation of Labor and the U. S. Chamber of Commerce, Taber proclaimed the first step to be an expansion of "legislative research" work; next there should be a director of extension, working under the master, to tend the fences of organization and recruit membership.

At the time of Taber's charge to his fraternity, Grange resources stood at a high of more than $180,000.

The nation's oldest farm organization boasts a sizable pile of accomplishments for farmers. The first-mentioned is always regulation of railroads and other public utilities, chief target for the radical granger movement of the old days which brought down charges of communism on its members. Beginning seven years after the Civil War, the grangers swarmed over state legislatures and Congress until the rugged individualists who ran the rail empire were made accountable in the form of rate regulation and abolition of such crude practices as giving free passes to politicians.

Four years later, in 1876, the Grange beat on Washington's door asking Cabinet status for the Department of Agriculture. Farmers were ridiculed for taking this position; even the Commissioner of Agriculture at that time opposed it, and the chairman of the House Agriculture Committee asserted that the principal function of the department was to distribute free seed, leaving Congress to do the important work. Thirteen years later the Grange won the fight, however, and saw one of its prominent members appointed first Secretary of Agriculture by President Grover Cleveland.

Rural free delivery of mail, the parcel-post system, and postal-savings banks were largely results of Grange demands, as were the birth or growth of land-grant colleges, experiment stations, vocational agriculture in schools, and the Extension Service.

The power of the Grange was thrown behind pure-food-and-drug laws, pure-seed legislation, eradication of contagious diseases among animals, and bans on the sale of oleomargarine colored in imitation of butter. According to its own words, "the Grange has been a stalwart champion of the dairy interests" in every legislative battle over imitation butter, filled milk and cheese, and the so-called cooking compounds. Yet one of its "goals for 1940" was to "reduce production costs by removing punitive taxation and unnecessary trade barriers between the states."

The Grange was a pioneer in conservation of forests, land, mineral resources, birds, and humans. Says the Grange *Blue Book:* "From its very beginning the Grange has advocated temperance and has used its mighty influence toward outlawing the saloon. It led the way in many a struggle to accomplish it and fearlessly stayed to the end in every such undertaking." The selling of liquor, narcotics, or dope long ago became sufficient cause for summary expulsion from membership.

On the subject of citizenship Grange opinions are far-reaching. Way back in 1879 it endorsed the short and secret ballot. Four years earlier it came out for woman suffrage patterned after that enjoyed by the feminine contingent in its own membership. It was not so tolerant with foreigners; for years the fraternity has stood against Chinese and Japanese immigration.

Similarly, the Patrons of Husbandry will have nothing to do with lowering tariffs on commodities which compete with them. On the other hand, it opposes tariffs on manufactured goods that are high enough to breed a monopoly. Its compromise with low tariffs for some imports and high tariffs on others is represented by an Export Debenture Plan which the Grange pushes to dump "surplus" crops abroad, while retaining a relatively high price on crops sold in America and walls against retaliatory dumping by other nations.

The Grange has always been aware of financial and tax matters. It supported the Sixteenth Amendment, which gave Congress power to levy income taxes, and worked for Federal estate and gift taxes. It opposes the sales tax, because that form of revenue raising "ignores the principle of ability to pay." Farm credit has always been a favorite subject of grangers, making them the spearhead of the move to consolidate all farm-lending agencies in the Farm Credit Administration, established in 1933. Two years later the Grange claims to have led the fight for a 3½-per-cent interest rate for agriculture, maintenance of which drains the Federal Treasury each year.

Foreign policy, to the Grange, has long been one of preparedness—coupled with the deportation of criminal aliens and the registration of all unnaturalized. It has consistently favored arbitration of international disputes, but opposes "unnecessary militarism and compulsory military training in the public schools."

After enumerating this historical list of achievements, Grange officials are wont to add that, "judging only from a dollar-and-cents standpoint, every farmer in America is under sufficient financial obligation to the Grange to pay his fees and dues for himself and his family." Stated another way, in a campaign pamphlet, "the Grange seeks to put dollars into the farmer's pocket and courage into his heart."

The Washington office of the Grange, on the twelfth floor of the People's Life Insurance Building, is something like the organization's program—mellow, utilitarian, and a little quaint. Four small connected rooms, full of desks and file cabinets, make up the national headquarters of the Grange as well as its Washington arm, for National Master Albert S. Goss lives in Washington. Thus the Grange is the only farm group which actually heads up in the nation's capital.

In the last room on the right sits the man who has been its Washington representative for over sixteen years, Fred

Brenckman. There is nothing fancy about Brenckman, unless it could be his $5,000-a-year salary. He is homespun in his talk, his mannerisms, and his presentation of Grange affairs. Seated behind a massive old mahogany desk, in a heavy, high-back swivel chair, his large body is framed by cases of musty bound volumes of rural journals and books dating back to the Civil War. The walls are punctuated with pictures of venerated Grange leaders in dingy frames, including a prized print of the first annual convention in 1873.

The Grange has maintained a Washington office continuously since 1919, when Dr. T. C. Atkeson, dean of West Virginia University's school of agriculture, assumed the duties. Brenckman succeeded him on January 1, 1927, which means that he has seen the formation of every policy of the Roosevelt Administration. He has also had a hand in much of that history.

Brenckman has spent the past twenty-six years in full-time Grange service. After spending his youth farming in Pennsylvania, roaming around the Northwest, where he worked on extension of the Milwaukee railroad to the Pacific, and working on a daily paper in Hazleton, Pa., where he wrote a thick volume on the history of Carbon County, Brenckman attended a business school in Philadelphia and became secretary of the Pennsylvania Grange. Besides having 975 subordinate granges under his care, he edited the state grange's monthly journal and acted as its representative around the Pennsylvania legislature.

In appearance and action, with his homey chuckle and whitish hair which creeps down toward one eye, Brenckman seems an unbelievable cross between Jesse Jones and the late Will Rogers. His speech is frank, earthy, illustrated liberally with anecdotes; yet he displays some shrewdness.

His clothes are plain and dark, except for a jaunty hat that accentuates a twinkle in his eyes.

Number-two man in the office is S. S. McCloskey, who came there after being released from World War I and went to work as a stenographer. Rather than being an assistant to Brenckman, as he was for years, McCloskey is now a general aide to Master Goss.

Besides having the national master in Washington, Brenckman and McCloskey have been eclipsed in relations with the outside world by two characters imported by Goss in mid-1942 to put punch in the Grange program. In quarters below the main office, with desks facing each other, sit Dr. E. W. Sheets and publicity man Charles Dana Bennett.

Sheets not only brought to the Grange a fund of knowledge acquired by many years of service to agriculture, but also brought connections with wool, livestock, and fats and oils interests, as elaborated elsewhere. Functioning as assistant to the national master, Sheets spends much of his time in the field among the membership, but part of his job is to lend a starting hand to the enterprise of newcomer Bennett.

For many years the Grange's publicity was mainly for its own consumption in the form of heavy journals. Under the direction of the quick, energetic Bennett, however, press releases are issued, Grange speeches are sent to the press in advance, and public relations are co-ordinated with those of the Milk Producers, the Co-op Council, and the Farm Bureau in strategy meetings where the most minute differences of opinion are reduced to the written word. Under Bennett, an excellent grammarian with a flair for catchy phraseology, the Grange office has become a source of opinion for newsmen to check frequently.

Also it is reaching out across the country through a

unique subsidiary called National Agricultural Research, Inc. As editor for this corporation, Bennett writes a weekly column, Washington Farm Reporter, in which he applies bright colors to usually drab farm news.

"Washington, D.C., Jan. 13," begins one of his copyrighted pieces. "This city was filled to the last cot for the opening of the 78th Congress. Hotel lobbies resembled a barn dance before the days of gas rationing. Hotel clerks were hoarse from telling room hunters that no accommodations were available. Meals were at a premium, with only one pat of butter per customer. Speaking to a capacity crowd which jammed the House chamber, the President delivered his report on the state of the Union."

Bennett's public relations are a composite of at least three kinds of experience in his interesting career. After studying journalism at Columbia University he traveled abroad off and on for seventeen years, wrote boys' books and, up to Pearl Harbor, stumped the country as a non-interventionist speaker.

By far the outstanding characteristic of press-agent Bennett is his amazing resemblance to GOP hopeful and governor of New York, Thomas E. Dewey—even to the black mustache.

Bennett is neither a professional publicity man nor farmer, but has a general background for both. The farming comes from a large country home facing beautiful Lake Champlain, in western Vermont, where he carries on agriculture partly as a· diversion and partly to maintain outside income enjoyed by him and his wife. Bennett was not a member of the Grange there, though he has since joined, but was introduced to his present job by working in the publicity end of Governor Aiken's successful senatorial campaign in 1940. Stopping occasionally in isolationist

Aiken's Washington office, thereafter, he met the farm leaders whom he now publicizes.

Because Goss only recently became national master, it is necessary to look back briefly at the man who guided the Grange for eighteen years, through 1941: Louis J. Taber. A former master of the Ohio Grange, and later Commissioner of Agriculture in that state, Taber kept national headquarters in Columbus, Ohio, though he made frequent trips to Washington. Upon retiring from Grange leadership at the age of sixty-three (he asked not to be nominated in 1941), Taber was made president of the Farmers and Traders Life Insurarce Company, an old-line agency launched years ago by Grange people but not officially connected to the Grange.

Taber's politics were solidly Republican, as are those of the Grange in general. Besides being a Republican, however, he joined several non-political movements of various kinds. He is still vice-chairman of the Advisory Council of the Committee for Constitutional Government, the group already mentioned which was established by Republican publisher Frank Gannett "to uphold free enterprise and the rights of free men." A few of Taber's colleagues on the advisory board of the committee are: Samuel B. Pettengill, former Democratic congressman from Indiana, who is now treasurer of the GOP; Colonel O. R. McGuire, wealthy Washington lawyer and moving power behind the abortive Logan-Walter Bill; novelist Booth Tarkington; Nebraska's ex-Senator Edward R. Burke, who fought many New Deal measures and is now representing the Southern Coal Producers Association and doing other lobbying in Washington; Judge John D. Miller, venerated ex-president of the Co-op Council; Mrs. Isabella Greenway King, former senator from Arizona, and Mrs. John R. McCarl, widow of the former U. S. Comptroller General who helped maintain the General Accounting Office as the right arm of the Republican party after the Democrats came back in 1932.

Taber's interest in movements like this one explains much of the Grange's hostility to the President's unsuccessful plan for shaking up the Supreme Court in 1937. One of the most recent blasts from the committee, sent to all congressmen, editors, radio commentators, and "other molders of public opinion," was an attack on the President's net ceiling of $25,000 on salaries.

"Let us be direct," wrote the Reverend Norman Vincent Peale, D.D., acting chairman and secretary of the committee. "Isn't the purpose [of the $25,000 limit] . . . to win and uphold support of radical labor organizers and to further a program to redistribute the wealth of America by executive decree and in contravention of the express will of Congress?" The committee called on Congress to knock out the limitation, which it baldly asserted was "sponsored by the CIO and Mrs. Roosevelt."

Although the Grange has no general counsel, which is not all-important but somewhat indicative of the soundness of an organization's opinions on legal matters, it is quick to detect what it regards as threats to the Constitution. Of current unconstitutionality, in its opinion, is the Administration's reciprocal-trade-agreements program, though it adds that the program is detrimental to agriculture as well.

As a general farm organization, the Grange is sometimes asked to send representatives to sit in with special groups. Past Master Taber's position as secretary of the National Highway Users Conference, the auto industry's front for getting better highways, has already been mentioned. In addition to Taber, Fred Brenckman represents the Grange on the Steering Committee of the conference. Last November, when the National Federation of the Fur Industry was formed as a supertrade association, Fred Brenckman was elected to the board to represent the estimated 2,500,000 farmers who are amateur or professional trappers.

The incumbent national master, Albert Goss, is a slender, white-haired man whose white mustache and quiet demeanor suggest at first sight the bashful Caspar Milquetoast. Beneath his dignified, neat appearance, however, is a firm and sometimes aroused personality. Though Goss scarcely reminds one of the old-fashioned militant grangers, he does exemplify the modern combination of ritualism and economic approach to affairs of the day. Before he became master in 1941, Goss was a self-styled "barnyard economist" specializing in farm credit. At the age of sixty, the self-educated Goss has acquired a working knowledge of many angles of farming, partly from trying a few himself and partly from long observation.

After moving to the state of Washington in 1889, he finished school in Spokane and Portland, Oregon. Dropping a try at bookkeeping, he entered the milling business as a sweeper in an elevator, then bought with his brother a water-powered mill in Walla Walla County of Washington. Death of his father postponed indefinitely his intention to become a mining engineer.

Goss operated the mill and a country store for about seven years before he decided that little mills were being squeezed out of business. About 1905 he bought a wheat ranch and embarked on his first farming experience. This he sold, also, and turned to the telephone business for nearly a year, having bought a 2000-phone exchange for two small Oregon towns.

From telephoning Goss went into dairying and milked cows for seven years on a 100-acre irrigated Washington farm. It was here that he became interested in the Grange and was president of a co-operative store. The crash of 1920 put about half of the Grange co-ops on the rocks, but because that run by Goss weathered the storm he was chosen to operate the wholesale end of the Grange enterprises for several years.

In 1921 the Washington Grange was ripped asunder by a small revolution. State Master William Bouck was suspended by the national master for urging his membership to refuse support to the government until a number of demands were granted. The smack of sedition, coming soon after the war, was too much for national headquarters, though the state grange at first supported Bouck because of its discontent with Eastern domination of the fraternity. Bouck's Western backing folded up, however, when he moved to form a rump group with almost the same name. Several Grange halls were burned to the ground, and fist fights were in order as grangers actually toted guns to meetings. State delegates to the national convention in 1921 approved Bouck's expulsion, but back in Washington the minority voters walked out of the hall as Goss was elected the new master. Bouck was later nominated for Vice-President of the United States on the Communist ticket, and Goss spent eleven years as state master healing the wounds.

Goss's work in rural credit in those years won him election as director-at-large of the Spokane Land Bank and set him up to help organize a production-credit corporation (for loans on seed, spray, fertilizer, and other out-of-pocket costs) in 1931 among Wenatchee applegrowers. When the

Farm Credit Administration was being charted by the New Deal two years later, Goss was called to Washington by its first governor, Henry Morgenthau, Jr., to be Land Bank Commissioner. In that high post until 1940, Goss supervised about one half of the $3,000,000,000 of loans made and was called "the largest holder of second mortgages in history."

In December of 1939, however, Goss offered his resignation in protest against the Administration's move to bring the independent FCA into the Department of Agriculture. In spite of Wallace's assurances to the contrary, Goss felt that the co-operative system he had helped build would be destroyed and the government would be running the credit business that his farm clients had been running. After sticking around for a couple of months Goss broke completely with the Secretary, and President Roosevelt finally accepted the Land Bank Commissioner's resignation.

That was not the end of the episode, though. The Administration-sponsored Jones-Wheeler bill was trotted out to effect the statutory change necessary to shift the program. Goss appeared before the House Agriculture Committee after a front-page story had thrown the bill into public controversy and told of his fears for the system. A few days later he told the Senate committee the same thing. The bill died in both committees after other farm organizations decided to follow the lead of Goss.

The Administration's countermove was to call a mass meeting in St. Paul, Minn., to rally support for the measure. Presence of a number of department officials in the crowded hall is still a source of irritation to the Farm Bureau Federation and others who maintain that government travel allowances were used that day for a political purpose.

After making several studies for the Grange, Goss was elected national master to succeed Taber. His feud over credit is not ended, however. On his own expense, or from finances raised by other groups, he continues to write local officers of the Land Bank system once or twice a year to "let them know the true condition" of their Farm Loan Associations. Part of his continuing sermon is a warning that government credit will become a political tool.

It took the barnyard economist only a short time to catch up with Grange affairs, as he had attended all conventions while with FCA. Meeting often with his three-man Executive Committee, Goss rules the Grange from a tiny room, complete with sink in the corner, in the Washington headquarters. The only decorations in his sanctum are pictures and calendars from the Canadian Pacific, Northern Pacific, and Union Pacific railroads—enough to make the old-time railroad haters of the Grange turn in their graves. A vest pocketful of pencils belies Goss's propensity for figures, but he does most of his calculating at home to avoid interruptions. Nevertheless his office is run democratically, and the master is nearly always accessible.

Whether purely by coincidence or not, the wartime battles of the Grange have been accompanied by a partial facelifting operation. The carpentering which Goss has ordered is nearly all based on the strategy of offense—publicity splashes and alliances with other organizations, except the Farmers Union—which foreshadows continuing activity.

The financial and membership backing of the organization has not been impaired in the struggle. With as much as $75,000 coming in annually as dues from its about 800,000 members, with a Juvenile Grange providing a new crop of active members each year, and with $123,000 set aside for a new building, the Patrons of Husbandry will stand solidly for years to come. Also the revenue from fraternal degrees granted will run into thousands of dollars so long as the secret, fraternal features of the order are attractive.

With special-purpose cash subsidies apparently here to stay in some form or another, the Grange's part in thrashing out national agricultural policy will be increasingly great, for Goss can write out at least ten arguments against subsidies faster than the Secretary of Agriculture can say "Triple A." Also the Grange's pot shots at Federal bureaucracy will continue to be popular, though a reading of Grange proceedings and the non-secret part of its ritualism makes one wonder why it should oppose bureaucracy as such.

Finally, more than any other farm-pressure group the Grange is an institution, meaning that its influence, however subtle, is constantly fallen back on in critical periods and that it seldom gets far enough ahead of the pack to become very vulnerable. Grangers seem to like it that way.

X

American Farm Bureau Federation

GOLIATH

THE FARM BLOC was born in 1921 at a meeting of a dozen senators in the Washington office of the American Farm Bureau Federation. The intervening twenty-two years have brought some new personalities, new issues, and alternate periods of fighting and resting; but the Farm Bureau is still the kingpin of the farm bloc.

Only two years before the historic meeting the federation had been created from an alliance of strange, semi-governmental units. An act of 1914 established co-operative agricultural work between the Department of Agriculture and state agricultural colleges. To put up their half of the Federal-state matched funds for the work, state legislatures passed acts granting the money outright or setting up "County Farm Bureaus" to co-operate with the agricultural agents. Twelve states named the Farm Bureaus, and several of those chose the technique of granting funds only to counties whose Farm Bureaus had a certain number of members. This made the extension agent, whose salary was being raised, practically an organizing agent for the Farm Bureau, to which there was little objection in those early days.

Since formation of the American Federation of these unusual organizations, however, the entrance of heated competition from other farm groups has made the statutory arrangements virtual closed shops in some key states. Also, before the AAA could set up its own machinery, the County Farm Bureaus were leaned on heavily to administer the radical new program.

Intrenched in this way, the Farm Bureau is the Goliath of the farm bloc. Certainly no description of the bloc is complete without a review of the AFBF record. That record, as used for recruiting purposes, has been summarized on slick yellow paper in a pamphlet called *Accomplishments of the American Farm Bureau Federation, 1919 to 1941.* Arranged in digesting paragraphs, seventy-four separate accomplishments are listed for the twenty-two years. A summary of those from 1920 through 1930, roughly up to the New Deal period, follows without editing for possible erroneous claims of sole credit.

The bureau secured reductions in railroad freight rates that have annually saved farmers $100,000,000, defeated proposed freight increases, and obtained farmer representation on the Interstate Commerce Commission. It secured passage of two acts regulating stockyards and grain exchanges, got power for the War Finance Corporation to lend up to $1,000,000,000 to farmers, achieved higher rates on various farm commodities in the Emergency Tariff Act of 1921, and "organized the first agricultural bloc in Congress in 1921 to give expression to farmers' demands for parity."

In 1922 the bureau secured passage of the Capper-Volstead Act to encourage co-operative marketing and passage of the bill that gave agriculture a member of the Federal Reserve Board.

It obtained the Rural Credits Act, establishing farmer banks and increasing the Federal farm-loan limit from

$10,000 to $25,000, got appropriations of $60,000 a year to each state experiment station for service to farmers, and obtained exemptions for co-operatives from taxes and regulations, which have saved co-operatives more than $1,000,-000 annually.

High lights of its accomplishments from 1931 through 1941 follow in the bureau's own language:

In 1932, secured establishment of twelve regional agricultural credit corporations to handle farm-loan functions of Reconstruction Finance Corporation, and secured appropriations of $10,000,000 for promotion of local agricultural credit corporations.

In 1933, secured passage of first Agricultural Adjustment Act.

Secured passage of Bankhead-Jones Act of 1935, authorizing additional Federal appropriations for support of state experiment stations and extension services and for establishment of Federal research laboratories.

In 1935, pushed through legislation enabling Federal Surplus Commodities Corporation to purchase surplus farm products for relief distribution.

In 1935, secured passage of Wheeler Amendment to Farm Credit Act, reducing interest rates on Federal farm loans to 3½ per cent, saving more than $40,000,000 annually for farmers. This rate has been maintained through subsequent extension of this amendment.

In 1937, secured passage of Marketing Agreements Act to promote orderly marketing of certain farm products.

In 1938, secured passage of the second Agricultural Adjustment Act.

Secured establishment of parity principle in national farm legislation and obtained appropriations of $212,000,000 for parity payments in 1939.

In 1939, obtained appropriation of $119,000,000 to restore impaired capital of Commodity Credit Corporation. Entire strength of organization mobilized to pass USDA supply bill providing $500,000,000 for soil-conservation payments, $225,-000,000 for parity payments, $205,678,812 for surplus disposal . . . $47,975,000 for administration of Sugar Act, $5,923,000 for crop insurance, $201,000,000 for road construction, and $54,225,000 for Farm Credit Administration.

Other appropriation measures in 1939 carried $49,635,730 for Farm Security Administration, including $40,000,000 for farm-tenant loans under the Bankhead-Jones Act, $42,970,000 for the Rural Electrification Administration, and $75,213,653 for grazing, reclamation, and vocational education programs.

Helped to secure an appropriation of $85,000,000 in addition to about $100,000,000 regularly available . . . for disposal of surpluses. An additional $50,000,000 was appropriated, with federation support, for Red Cross use in feeding war refugees, and later another $50,000,000 for surplus disposal was obtained.

Obtained appropriations of $212,000,000 for parity payments in 1941.

The federation supported the Agricultural Appropriations Bill providing $918,603,918 for programs to be administered by the USDA during the 1941 fiscal year, including $498,560,000 for Soil Conservation Program.

Woven into these tangible steps is a grist of annual resolutions, passed in convention duly assembled and run off on the printing press as a guide to any who want to consult the official position in the next twelve months. There are, of course, untold stories behind most formal resolutions, involving smoke-filled hotel rooms, trading blocs of votes, parliamentary strategy, and personal appeals; but withal, a summary of resolutions of the Farm Bureau, like those of other organizations, is the quickest key to its fundamental policy.

The Farm Bureau meets annually in early December, together with its Associated Women's auxiliary, whose resolutions are incorporated into those of the menfolk. Starting arbitrarily with the twenty-first annual meeting, held in Chicago in 1939, here are the high lights, edited to avoid repetition elsewhere.

Parity: Reaffirming its traditional support of parity as a goal, the bureau resolved that "either there must be a readjustment of industrial and labor policies to bring industrial prices to a level in relation to farm prices which will insure maximum consumption of the products of both agriculture and industry, or agriculture will be forced to demand of Congress appropriations adequate to make the AAA fully effective in bringing farm income to a level which will permit farmers to buy the products of industry in normal volume."

After reiterating the Agricultural Adjustment Act of 1938, as its statement of the parity concept, the bureau then complained that "control of production has not been rigid enough to raise market prices to parity levels" and "appropriations for parity payments have been inadequate to bridge the gap between open market prices and parity." Failure to raise agriculture's income to parity was assessed the major blame for "the unemployment which has cost the Federal government billions of dollars in relief appropriations."

A 1942 plank on this subject which has left many observers puzzled, in view of later fights for superparity, went like this in part: "We deplore efforts that are being made to raise the parity prices of farm commodities through a revision of the formula upon which parity prices are determined. If these efforts are successful, the sound and defensible basis of present parity . . . would be destroyed, and agriculture would be breaking faith with the masses of the people."

Tariff: The Farm Bureau stood against any reciprocal-trade agreements which might "force or hold domestic prices for any farm commodity below parity level." To this end, members asked an amendment to the Trade Act "to provide that no agreement be consummated unless unanimously approved by the Secretaries of State, Commerce, and Agriculture."

Labor: "The American Farm Bureau Federation has always supported organized labor in all reasonable and legitimate efforts to improve the income of workers . . . however, we deplore the use of violence, boycotts, lockouts, failure to recognize duly constituted governmental authority, disregard of contracts, and other irresponsible acts, or any form of intimidation or coercion, either by labor or employers, any or all of which may result in the obstruction of the orderly flow of goods and services to the detriment of the public."

Another year the federation asked equal control for industrial prices and wages and declared that "there are not now and there will not be any bottlenecks in agriculture," and challenged labor to announce a moratorium on all work stoppages and strikes.

In other labor statements the bureau branded overtime pay as having "no justification," opposed efforts to include agricultural labor in wage-and-hour and labor-relations legislation, and expressed resentment of labor groups attempting to organize farmers or farm labor, obviously referring to John L. Lewis.

Antitrust: The federation heartily commended and supported the Department of Justice in its efforts to enforce the antitrust laws.

War: One year before Pearl Harbor the convention recognized the threat of Mars. Whereas the year before in

Chicago the federation had stated that "Federal income and credit must not be dissipated in expenditures for unnecessary implements of war," the 1940 plank on foreign policy was considerably modified.

"While this is no time for unreasonable national fear," it read, "we insist that the experience of many nations furnishes conclusive proof that the interests of America demand that the full energies and resources of our nation be devoted to the perfection of all our national defense with the utmost speed and efficiency until this country is made absolutely impregnable to foreign attack."

"No good purpose" was seen, however, in entering the conflict.

The Good Neighbor Policy: The federation decided that "it is not necessary that a sympathetic Latin-American policy be any threat to the welfare of American agriculture." Favoring financial assistance to Latin-American countries for storing and controlling surplus crops, the bureau resolved that "no useful purpose would be served by bringing commodities to the United States which are already in surplus in this country."

Department of Agriculture: In 1940 came a bombshell. Secretary Wickard had succeeded Henry Wallace as Secretary of Agriculture just three months before the meeting, and considerable speculation on possible changes of policy and administrative techniques was in the air. Against this background the Farm Bureau threw into the arena a demand that the department be thoroughly decentralized in such a way that all its sundry programs be administered in the field by Extension Service agents. To "unify" what it regarded as "too much overlapping and duplication" of these programs, the Farm Bureau asked for creation of a five-man, non-partisan governing board within the Department of Agriculture. Further, the board was to be representative of the nation's agriculture.

This ambitious plank, which would have substantially changed the Cabinet system of government and delivered the guts of the department into the hands of persons amenable to the federation, was brushed off in Washington. The recommendation that funds should be transferred to the Extension Service and to the state AAA committees for decentralized administration along these lines was likewise ignored. But the Farm Bureau had willfully widened, by one more big notch, the breach that had slowly been growing between it and its old friends in the department.

Food: After baldly stating that "American consumers need fear no rationing of food or fiber," the federation went on record for commodity-loan supports at 85 per cent of parity, then lit the fuse on another, smaller bombshell—this time under the Food Stamp Plan. In hedging language the federation demanded that appropriations for this program be charged up to relief rather than to disposal of farm surpluses:

"We endorse the broad, humanitarian objectives of the Stamp Plan for disposing of agricultural surpluses. We urge the continuation and extension of this program. We draw attention to the fact that in this program benefits are shared between the underprivileged and the undernourished, businessmen, and the producer of agricultural surpluses. It should not be considered exclusively an agricultural measure. In making agricultural appropriations, we ask the Congress to recognize that it is not a substitute for direct purchase in especially distressed markets or for the other agricultural programs."

In interpreting this move the following resolution on relief, passed by the Associated Women, is pertinent: "We must have legislation of such a nature as will tend to decrease dependency rather than promote its growth. We urge the enactment of a comprehensive work-relief law requiring every able-bodied person to perform some constructive service in return for relief assistance."

Social Security: The federation opposed extension of old-age benefits to farm workers "until such time as agricultural prices are restored to parity levels."

Wartime Prices: The 1941 convention, held in Chicago, met just three days after war had been declared by America. The extent to which the Farm Bureau was shaken by the blow is particularly significant in the light of the congressional battle over prices that was yet to come.

"The farmers of the American Farm Bureau Federation," it was resolved, "here and now, throw themselves into the struggle that will be waged upon the battle front by our army and our navy. . . . We commit ourselves to the stern labor and unselfish sacrifice required if our hallowed Christian heritage is to endure. We pledge ourselves wholly and unreservedly to the victory that must be won, so help us God."

To implement this all-outness, the federation urged "prompt action by Congress to establish . . . a Federal authority to establish maximum prices for commodities on a selective basis to the extent necessary to prevent inflationary price increases."

A clue to the way this declaration was later to be badgered, in large part, by Farm Bureau maneuvering on Capitol Hill was given farther down in the same resolution. After insisting that the principle of parity be "recognized," the joker was inserted: "In order to prevent the average price . . . being depressed below parity . . . no price ceiling should be established on any agricultural commodity . . . at a price less than 110 per cent of parity."

The resolutions closed with notes on the importance of keeping experienced farm hands on the land and of getting high priorities of farm machinery. Also centralization of control of the farm-credit system was opposed.

The December 1942 convention, held just after partial rebuke in the price-control fight, was marked more by the star-studded guest list than by new and different resolutions. Besides big-name farm leaders, the assembly applauded speeches by Chamber of Commerce President Eric Johnston, Senator Elmer Thomas, Representative H. B. Steagall, War Manpower Commission expert Collis Stocking, and columnist Dorothy Thompson.

The federation went on record as being impatient with government red tape, "unrealistic" farm-price policies, labor-union restrictions, lack of recognition of agriculture as a war industry, the Administration's policy of "using subsidies to keep food prices down" and its "flouting" of the Price Control Act strictures on ceilings for farm prices. It favored preservation of constitutional government, justice for Puerto Rico, postwar planning, unity in agriculture, and registration of groups seeking to influence national policies.

No position was taken on sin.

In addition to its resolutions the Farm Bureau is blessed with a number of pamphlets, speeches, and statements to furnish more low-down on tactics and between-the-lines policy. For example, there is material used in the heat of recruitment. Two documents, running about twenty pages in all, but not publicized, have been circulated in Florida, Arkansas, and Louisiana at least. Replete with gross inaccuracies and smacking of smear campaigns, the appeals make very illuminating reading besides revealing the Farm Bureau's approach to farmers in the field.

First, the one from Florida, entitled: *FARMERS UNION AND CIO UNITE—Radical Group in Department of Agriculture Urging Triple Alliance of FSA—Farmers Union —CIO.*

"As further evidence of unity between the Farmers Union and the CIO, let's check the records of how they line up on national issues to date," begins the paper, listing five points which are here excerpted.

I. *Congressional Record,* March 11, 1942, Page 2353: Letter from Farmers Union opposing appropriations to Dies Committee. Quote· ". . . We agree with the CIO statement, urging the refusal of its request for further continuation . . . At its Omaha convention National Farmers Union passed a strong resolution condemning the unpatriotic character of the Dies Committee . . ."

It is interesting to note that in addition to the CIO and Farmers Union, the others opposing the Dies Committee are the German-American Bund, the Silver Legion of America, National Workers League, a Nazi anti-Jewish group, the Communist party, etc., while those who defended the work of the Dies Committee, investigating un-American activities, were the American Legion, the Veterans of Foreign Wars, Federated Womens Clubs of America, the D.A.R.s, Knights of Columbus, and officials of American Farm Bureau Federation.

II. Farmers Union and CIO united to oppose extension of 40-hour work week and also the Smith Anti-Strike bill.

III. The CIO and the Farmers Union united in an effort to expand the bureaucracy of the Farm Security Administration.

IV. The Southern Tenant Farmers Union, a CIO affiliate [false], has received a boost from Bishop Francis J. McConnell in his letter addressed to hundreds of civic leaders in the Northern and Eastern states.

The letter, which was attached, was on stationery of the New York City Committee, National Sharecroppers Week —March 1 to 8, 1942—and listed Mayor LaGuardia as honorary chairman, with the bishop as chairman. Here are a few excerpts from the eminent bishop: "I appeal to you on behalf of nearly two million sharecroppers and tenant-farmer families who live lives of despair and of degradation in the midst of our democracy. . . . Under cover of the false cry of 'economy,' the economic group which would condemn the sharecroppers to perpetual serfdom has demanded the abolition of the government agencies which have tried to help them. This group demands the retention of the poll tax, the political means by which the Southern agricultural population has been disenfranchised."

V. The Farm Security Administration has recently hired the executive secretary of the Farmers Union in Arkansas, and the all-out campaign is on to organize the clients of the Farm Security Administration into the Farmers Union in that state.

Conclusive evidence points to an all-out drive to organize the *working farmers* of the South through the alliance of Farm Security Administration—Farmers Union and CIO.

Under the heading "WHY HAS FARM BUREAU OPPOSED FSA?" the document dragged in a number of equally unconnected and exaggerated gossip items to damn the FSA further. One of six will illustrate:

V. The Farm Bureau is very definitely opposed to the radical leaders of FSA who have joined hands with the radical labor leaders of the nation and "sell Agriculture down the river" in order to gain their own selfish, bureaucratic aims. . . .

The paper wound up with the familiar blast at FSA for seeking to "duplicate" the Extension Service, and a word of praise for parity.

The Arkansas and Louisiana document—dubbed a "white paper" by some—was longer, overlapped with that already quoted, and was even more of a catchall. But a glance at the unduplicated parts shows the extent to which the gullibility of prospective Southern Farm Bureau members was played upon by mixed fact and innuendo.

Declaring that a group of individuals in the Agriculture Department are working toward "State Land Socialism," the document denounced "a program to smear owners of land in excess of acreage sufficient for subsistence, or non-commercial farming."

"Confiscation of farm lands is openly advocated," the Farm Bureau charged, adding that "private landowners have come to regard this group as 'Modern Carpetbaggers' because they come into the South, attempt to find evidence to substantiate preconceived ideas about Southern conditions, view our economy through social-reform eyes, and attack the result of 'The Nation's Number One Economic Problem' rather than give consideration to the causes.

"They are the same individuals who are the first to holler when farm prices approach parity," the document complains, and "there is also indisputable evidence that they have preached class distinction, racial distinction, and economic distinction in their efforts to bring about dissension among Southern farmers and divide them on a racial basis. . . ."

CIO President Murray's statement, at his 1941 convention, that the slogan for the coming year must be "Organize the South" was spread thickly by the Farm Bureau. Likewise, several pages related details of Lewis' dairy-farmer drive and the plan of West-coast teamster czar, Dave Beck, for extending AFL membership geographically, eyeing particularly the unorganized South.

After several pages of haranguing at FSA and the Farmers Union support of it, the Farm Bureau document exploded for three pages at Rex Tugwell's administration of Puerto Rican affairs. Hung on the vague connection that Tugwell had once been chief of FSA's predecessor, the Resettlement Administration, it repeated paragraph after paragraph of editorial echoes of Puerto Rican attacks on the hapless governor. Those who understand the Puerto Rican situation know that Tugwell's opposition stems mostly from feudal landowners' fights against his enforcement of a land law which would break up all ownership in excess of 500 acres—a law passed several years before Tugwell's regime. But no effort was made in the vicious pamphlet even to name the issue, much less to explain it. Obviously the 500-acre law, designed to give more of the population a chance to eke out a private living instead of working for someone else, strikes at the Puerto Rico Farmers Association, an affiliate of the Farm Bureau.

Partly because it was so hot, partly because it was uninhibited by script, and partly because it came in answer to a specific challenge, the speech of Ed O'Neal in early October of 1942 at Des Moines, Iowa, should be added to the Farm Bureau policy collection. Twelve days earlier, as is detailed in the next chapter, Farmers Union chief Patton had given a keynote speech in Des Moines to a crowded hall which included high department officials who attended in a good-will effort. O'Neal was storming the city to accept Patton's implied challenge and deliver a full-dress blast at the Administration and organized labor as well.

Seated on the Shrine Auditorium platform with the smoldering veteran were J. R. Howard, first Farm Bureau president; Francis Johnson, president of the Iowa Farm Bureau, who introduced O'Neal; Allan Kiline, vice-president of the same organization; M. E. Cadwallader, vice-president of the Nebraska Farm Bureau; Hassel E. Schenk, president of the Indiana Farm Bureau; Coe Prichett, secretary of the Missouri Farm Bureau; George E. Metzger, secretary of the Illinois Farm Bureau; J. J. Lacey, director of information for the American Farm Bureau, and Murl McDonald, assistant director of Extension Service, Iowa State College.

As reported by the Des Moines *Register,* O'Neal started to work on his 2,500 listeners by putting aside his prepared manuscript and turning to old-school oratory. Defending the farm bloc from the criticism that it had been a major factor in inflating prices, O'Neal said, "The laboring man's wages are the answer for that."

Chiding the American worker, particularly for time and one half for overtime, O'Neal charged: "He has so much money he doesn't know what to do with it. In the last war he bought two silk shirts and two quarts of whisky. Now he has four silk shirts and a half case of whisky."

With his audience laughing uproariously at such jibes, O'Neal kept beating the drum: "Let us issue a challenge to American labor on this point. They want to work 40 hours a week, while the farmer—often a man who has been retired but has gone back to work—labors 70 and 80 hours a week."

Attributing the production woes of his farmers to high wage levels, O'Neal asked: "How can the farmer compete for labor when these high factory wages are paid, with the country going deeper and deeper into debt to do it? The farmer would take a lower level of prices if wages and the prices of things the farmer buys were in balance with the amount he received for the things he raises on the farm."

Although the meeting was frankly an answer to the Farmers Union, O'Neal alluded only casually to the rivals, mentioning them at one point as an "organization with few members—probably a shirttail of them here in Iowa."

Poking frequently at President Roosevelt and the New Deal, O'Neal recalled the farm bloc's fight through depression years and his visits to President-elect Roosevelt at Hyde Park, saying that he believed his suggestion of Iowan Henry A. Wallace as Secretary of Agriculture had led to Wallace's selection at a time when an Easterner was being considered. He then revealed that he had hesitated in accepting appointment the week before to Byrnes's Board of Economic Stabilization, the agency whose creation climaxed the September farm-bloc fight.

"I was afraid I might not be able to serve agriculture so well if I did. Sometimes things like that mean a kiss of death," he drawled.

Explaining why he had finally decided to accept the advisory position, O'Neal declared that if he sees that "things are not going well for agriculture" he will "raise hell about it."

Finally, he urged agriculture to maintain a united front and assailed the bureaucrats who, he insisted, are trying to take away the right of the farmer to protect his own rights by appealing to his duly constituted representatives. The greatest hope of the farmer in keeping these rights, he concluded, is the American Farm Bureau Federation.

Lost in the oratory was the introductory remark of President Johnson of the Iowa Farm Bureau that the farmers in their mass meeting must not give the appearance of "rabble rousing prejudice," as President Roosevelt and many of his agricultural advisers had helped in early fights for much of the progressive farm legislation.

One answer to O'Neal's one-man tornado came in a joint statement issued a few days later by A. A. Couch, president of the Iowa Federation of Labor, and Ben A. Henry, president of the Iowa-Nebraska States Industrial Union Council.

"Iowa farmers and laborers will not permit outside influence and selfish politicians to drive a wedge between them," said the AFL and CIO leaders. Charging that O'Neal had "deliberately insulted every man in America who toils for a living," the two spokesmen challenged the good faith of O'Neal in coming to Des Moines "on the pretext of discussing farm problems." Exploring what they believed to be the true purpose of O'Neal's rally, Couch and Henry stated that "further light was cast on the purpose of the meeting when Iowa President Johnson called for election support for Iowa's eight congressmen."

"Could there be any significance in the fact that seven of these congressmen are Republicans?" they asked rhetorically.

An equally vigorous protest was lodged publicly by former Governor Nelson G. Kraschel, running at the time for a comeback on the Democratic ticket: "Mr. O'Neal lowered himself in the high esteem in which he has always been held by Iowa people," Kraschel asserted. "His words and demeanor were not becoming to the dignity of his position as a national farm leader. I am a charter member of the Farm Bureau, but I deplore such an unfortunate display of bad manners."

After a personal attack on O'Neal as "an aristocratic Southern planter who wants to continue the feudal land system of the South," the livestock auctioneer and politician said that the "farm bloc's threat against national unity by demanding concessions not generally sought or expected by farmers is the outgrowth of overzealous farm leadership."

Who are the officers who formulate and execute the Farm Bureau program?

The history of President O'Neal is almost the history of the American Farm Bureau Federation. Not only has he been one of its leaders from the beginning, but his roots and growth are typical of the source of the organization's real strength. Not all of the parallel is coincidence; much of it was planned that way.

Briefly stated, the career of the sixty-seven-year-old rural leader has been a transition from a large, inherited plantation to full-time organizing. He was born near Florence, Alabama, into a family of first settlers of Tennessee. His birthplace was the large cotton plantation of his grandfather, a brigadier general in the Confederate Army who marched toward Washington with Lee's army in a little different way than O'Neal now does and who later served two terms as governor of Alabama. One of O'Neal's uncles, Emmett O'Neal, by also becoming governor, made the family name well known to Alabamians.

In 1898, O'Neal was graduated from Washington and Lee University with an A.B. degree, including one year of law. He returned immediately to his grandfather's plantation and set out to apply scientific, progressive farming methods to the soil as a necessary hedge against the vicissitudes of one-crop economy which so long plagued the South. At the present time O'Neal operates, though by remote control, a 1,200-acre plantation which was inherited through his mother from Andrew Jackson Hutchins, a ward of President Andrew Jackson and a nephew of General John Coffee, O'Neal's great-grandfather. The land lies on the Tennessee River, near O'Neal's birthplace and the point at which the Tennessee volunteers, under Andy Jackson and General Coffee, crossed the river on their way to the Battle of New Orleans and the Creek wars. O'Neal is proud of relating the close association between Jackson and Coffee and how the deed to the Coffee farm (now O'Neal's) was written by Jackson, while that of Jackson's famous home, the Hermitage, is in the handwriting of and witnessed by the general.

The ancestral plantation is only two miles from Muscle Shoals, scene of the controversial Tennessee Valley Authority birthplace. Years later, as a member of President Hoover's Muscle Shoals Commission, O'Neal put his organization against use of the huge facilities for anything but fertilizers—no public power.

In 1921, as a charter member and first president of the Lauderdale County Farm Bureau, O'Neal began his long period of activity in the AFBF. A year later he was elected vice-president of the Alabama state unit, becoming president in 1923 and serving for the next seven successive years. While climbing rapidly in the Alabama federation, he had also become important in the national. He was made a member of the Finance Committee in 1922 and the Executive Committee in 1923. In 1924 he became vice-president of the national body, a position he held until 1931, when Sam H. Thompson was appointed to the Federal Farm Board and O'Neal succeeded him as president. Besides all these positions, he had served for several years as a director of the organization, as chairman of its powerful Committee on Resolutions, and as a member of the Committee on Legislation and Taxation.

Although the press of organizational duties took O'Neal from active management of his own farm in 1923, he has been recognized several times since for service to agriculture. According to an official biographical sketch, one of O'Neal's most precious possessions is the gold medal attached to his watch which bears the inscription: "For Distinguished Service in Farm Leadership." The medal was awarded to him in 1927 by the *Progressive Farmer* and the Alabama Polytechnic Institute at Auburn. In May of 1933, O'Neal received the honorary degree of Doctor of Agriculture from the institute, and in 1939 was selected by the *Progressive Farmer* as the South's "Man of the Year" for outstanding leadership in farm organizational work.

As president of a major association, O'Neal naturally has been called in by the government frequently. Most recently President Roosevelt put him on the Management-Labor Policy Committee of the War Manpower Commission. In 1935 he was appointed to the Allotment Division which was set up under the Works Relief Bill to distribute $4,000,000,000 through work-relief projects. Some observers believe that O'Neal, instead of his powerful vice-president, Earl Smith, is head of the Farm Bureau only because it is smart to have a Democrat there during a Democratic administration. But O'Neal's full-time devotion to the federation is not doubted.

Since the appearance of war clouds over Europe, O'Neal has spent even more time in Washington than usual. As early as 1939 he was made a member of the Agricultural Advisory Council appointed by Secretary Wallace to aid the department in handling war-created problems. In 1940, when Chester C. Davis was representing agriculture on the National Defense Advisory Commission, forerunner of OPM, SPAB, and WPB, he was appointed to the committee set up by Davis to advise with him on defense matters.

Most of his many trips to Washington include a look at congressional matters, and when a fight is on in the chamber the veteran's white hair can nearly always be spotted in the gallery. Congressmen long ago learned that he watches them vote.

The unceasing legislative drive of the Farm Bureau centers in its Washington office in the Munsey Building—the same building in which it rented space when the farm bloc was organized twenty-two years ago. Now on the eighth floor, the federation's suite of rooms is little different from any others, except for the noticeable contrast between its snappy fluorescent lighting fixtures and its bare wooden floors.

On the right of the reception and stenographers' room is the office of lawyer Hugh Hall. The walls around Hall's cubicle are lined with official documents and loose-leaf legal services, tools in his trade of fretting with government rules and regulations.

On the left is the larger office and huge light oak desk of W. R. Ogg, director of research and general Washington representative. Behind the diminutive, conservatively dressed Ogg is a symmetrical display of autographed portraits of Roosevelt, O'Neal, Herbert Hoover, Calvin Coolidge, and miscellaneous public figures. Hung low along the wall on Ogg's right is a row of more pictures, including farm-bloc chieftains of present and past.

Speaking ever so softly and hardly moving his lips, Ogg can recall most of the Farm Bureau's history, as he joined its staff in 1925. His association with the federation was quite accidental. As a tobacco farmer in Virginia, where he had moved from Kansas after the World War, Ogg threw his lot in with that of other distressed tobacco growers who found only low prices for their bountiful crops.

Out of a mass meeting emerged the Virginia Tobacco

Growers Association, of which Ogg was made secretary. Soon the two Carolinas were brought in to make it a tri-state organization pledged to reduce tobacco acreage by one third. Because membership was not 100 per cent, however, the voluntary restriction failed to force prices upward. That experience, thirteen years before a similar feature was written into the AAA, taught Ogg the value of total compliance and threw him in contact with Farm Bureau officials who employed him as assistant Washington representative. While in the capital he completed his college education at George Washington University, receiving a master's degree in psychology—a valuable asset for an influencer of legislation.

In 1933 he served in the Chicago headquarters as assistant to the president and secretary of the federation, then moved back in 1938 to Washington to replace Chester Gray, who gave up the rigors of active lobbying to become director of the National Highway Users Conference.

As the Washington spokesman it is Ogg's job not only to anticipate legislation and administrative decisions which might affect the Farm Bureau adversely, but also to explain to all inquirers the organization's official positions. Even though the AFBF is supercritical of Washington bureaucracy, Ogg often has to sit around the table with government officials who are targets of his attacks. Also he must convince the doubtful that the Farm Bureau really represents the cross section of farmers—big and little alike—that it claims to represent. He asserts that it is libelous to charge that his group or the Grange is composed of large, commercial-type farmers as against small, family-type farmers. What is more controversial and harder to prove, however, is that the Farm Bureau does not represent the *viewpoint* of commercial farmers, regardless of what its *membership* claims may be.

The ace in the hole for Ogg and other federation officials on this point is that their membership figures show an increase in spite of continuous attacks. According to the latest secretary's report, paid membership rose to 591,230, an all-time high and an increase of 14 per cent over 1941. Counting members of families, the organization estimates a total of 2,500,000 rural people behind its program. National dues of 50 cents a year are taken from assessments which range locally from $2 to $5 in most states and up to $15 in Illinois, where $10 stays in the county to pay a share of the extension work.

Ogg keeps in close touch with President O'Neal, whose main office is a more comfortable layout in Chicago where the central staff of about ten, plus stenographers, carries on the daily burden of federation work, including the publication of a four-page weekly tabloid called the *Official News Letter* and a slick-sheet monthly, *The Nation's Agriculture*, which boasts a circulation of over 475,000.

Chicago is also the home of the Illinois Agricultural Association, the Farm Bureau affiliate in that pivotal state. Since 1926 Earl C. Smith, vice-president of the national body, has been president of the Illinois unit; today he is easily the outstanding state president. Smith's general counsel in the IAA is Donald Kirkpatrick, who also serves as general counsel of the AFBF. Smith, as a veteran of legislative fights, is a man of acknowledged power among congressmen and downtown signal huddles as well. He has little in common with the New Deal and peddles his opinions strategically from his additional position as chairman of the AFBF Resolutions Committee. By profession he is a large operator; by political faith, a Republican.

Among the forty-two states in which the Farm Bureau lists affiliate federations there are often differences of policy. For example, Illinois and Ohio, only one state apart, are almost opposite poles in policy. Murray Lincoln, Ohio secretary and kingpin, frequently leads his followers into joint positions with the Farmers Union, while Earl Smith's course is far in the other direction. Also there are spasmodic rebels in the big family. Besides that of Ohio, the federations of New Hampshire, Vermont, and sometimes Utah occasionally stray from the fold and say so.

The AFBF is governed between conventions by O'Neal, Smith, and a Board of Directors composed of several state presidents from each of four regions plus the president of the Associated Women of the AFBF. One of the state presidents on whom so much of the policy forming falls is Ransom Aldrich, of Mississippi.

Two speeches on October 27, 1942, before a county Farm Bureau assembly in Greenville, Miss., showed that state to be following the lead of President O'Neal's biting Des Moines pronouncement. One was by Aldrich, the other by his friend Oscar Johnston, president of the National Cotton Council and operator of the second largest cotton plantation in the country.

According to the Memphis *Commercial Appeal*, the speakers charged that "the Agriculture Department is directed by the CIO," and called the Administration a "Labor party."

"If there ever was a time," Aldrich said, "when we should pull together as farmers and have one tongue, it is now. We must realize that the present administration is not a Democratic party. It is a New Deal party, a labor government. We are letting creep in with the labor policy of the government a lot of communism and state socialism."

Johnston, who works hand in glove with the Farm Bureau in the South, touched on the military situation, then told his enthusiastic audience: "We should go shoulder to shoulder to win this war and exterminate our adversaries. We will, but while we are fighting this war in the Orient and in Europe, this magnificent edifice we call our homeland is being undermined—gutted from within."

Commending the cotton farmers of Arizona for holding out against the efforts of the "Farm Security Administration and the CIO to organize the Mexican labor brought into Arizona to pick cotton," Johnston said the planters rightly refused to deal directly with an agent of the laborers.

"The Arizona farmers," he told their Mississippi brethren, "were condemned for holding out, but they were doing it for us. Had they accepted the CIO pickers, next year we would all have to be dealing with the CIO to get our farm labor. Unless the farmers—the sensible farmers—organize and fight their own battles, we will all be in a hell of a fix."

"Mr. Johnston said the Arizonans were good Farm Bureau Federation members," the *Commercial Appeal* reporter added.

Another big name among state Farm Bureau presidents is Walter Randolph, from O'Neal's Alabama. Randolph's recent build-up hints a move to make the huge man a high national officer soon. Meanwhile he travels to Washington often.

Randolph resigned as assistant to I. W. Duggan, chief of AAA's Southern Division, to become president of the Alabama federation. He was helped by being a protégé of the head of Alabama Polytechnic Institute, under whom the State Extension Service is operated. The friendliness of both men for Aldrich helps to explain the tie in that area between the Extension Service and the Farm Bureau.

One of the most recent state units to be established is in Oklahoma, a particular stronghold of the Farmers Union. In fact, the more radical union is so strong there that it took E. K. Gaylord, wealthy publisher of the *Farmer-Stockman* and other papers, to get the Farm Bureau started there. In his rural paper Gaylord announced that if 500 candidates for membership signed up at $5 per head, an organizer would be brought in to clinch the beginning. In a short time he claimed 1,000 names on the line and got O'Neal to come from Chicago for the inauguration of permanent organization.

It was also Gaylord who started the short-lived but famous "prairie fire" under Congress in the midst of the 1942 fight over labor legislation. Readers of his *Daily Oklahoman* were asked to clip protesting coupons from the paper to send to congressmen. It was several days before newsmen in Washington discovered the inspired nature of the conflagration.

The Farm Bureau does not always get its main help from top citizens like Gaylord, however. More often its friend is the Department of Agriculture. Complete documents on the old practice of using official Extension Service backing for the farm organization, especially in the South, were spread on the record in February of 1942 when the Joint Committee on Reduction of Nonessential Expenditures was probing the Farm Security Administration. Farm Bureau officers were the chief complainants; Virginia's Senator Harry F. Byrd, whose main interest in the farm problem is Virginia apples, was chairman.

President O'Neal and others had lambasted FSA's conduct on familiar charges of "socialization of the land," bureaucracy, and subsidization of uneconomical farmers. As a sensational buttress to the Farm Bureau's attack it employed a half dozen men to go into the field to probe the FSA. The long, vague, and only sketchily documented report of William C. Carr, Chicago attorney who went deep into the South, proved to be the most interesting. After the committee had given FSA an inhumanly short time to check each charge of Carr's and the fur was flying around the committee table, Senator Robert La Follette asked FSA to supply him with any information available on instances of governmental encouragement to the Farm Bureau.

The result was two pages of fine print detailing brazen use of the government franking privilege, county agents' offices, and outright Extension Service appeals to help the federation. The principal time for collaboration was shown to be just as AAA money was being distributed, and the technique was to let Farm Bureau representatives cash checks for farmers while they talked them into paying dues then and there; but the county agent of Perry County, Alabama, was not so subtle. Excerpts from his letter of March 15, 1939, to all farmers in his area illustrate:

We will begin delivering 1938 agricultural-conservation checks Friday of this week. Since 1933 farmers in Perry County have received $1,532,780 in Agricultural Adjustment Administration benefit payments. . . . There is only one way to continue to receive these payments; it is through the membership in an organization which is strong enough to tell Congress what you want. The American Farm Bureau Federation is the largest farm organization in the world, and only through this organization have you been able to receive these payments. . . .

The close link between the Farm Bureau and the AAA is a traditional bone of contention among farm organizations, not only because of the favored position it has given one organization compared to the others, but because it is felt by small fry around the table that AAA payments have been made too often and too large to big operators who operate their holdings from a city office building—usually an insurance company's headquarters. Agitation from the little fellows resulted in a legislative requirement that the department submit a report each year on all payments over $1,000.

To offset the length of this document the department sends along with it statistics showing the breakdown of payments by size. For example, in the 1940 program 1,650,-000 farmers, representing 27 per cent of all recipients, got *conservation* payments of $20 or less; 1,500,000, representing 25 per cent, received payments ranging from $20 to $40; and 448, representing .007 per cent, received payments ranging from $5,000 to $10,000. Roughly the same distribution applied to *parity* payments that year. However, the small voices against AAA still point to the fact that in the same year more than 13,000 conservation payments of over $1000 in size were made.

Challengers of the Farm Bureau, in and out of the department, invariably connect its alleged spokesmanship for big commercial farmers with charges that most fat AAA payments fall into its hands. This is always denied by the Farm Bureau and cannot be written down as a fact, but until solid research in the field settles the point it is at least a controversy. So long as the militant Farm Bureau is king of farm organizations it will continue to be harried by such charges. Also stories will continue to be told on it like the one brought back by a competing organizer who stopped in at a tavern and found this sign over the bar: "Member of the American Farm Bureau Federation."

Proverbially speaking, "Uneasy lies the head that wears a crown."

XI

National Farmers Union

DAVID

IT WAS OLD Isaac Newton Gresham, sitting on a log in front of a plank storehouse in the village of Point, Texas, who planned the Farmers Educational and Co-operative Union. Borrowing the only typewriter in town, Newt Gresham pecked out his ideas for building a new farm organization on the foundation of Rochdale co-operation, plus an educational program. He had belonged to the Grange and had been an organizer for the National Farmers Alliance in Lauderdale County, Alabama—also the home of Ed O'Neal.

In 1887 the alliance, merged with a Louisiana group called the Farmers Union, had become the Populist party and never survived its political fling. With a dream of avoiding past mistakes, Gresham corralled nine farmer friends and formalized a charter for the Texas Farmers Union. On September 2, 1902, the first local unit was set up at the Smyrna Schoolhouse, near Point, and Gresham, who had been made organizer of the state organization, soon was flooded with requests for information on his new movement. His correspondence became so heavy that extra help had to be hired for the Point post office. By 1905 there were 200,000 members in eleven Southern states. In 1906 national officers were elected.

In the next twenty-two years, up to the depression, the Farmers Union grew northward under the vigorous leadership of Charles Barrett. Moving right up the Mississippi Valley to the Canadian border, union records showed 935,837 members in good standing. The economic and political grips of the World War caused casualties among several state unions, but the nucleus held tight. When Charley Barrett retired in 1928 to become the union's Washington representative and write a weekly column, he could look back on the building of a major, general farm organization. What he could not see was the way his colleagues were to be almost fatally split by issues of the great depression.

Three top leaders of the Farmers Union had been instrumental in calling the conferences which led to the ill-fated McNary-Haugen Bill and Hoover's Federal Farm Board, but within the union there was bitter difference of opinion as to whether the Farm Board was worth struggling along with. At the 1930 convention John Simpson, fourteen years the president of the Oklahoma union and twice vice-president of the national, was elected president. The faction opposed to the Farm Board had won control on a platform demanding more radical legislation. Until his death in 1934, Simpson kept things hot for even the Democrats who had swept into office.

Meanwhile, in 1931, Edward E. Kennedy was elected secretary and started waging a relentless fight for legislation, including the drastic Frazier-Lemke Bill to scale down interest rates to farmers and refinance the farm indebtedness which was bringing bitterly resisted foreclosure sales in most counties. One of the media of Kennedy and Simpson was the Farm and Home Hour, a national radio program sponsored by the Department of Agriculture and the National Broadcasting Company. Farm organizations were—and still are—given time to air their views on this program, which fact led to the interesting picture of the Farmers Union often spending theirs for merciless lambasting of the department.

At the same time, in Minnesota, the Dakotas, and Wisconsin, desperate farmers were organizing the famous Farm Holiday Association, pledged to strike against starvation prices by keeping their products off the market. Many heads were bashed in as Holidayers upset milk trucks and otherwise took economic ills into their own hands. In many areas the movement was actually sponsored by state Farmers Unions. In Iowa the fiery veteran farm leader and state president, Milo Reno, led the violence and became national president of the Farm Holiday.

Those members of the Farmers Union who did not join in the show of force dug in on the front of lifting themselves by buying and selling co-operatively, but even after Simpson died control of the organization continued in the direction of political action in the hands of E. H. Everson, South Dakota president. Under him, as under Simpson, Kennedy was national secretary. In addition, the militant Kennedy became editor of a new and official paper, the *National Union Farmer*.

Kennedy's insistence on flaring into national issues widened the gulf between those of his belief and those clinging to co-operation. Then, according to a union historian, Kennedy began to take sides with Father Charles Coughlin, the Detroit radio priest. In 1936, Representative William Lemke, of North Dakota, ran for President on the ticket of the new Union party, with ardent support of

Father Coughlin and Kennedy. In the north-central states the issue was hot enough to tax the Farmers Union precept, written into its constitution and bylaws, that partisan politics and religion were not to be discussed in its meetings. Violaters could be expelled, in fact. With Southern members of the union being staunch Democrats and those of the North being nearly as staunch Republicans, a great fuss was understandably raised over Secretary Kennedy's activity.

At the national convention of 1936, after the re-election of Roosevelt and miserable defeat of Lemke, Kennedy brought Lemke in to address the meeting. The display was not well taken, as Kennedy was defeated for secretary a few days later by a one-vote margin. Followers of Kennedy disgruntledly attempted to disaffect the state organizations of Michigan, Ohio, Illinois, and Pennsylvania, which they partly succeeded in doing, and formed the Farmers Guild. Kennedy was made its executive secretary and continued his program of legislative action through pressure.

The guild gradually grew weaker, after working mainly for some form of cost-of-production legislation, and in 1942 Kennedy turned up in the most peculiar of farm organizational jobs: director of research for John L. Lewis' United Dairy Farmers Division of the United Mine Workers.

The rift left the Farmers Union admittedly weakened in numbers but standing solidly behind its program of co-operation and education. After two or three years of consolidating gains there emerged a vigorous young group of officials who were capable of adding the necessary personality, drive, and leadership to build up the Farmers Union once again. Coincidentally, war clouds over the isolationist West rallied scattered members behind the energy of James G. Patton, formerly president of the Colorado Farmers Union and, at thirty-eight, youngest man to be elected national president. Significantly, the resolution of brotherhood with organized labor was the strongest ever passed by a Farmers Union convention.

Whatever else may be said of Jim Patton, he is a son of the soil. Born in the same year as the union at Bazar, Kansas, Patton's parents moved him at the age of two to Amity, in eastern Colorado, after which he moved from one small Colorado town to another. After leaving Trinidad, where his father, an electrical engineer, worked for the Colorado Fuel and Iron Company, the Patton family crossed the Continental Divide of the Rocky Mountains. Here they took a homestead in a co-operative colony of farmers at Nucla, in the San Juan Basin. Young Jim stayed there until he was seventeen, learning at a most impressionable age the rudiments of economic co-operation.

Although land in Nucla was held individually, it was pooled for some purposes, and the citizenry daily shared its co-operative laundry, mill, creamery, and store. Before the seventy-five families of Nucla were supplanted by newcomers who did not fare so well, Patton had learned lessons like this one in land utilization: At the customary meetings in Town Hall, after due deliberation and debate on the subject of where to build the town buildings, it was decided to perch them atop the rockiest hill in the settlement so that the land of no member would be increased in value by adjoining them.

Patton fondly recalls such lessons, but other recollections are not so fond. When his father developed a cancer that required the expert medical care which the Pattons thought they could get at Glenwood Springs, they moved back to a farm near there. The years 1920 and 1921 were hard ones for the Pattons, never to be forgotten by the only boy in the family. The postwar depression not only caused general price slumps but also the loss of the family's herd of cattle. In 1921 his father died and Patton turned to school teaching for the support of his mother and three sisters, although he had had no college training at that time. For four and one half years he taught at the small schools of Nucla, Grand Valley, and Eckert.

Then came the realization of his desire to go to college. After six months at the University of Colorado, where he started out to be an engineer, Patton transferred to the smaller Western State College at Gunnison. At Western State it was easier for him to work his way through and be nearer his dependents. His record there foreshadowed later success as an organizer and salesman. In three years he was president of the student body as well as of his local fraternity, assistant editor of the yearbook, and assistant business manager of the school. Also he played right halfback or guard on the football team, ran the mile for his track team, played basketball, and boxed.

Although he majored in business administration and economics, which became useful to him later, Patton's fondest recollection of Western State comes from the honorary LL.D. degree it bestowed on him in 1942.

In July of 1929, just a few months before the devastating crash, Patton went to Denver to work. After a time with the Burroughs Adding Machine Company he became regional representative for the L. C. Smith Typewriter Company, for whom he had sold portables to fellow students at college. However, the ways of corporate life were not appealing to Patton. As a regional representative he did not like the way a big company operated; so he sought the more independent existence of an insurance salesman, joining up with Occidental Life, another company whose wares he had peddled at college. It was while dealing for this firm with the Farmers Union on group-policy plans that Patton put private enterprise aside and joined the union for the purpose of setting up its own co-operative-insurance agency. He is still its president.

Both Patton and his father had been farming members of the union for years; it was natural that the son became active in aspects of the program other than co-operative insurance. In 1934 he was elected secretary of the Colorado Farmers Union; in 1937 he was elected to the national Board of Directors; in 1938 he became state president, and in 1940 he was given the union's highest honor. As national president he gets a salary of $5,000, but he receives nothing as head of the insurance co-op.

The young farm leader earns every penny. An average of 200,000 miles on the road each year takes him away from his wife, their sixteen-year-old daughter, and their nine-year-old son nine tenths of the time. Though Denver is the union's national headquarters, the president must look in on thirty-five states at least once in a while.

In 1941 he and a small group of other agriculturalists were sent to South America by the Carnegie Endowment for International Peace as general agents of good will. It was a big trip for Patton, as his hobby, besides fishing and woodworking when time permits, is international affairs. Someday his international avocation, he hopes, will be much more than an avocation, for he is trying to establish an International Farmers Union.

To that end he maintains correspondence with farm leaders of India, England, China, and other countries where he feels that farmers will need an aggressive union in the dubious postwar period. He also keeps in touch with the Canadian and Mexican leaders and is a member of various international-study committees, such as that of James T. Shotwell.

On foreign policy Patton was behind President Roosevelt from the beginning. In fact, he risked his neck at the hands of traditionally isolationist farmers to join William Allen White's Committee to Defend America by Aiding the Allies.

Traveling so much of the time, correspondence is difficult for Patton, but he does get considerable reading done. Among his favorite topics are such books as Lewis Lorwin's *The Economic Consequences of the Second World War.* Also he meets many, many people—which is one of the things he likes most.

It is difficult to say how much of the Farmers Union's success in finding at least a small place in the sun is attributable to the organization's policy and how much is attributable to Jim Patton's personality. He is a good speaker, an educated meeting attender, carefully groomed, and an expert salesman. He looks neither as radical as some union resolutions nor as conservative as most professional farm leaders. Accenting with his big head and husky hands, Patton is not afraid of hurting feelings, yet he is not undiplomatic. He is the maverick of bureaucratic government advisory sessions and a cutter of red tape.

Appointment of the youngest of the top-flight farm leaders to the Economic Stabilization Board, headed by ex-Justice Byrnes, caused much headshaking among the remainder of the farm bloc. The fact that the other agricultural seat on the board is held down by the Farm Bureau's O'Neal is a comfort to them, and they try to explain away Patton's success with President Roosevelt by calling it a political deal. A disinterested judge, however, cannot help thinking that Patton's combination of charm and forthrightness had much to do with the victory, for there is something about him that says his career lies ahead of him. Maybe it is his liking for the future tense.

Of course it cannot be said that the challenging David has toppled a Goliath yet, but he has a stone and a slingshot and has issued the challenge. It may be years before he lets fly, but he has the years.

Vice-president of the union is a Montana wheat and stock farmer in his fifties, Herbert Rolph. By virtue of ten years in the State Legislature, being speaker for two of them, Rolph is the union's parliamentarian. Also his political acumen and ear for gossip make him the ace crossroads organizer. Though he is no firebrand whipper of enthusiasm, Rolph is kept on the road for the union much of the time.

Emil Loriks, one of the youngsters who recently entered officialdom, is secretary. Loriks actively manages a substantial farm in South Dakota, was a leader in the Holiday strike in that state, and was once president of its Farmers Union. After a narrow defeat for Congress, Loriks became state director for the Farm Security Administration until elected national secretary in the fall of 1942.

An Oklahoma homesteader, Tom W. Cheek, who has been active in the union since 1904, is chairman of its Board of Directors. Cheek organized nearly 100 co-op cotton gins and worked eleven years as a mechanic in a railroad shop while farming on the side. In 1930 he became president of the Oklahoma union, the largest state branch in recent years. Cheek is a corncob-pipe-smoking, battle-scarred warrior of the plains—an agrarian socialist of the old type; he has also been active in a labor union and tried to develop farmer-labor consumer co-operatives.

The strangest officer of the Farmers Union, one of its biggest assets and liabilities at the same time, is M. W. Thatcher, vice-chairman of the board and for years chairman of the Committee on Legislation. A fifty-nine-year-old, high-pressure operator, Thatcher is a hated person among competing grainmen in the Northwest, where he is general manager of the Farmers Union Grain Terminal Association. Yet he is admittedly one of the best grainmen in the business.

Thatcher's father was a leader in the old hell-fire granger movement, but the son went into accounting after a brief shot at engineering in Purdue University. While attending school in Chicago, Thatcher earned a living playing the piano here and there, and today has an electric organ in his home. In 1904 he joined a large accounting firm, with which he traveled widely and learned the business end of the grain game. By 1911 he had his own firm and ran a grain business on the side. In the following years he was on the financial or managerial end of a number of co-operative ventures, some of which fared badly and left clouds over his name. What actually happened is highly controversial, but today his Grain Terminal Association, to which 52,000,000 bushels of wheat were fed from local co-ops last year, is a thriving enterprise—perhaps the largest in the country. Five per cent of its net earnings goes each year into the Farmers Union for organizational and educational work, meaning that Thatcher holds many of the chips which President Patton plays. An outstanding Thatcher achievement has been gaining seats for co-ops on the grain exchanges from which they were excluded for years.

From 1931 through 1937 Thatcher was in Washington

representing the largest of the old Farm Board wheat co-operatives. As a lobbyist he earned a reputation for being ruthless and shrewd, and he is still able to dip into town when the union is interested in legislation and practice a few tricks of the trade.

Two old-timers of interest who still have a big hand in union affairs are A. W. Ricker and C. E. Huff. Ricker started being an agrarian rebel back in the 1880s and has been the pamphleteer and propagandist of many farm movements, including the Populists. He is now editor of the *Farmer's Union Herald*, located in St. Paul and serving about 140,000 farmers in the Northwest. Ricker is not only a revered elder of the union but is still its best grass-roots fund raiser. Huff, national president in 1928 and 1929, is a versatile farmer and elevator operator. Self-training has made him a minister, businessman, and master of the classics. After leaving the managership of the largest grain co-op under the Farm Board, for which Thatcher was Washington representative, Huff went to Denver to become manager of the Colorado union's co-operative enterprises, especially insurance.

One of the big sparks in the Farmers Union is a brother-and-sister act. The duo consists of Mrs. Gladys Talbott Edwards and Glenn J. Talbott, children of the late North Dakota president, C. C. Talbott, and both leaders in their own rights today. Son Glenn was left to operate the 1,400-acre family farm when his father turned to full-time organizing for the union. When the elder Talbott died Glenn succeeded him as North Dakota president, but before that he had put in more than ten years traveling the state as fieldman for a grain co-op. Even though he has had no college education, he has risen in union counsel to become chairman of the national union's Economic and Social Planning Committee. In that capacity he frequently prepares and brings to Washington the official union statements which he, Thatcher, and Patton present to Congress on major issues.

Mrs. Edwards is the capable and energetic chairman of the Education Committee and one of the few women exerting influence over both men and women in a farm organization. Besides being in charge of the junior work, she is interested in international relations and peace movements.

The year of 1942 was a banner one for the new crop of union officers. Working against what seemed to be overwhelming odds, they helped win a big victory and a new lease on life for the Farm Security Administration. Of more lasting importance, however, is the fact that the Farmers Union for the first time was given a hearing before a congressional committee on a par with the Farm Bureau. The sincerity of union spokesmen and their refusal to indulge in personal invective contributed greatly toward getting the Farmers Union foot in the congressional door and attracted attention from New Dealers downtown who needed a spark to remind them of the FSA's problems. Thus hearings on FSA were a gateway to greener pastures for the small fry of organized farmers.

The next issue was price control. After blasts from the Farm Bureau, in the face of skyrocketing food prices, had made the lengthy inflation debate front-page news, the Farmers Union laid low for a while. Then, when militant farm-bloc resistance to national policy became completely uncompromising, the union threw its small but temporarily decisive weight with the Administration inflation controllers.

Thereafter, at meetings, congressional hearings, White House calls, and in public debate, the Farmers Union not only supported control but actually lashed out against opposing factions, branding them as commercial tools for riding roughshod over little fellows. Agriculture officials, many of them at least, welcomed the chance to deal with comparatively new faces from the hinterland; other farm-bloc leaders retaliated by labeling their rising competitors as "kept by the Administration" and not genuine representatives of the hard-hit farmers.

One of Patton's first shots came just after O'Neal had based much of an Administration attack on the assertion that parity was being denied farmers. The President had just delivered his "October first, or else" ultimatum to Congress, and the lines were forming for battle on the 110-per-cent-of-parity proviso. Noting that O'Neal, the day before, had called upon American farmers to "wake up to what is happening in this country," Patton answered:

"Mr. O'Neal's trouble is that farmers are already wide awake. They know, particularly since Pearl Harbor, that this war is being fought for keeps and that this is a time for firm unity of all believers in political and economic democracy, not a time for partisan hog-trough tactics by farmers, labor, or big business. They want parity for the foods and fibers they produce—and no more."

Patton then listed the percentage of parity returned to farmers each month from September of 1941 through July 15, 1942, as follows: 101, 99, 94, 100, 102, 99, 97, 99, 100, 99, and 101 per cent.

Declaring that O'Neal's charge that labor and the Administration worked "hand in hand" against farmers is a ghost story, Patton countercharged. The working farmers of the nation know, he said, that "they themselves and many of their own organizations, including the National Farmers Union and state units of the Farm Bureau Federation and of the Grange, opposed the high-price-through-scarcity program urged by Mr. O'Neal and his one-man brain trust, Earl Smith of Illinois. . . . It is Mr. O'Neal who should wake up."

In sharp contrast to other elements of the farm bloc, the Farmers Union stands on the premise that Mexicans are people and should not be brought into this country as mere chattels. The day after Vice-President Wallace, speaking in Los Angeles, called for abolition of discrimination against Mexican labor in the Southwest, Patton issued a press statement carrying Wallace's demands one step further. Observing that Wallace's position on the Mexicans was the logical next step from his famous Free World speech, setting war goals for free people based upon equal opportunity, Patton said that Wallace's statement called for action. He then charged some kind of sleight of hand in delay of a public hearing on racial discrimination that was to have been held in El Paso, Texas, late in July. Postponement, Patton charged, did not jibe with his impression of the Mexican government's attitude as he had gathered it while attending the Inter-American Conference on Agriculture in Mexico City. Demanding a full public hearing immediately, Patton closed by saying that "the situation requires a down payment on some of the Four Freedoms."

A recent statement of Farmers Union beliefs on general issues came at a highly significant but undramatic meeting of the Iowa Farmers Union at Des Moines, September 29, 1942. Although it was not apparent on the surface of the program there, the gathering marked the first time in history that the high moguls of the AAA had gone out of their way to lend moral and physical support to the union, which has traditionally attacked them for running a program in which cash payments increase in size proportionately with the size of the operator.

Weeks of behind-the-scenes preparation preceded the Des Moines session. Department personnel was in the unknown position of finding its old reliable pressure groups in the hinterland and on the Hill at sharp odds with the Administration. While this picture was in the darkroom for developing and a foggy result was being expected, the lowly Farmers Union, befriended before only by the also lowly FSA people, emerged as the Administration hopeful. At the same time, but far from coincidentally, the department's Food for Victory campaign had brought out nearly all increases possible among farmers represented by the old guard.

Detached farm laborers were pouring into fatter factory jobs, leaving the alternatives of jacking up prices to allow offers of higher wages to the departers or extending a bit of help to Ma and Pa Jones who had been clinging to 40 acres and a mule. Ma and Pa were hardly eligible for a riveting job and could be counted on to go right on doing their own chores if they were only given a fragment of credit and assurance of a few pieces of small equipment. To reach Ma and Pa, and others on the borderline, the department had to talk turkey with Patton. Talking turkey with Patton is easy; he has been doing it for years with those who will listen, has developed as a conversationalist, never throws temper tantrums, and is forthright in his dealings.

So high AAA officials began wooing Patton and laying the groundwork for collaboration. It was not the kind of activity which attracted public attention, but the presence at Des Moines of such persons as Clifford M. Townsend, then chief of the Agricultural Conservation and Adjustment Administration and formerly governor of Indiana, was planned as the beginning of an era of better feeling. In the light of later developments it appears to have been a shotgun wedding, but everyone involved tried.

Patton's address that day to union members in a state of great Farm Bureau strength was not world-shaking, but furnishes a recapitulation of beliefs of the modern Farmers Union. Prefaced by the remark that "as goes agriculture in Iowa, so goes agriculture in the nation," Patton applauded the Ever-Normal Granary as "a monument to one of the greatest liberals of our time, Henry A. Wallace," and "the very cornerstone of abundance."

Denying that war requires the suspension of democracy, Patton admonished that farmers must "join with all other Americans in accepting—yes, in insisting upon—democratic discipline." "If we are to win this war," he said, "the public interest must come first. Concretely, this means that we will not selfishly seize the needs of our nation's armed services and civilian population and of our allies to jack up prices far beyond parity and thereby bring on an inflation. We can only ruin ourselves by such tactics. . . . It means that we will pass up the chance to make a 'killing.' . . . It means we will pass up a chance to commit suicide."

Next Patton made a bow to guests from the Department of Agriculture and handed a bouquet to the AAA. "It was the Triple-A committeemen who fought down the criticism of certain organized groups who last year opposed increased production of hogs, for example, and as a matter of national welfare went right on to stimulate such an increase at a time when hogs were selling below parity," he said.

Calling for conversion of all agriculture to the war effort, he stated briefly the Farmers Union position on some of the major problems of agriculture:

"We believe profoundly in production for abundance.

"We are committed to the maintenance of family-type farming in America.

"We believe in parity for agriculture. We go beyond the narrow view that price parity is the answer to the farmers' needs to say that parity of food, clothing, shelter, education, and health for all who produce in agriculture is desirable and possible.

"We are for parity of sacrifice right across the board, stabilization of farm prices at parity, stabilization of wages, a sound tax program that will close present loopholes and will be based upon the ability to pay, with a top limit on net incomes of $25,000 a year."

The speech was closed with a few words about the need for farm organizations. "In our war economy," Patton said, "we have compact and powerful organizations of finance, industry, and business; we have 12 million out of 50 million wage earners organized into unions for the protection of labor's interests; we find less than 4 million of the 24 million farmers organized."

Agreeing that the Department of Agriculture is a most efficient agency, Patton warned: "But we cannot rely wholly upon a government agency to maintain our rights against the powerful pressure groups which have always exploited the farmer. Only a strong and wholly independent organization of working farmers can accurately and forcefully represent their interest. Such an organization can cooperate with and support government agencies without in any way becoming linked to, dependent upon, or in control of a government agency or service."

The Farmers Union, Patton claimed, has a membership

of 125,000 working farm families, is affiliated—through Farmers Union co-operatives—with some 400,000 farm families, and represents "the interests of the majority of family-type farmers of the nation." According to news correspondents, 1,000 farmers from all over Iowa cheered Patton's talk.

Next day the Senate passed part of the price-control amendment, but not the main part. Two days before that Legislative Chairman Thatcher had sent to all senators, just as their noses were being counted for the big showdown, a letter asserting that "the crisis in agriculture is a manpower crisis, not a price crisis."

Calling for a "master production-manpower program" in which essential workers could stay on farms, Thatcher asserted that "increased prices for farm products cannot hope to secure the manpower to assure agricultural production. A change in the formula for determining parity price will not solve the production problem."

Citing his organization's cross-section report from the Great Plains and part of the corn belt, Thatcher declared that rank-and-file farmers wanted no more than parity, "provided that their sons and hired men can be assigned to war duty on the farms" and that they can have the protection of parity prices for a period of years following the war.

The day after the Senate passed its version of the amendment Thatcher commented publicly that "the hullabaloo raised by some farm-organization spokesmen has petered out."

Six weeks later Farmers Union Washington secretary, Robert Handschin, took up the battle of the mimeograph machines, lashed out at the farm bloc, and advanced affirmative proposals for meeting the manpower problem.

"The National Farmers Union," said Handschin, "does not join in the threat of a sit-down strike in 1943 made explicitly in a statement attributed to the president of the American Farm Bureau Federation and implicitly in the joint statement published November 3 by spokesmen for the Farm Bureau Federation, the National Grange, and the National Council of Farmer Cooperatives.

"We dissociate the National Farmers Union from such statements as this quotation from the joint statement: 'Under guise of the war effort a social revolution is being perpetrated upon the American people.' "

Returning to differences of opinion about treatment of transported seasonal workers, Handschin said: "We note that the President of the Farm Bureau Federation is quoted as foreseeing farm wages of $1.50 an hour . . . and . . . that the Department of Agriculture is 'trying to force the farmers to provide toilets, baths, hot and cold water, and all that red-tape stuff . . .' The National Farmers Union believes that farm workers are people and that they, no less than members of working farm families, are entitled to 'toilets, baths, cold water,' and perhaps even hot water, 'and all that red-tape stuff.' "

As its name shows, the Farmers Educational and Cooperative Union emphasizes education of its members. The reason for this historical emphasis has been explained aptly by Mrs. Gladys Talbott Edwards, National Director of Education. In her 165-page booklet on the organization Mrs. Edwards writes:

Farmers organize under the stress of emotion. They are usually concerned with some specific injustice which they expect to correct in a short time by force of numbers. Economic injustice is the result of social conditions which have been a long time in the making, and it cannot quickly be remedied. But when people who have joined an organization for the purpose of stopping a mortgage foreclosure find that they haven't been able to accomplish this particular thing, they blame the organization and not the mortgage system. The result is that the organization dies while the mortgage system continues to flourish.

Core of the union's educational program is the old saying that "as the twig is bent, so the tree inclines." Since 1930 the national organization has nurtured its junior department, consisting of the sixteen- to twenty-year-olds in Farmers Union homes who are covered by the family-membership system.

Juniors who prove themselves proficient in the art of public speaking are made Minutemen and stand on call for speaking work throughout their states. Each year juniors elect two of their comrades to receive the convention-bestowed honor of being named Torchbearers. General success of the union in keeping interest high among its youth by maintenance of camps and other projects is attested by the fact that frequently there are an equal number of juniors and adults in attendance at the annual conventions.

The founding principles of the Farmers Union, run off by Newt Gresham over forty years ago on a foot press, have a quaint ring today but are still cited in the organization's literature. The preface of the union's constitution and bylaws has contained this assertion from the beginning:

Today we stand amazed as we watch the organized world do business. It is next to an idle tale to say that every line of business, from the bootblack to the money kings, of the new and the old world, is organized, save and except the man who raises the raw material for our food and raiment. Time was when the great mass of the people owned the great mass of wealth of the nation. But today less than 10 per cent of our population owns 90 per cent of the nation's wealth.

The closing sentence of the preface reflects the conscientiousness of the ten men who signed it: "May the Supreme Ruler of the Universe help us to lift the burdens from our people, by causing them to unite in one solid phalanx for the betterment of our condition and that of our posterity."

In 1937 the Farmers Union program was restated in terms of modern problems. Taking an inventory of 250 years as a nation, the union found 53 per cent of the farms operated by tenants or sharecroppers, with mortgage foreclosure facing some of those listed as owners; 500,000 farm families existing on land whose fertility had been entirely depleted, and 750,000 sharecropper families in the South on a subsistence basis below that of peon labor.

On the subject of taxation it found a "system so ruthless that it leads to inevitable expropriation of lands and home, even (through that most vicious of all taxes, the sales tax) to deprivation of the actual necessities of life."

Millions of persons, the union found, were unemployed; youth, "hopeless and disheartened," faced a future without opportunity, tramping the roads or enrolled in CCC camps, and the aged were "a liability to society and a burden to themselves." A major percentage of the population was found to be suffering from lack of proper medical care, and "large numbers of Americans were in imminent danger of losing the civil liberties so necessary and so precious to democracy."

Summarizing, the Farmers Union pointed to "the paradox of a land containing vast natural resources and raw materials, modern productive machinery, and mental genius sufficient to provide abundance for all, and within this land countless millions underfed, inadequately housed, and poorly clothed."

Unless there was a rededication of the Farmers Union to its original aims and purposes, it warned itself, "America will become the victim of fascism and dictatorship, the prey of war lords and munitions makers; a shackled and desecrated ghost of Democracy."

The gigantic economic problem, the union declared, "has been created by and must continue to become more serious under the 'Profit System' by which our business structure is operated. A profit system must be predicated upon the theory of scarcity, which necessitates controlled production and controlled distribution for the specific purpose of fixing price."

The co-operative system of business, owned by producers and consumers, was advanced as "the only means by which the potential abundance of this nation may be made available to all its people and by which true Democracy may be maintained and safeguarded. . . ."

That was the restatement of 1937, the year in which the Farmers Union moved over and left behind the dissenters who were howling for red-hot political fights. The co-operators and educators gained the upper hand that year, and new blood came into the Board of Directors.

Three years later came another historic convention which wound up with Patton in the presidency. Meeting in Denver in the fall of 1940, the union adopted six basic aims, which Patton reiterated in his Des Moines speech, and passed the usual run of resolutions, only some of which are of current interest.

On Soil Conservation payments, the union demanded that payments for preservation of the soil be made only on the basis of soil needs, not as a means of supporting commodity-income programs. Also it recommended a reduction in maximum size of benefit payments, together with increases in small payments.

The commodity-loan program was supported with the important exception of a demand that the Commodity Credit Corporation get out of the field of warehousing and direct handling of cotton and corn, and that it utilize co-operative-association facilities as directed by law.

The union wanted dairy products brought under AAA, more research for new uses of farm products, removal of interstate trade barriers, and adequate appropriations for Farm Security. Federal aid for rural health services and co-operative hospitals, as well as a program of low-cost rural housing to clear rural slums, was favored.

In sharp contrast to competing organizations, the union struck at payment of poll taxes as a condition for voting in seven Southern states and opposed the principles of the Walter-Logan bill, which would have strait-jacketed administrative agencies in the name of additional court appeal.

On the subject of the then slowly fading peace the union declared: "We reassert our historic position of opposition to the sending of American boys to fight on foreign soil, and demand that the Congress of the United States limit military action of this country to a strictly defensive policy, dedicated only to the preservation of our democracy." In 1937 the union had stood solidly on neutrality, an economic boycott of warring nations, and limitation of armaments.

The most significant plank of the 1940 platform, from the standpoint of cataloguing farm organizations, came under the heading of "Co-operation with Organized Labor." Notably absent were the Grange and Farm Bureau standard clauses, "We believe in the right of labor to organize, *but* . . ."

"In the emergency that confronts the common people of America at this time," the Farmers Union resolved, "the need for active co-operation between organized labor and organized agriculture becomes of the greatest importance.

"We, therefore, reaffirm our historic position toward organized labor in expressing a continued desire to co-operate with the organized workers in mine, mill, and factory."

After expressing appreciation for labor's support in Congress, the union assured organized labor that it "may count on the Farmers Union for the fullest support in the fight for legislative justice to wage workers. From this position we shall not retreat. We ask labor's support of our legislative program."

It is the support of organized labor, of the President's anti-inflation program, and of the smallest, most down-trodden farmers that sets the Farmers Union apart from the Grange, Farm Bureau, and Co-op Council. Other differences among the four are, in general, counterbalanced by a number of similarities; but the union constantly moves away from its three more conservative brothers, just as they are constantly ganging up on the union.

Though farmer-labor co-operation is well distributed throughout the Farmers Union membership, it reaches the peak of strategy and articulation in the Washington office. Not only do the leaders involved tend to congregate there, but much of the reason for the loose alliance is joint action in Congress.

The Farmers Union has never been hostile to organized labor, but its definite prolabor activity is young and still growing. The financial impetus for effecting it came at the 1941 convention when the union received $30,000 from the

Robert Marshall Fund, earmarked for enlarging the Washington office to include a public- and labor-relations officer. The gift was duplicated in 1942, after other members of the farm bloc seized with glee on the smear attack against the fund by Representative Martin Dies in one of his periodic, irresponsible fulminations at allegedly subversive movements.

It was not the deceased Marshall that Dies was worried about—he was an author and career conservationist in the Bureau of Indian Affairs and in the Forestry Service. Target of the attack was Gardner Jackson, former newspaperman, official in the old AAA Consumers Counsel unit, Washington representative for a while of the destitute Southern Tenant Farmers Union, head of John L. Lewis' Labor's Non-Partisan League until Lewis plumped for Wendell Willkie in 1940, and economist attached to the Under Secretary of Agriculture, Paul Appleby. Jackson's close friendship with Farmers Union leaders, the CIO, and the Farm Security Administration naturally made him distasteful to witch-hunter Dies, who never asks questions of those he wants to smear—or of anyone else. It was Jackson, as one trustee of the Marshall Fund, who presented the Farmers Union with the check. His private opposition to other farm groups, and the breech between Secretary Wickard and people who urged him to give Farm Security a prominent place in the food-production drive, led to the ousting of Jackson in January 1943—again to the delight of the Big Four.

Before the Washington office was enlarged it was run alone by Robert Handschin, thirty-two-year-old professorial tall man of the capital's farm leaders. A graduate of the University of Illinois in mathematics and rural sociology, Handschin is an expert in digging out heavy statistics and keeping track of the heavy thinking in the Department of Agriculture. His effectiveness in conferences is his ability to cite chapter and verse of background data and to let opponents know in a booming voice when he thinks they are cockeyed.

Handschin's father was an agricultural economist at Illinois University and a leader in farm-management studies and extension work. Son Bob spent summers on farms and worked on experimental farm projects in later years. In 1933 he went with the Workers Alliance of Illinois, a union of unemployed; in the next two years he directed rural-relief studies at the university. Besides farm subjects, Handschin has always been interested in labor economics. In 1936 and '37 he was a paint sprayer for the Ford Motor Company, until he was fired with others for union activity. In 1938 he studied farm income at Illinois University and came to Washington for the Farmers Union, where he still does much of the pressure group's brainwork.

In the summer of 1942 the staff was doubled by the addition of Public and Labor Relations Director Paul Sifton, playwright, journalist, and labor administrator. As an assistant to President Patton, Sifton writes a periodic news letter to the membership, articles for the *National Union Farmer*, and occasional press releases, besides working on all matters in which the union takes joint interest with organized labor.

Sifton was reared on Wisconsin and Michigan farms, graduated from the University of Missouri School of Journalism, and took graduate work at the London School of Economics, where he studied under Sir William Beveridge, among others. Action in France with the AEF in 1918 made him a disabled war veteran.

With the United Press, the Des Moines *Register*, and the

old New York *World* Sifton rolled up about fifteen years of news experience, during which he and his wife started writing plays with considerable success. *The Belt*, in 1927, portrayed the Henry Ford type of assembly-line production; "*1931——*" dramatized the depression, and *Midnight*, in 1930, was later made into a motion picture.

In 1934 Sifton became a civil servant with the New York State Department of Labor, first in the publication, then in the administrative end. Four years later he was made deputy administrator of the infant Wage-Hour Administration. In 1939 he became assistant director of the Consumers Counsel unit in the administration of the Bituminous Coal Act. The Farmers Union was next.

With Sifton has come a popularization of union statements and a departure from stodgy terminology. Most of his press releases show a sense of humor and a punch, rather than the usual seriousness and gravity which have marked farm publications for years. That is not to say, however, that the Farmers Union is taking its battle lightly. It merely refuses to be downed by pedantics and to take itself deathly seriously.

Sifton has not had to be indoctrinated with the cause of small farmers, or even big ones; but because he did not come to the union in overalls he has been sent into the field to attend meetings and rub blue-denimed elbows with the tillers for whom he is speaking. To his playwright wife, also devoted to the organization, went the assignment of finding a muralist to paint the walls of the North Dakota union's new center in Jamestown. In January of this year she selected William Calfee, a leading Washington artist, to get out to the plain country and meet the farmers whose history he will depict.

Perhaps the high point in the union's public-relations

strategy came in late June of 1942, when it drafted a lengthy letter to the President and joined with a powerful coalition in signing it. It was a propitious moment, for the Administration and the public were just becoming aware of the Farmers Union voice in the farm-bloc wilderness. Signers, besides Patton, were Murray Lincoln, executive secretary of the Ohio Farm Bureau Federation (which nearly always defies the Farm Bureau national leadership on such matters); William Green, AFL president; Philip Murray, CIO president; J. G. Luhrsen, executive secretary of the American Railway Labor Executives Association; L. G. Ligutti, executive secretary of the National Catholic Rural Life Association, and Benson Y. Landis, for the Federal Council of Churches.

The letter urged President Roosevelt to take to the people the issues of cutting down Farm Security appropriations and preventing sales of corn and wheat at less than parity. Asserting that FSA had been smeared by "farm interests committed to the high-price-through-scarcity concept," the seven outstanding signatories told the President that his people did not understand that by giving full help to low-income farmers enough additional food production would be obtained to supply an army of 2,400,000 men with milk, cheese, and eggs for a year, and potatoes, pork, and butter for six months. Referring again to the difference between FSA clients and "corporate and large-scale commercial farming," the letter ended with an appeal that "what happens now in agriculture will shape what happens after victory has been won."

The historical document was widely publicized and could be interpreted as nothing but a roundhouse swing at the remainder of the farm bloc—if acknowledged in full by the President, which it was.

On July 3 he replied that the unity shown by the seven signers was "heartening" and that authority to sell some government-held grain for feeding purposes at 85 per cent of parity was "essential if the armed services and the civilian population are to be assured adequate supplies."

"I am certain," he wrote, "that pressure-group tactics will not prevail."

Agreeing with the plea that farmers must be assisted to stay on the land "and to have or to get a life's stake in it," the President expressed belief that the Senate recommendations for FSA appropriations would do that in a measure and would be "infinitely better than the inadequate proposals that are being mistakenly urged on the Congress by certain selfish and power-hungry groups."

Finally, the President stated that if resistance to the proposals persisted he was "confident that the people will hold those responsible to strict account." Nearly a year later there was still some strict accounting to be done, according to the President's standard, but the Farmers Union had received a big boost.

XII

The Commodity Boys

While the general farm organizations get the spotlight at the center of Washington's revolving stage, a score of special-commodity lobbies scurry around in the shadows and corners where their particular kinds of concessions are handed out and their favors have the most effect. Technically, the Milk Producers' Federation is one of these, but its inclination and size have made it much more. In sugar, vegetables, nuts, grain, fruit, and even fertilizer, however, there are a number of associations that either do not fit into the Co-op Council or maintain separate offices in the capital. Outstanding among these is the sugar bloc.

If this country were left to the devices of the sugar lobby it would be in a sweet mess. The sprawling industry includes many feuding factions, such as Western beet sugar against Cuban cane sugar, and never fails to put on a good show when sugar legislation lies on congressional desks.

At the core of the intraindustry battle are three main elements. First, the entire tariff policy—protective walls versus free international movement of goods—is wrapped up with a few sticks of dynamite in the geographical situation of the industry. The Puerto Ricans, Cubans, Hawaiians, and Filipinos are all American brothers during the war, but they were just so many foreigners until Pearl Harbor so far as American sugar growers and processors were concerned. Second, the industry has been characterized by the poorest of labor conditions until recent improvements. All the economic and social ills of plantation farming, plus the squalor of hutted family workers who know nothing but tending sugar beets, saddled the industry for generations. Third, the industry is both highly concentrated and economically inefficient. Its spokesmen have always been the biggest operators, though there is some representation among farmers, and the entire industry is fighting for a life which would almost be snuffed out if free competition with "foreign" producers were allowed.

In 1934, with passage of the Jones-Costigan Act, a balance was struck between domestic and foreign sharing in the great American sweet tooth. By setting up quotas, American producers were given roughly 30 per cent of the market. Although this amount was artificially handed out, it left the United States with enough of an industry to furnish a minimum sugar supply against any eventuality. That minimum is now about the rationed amount, as shipping problems knocked out most of the island potentiality.

Current sugar-bloc activities largely concern jockeying for favorable places in this divided picture, but come far from their prewar fervor. Worry over price ceilings, transportation orders, and rationing has taken the place of fights with the Administration over subsidy provisions of the Jones-Costigan Act and its successor, the Sugar Act of 1937. For fiscal '43 this subsidy, in the form of cash payments for complying with planting restrictions and other conditions, amounted to nearly $50,000,000.

Spending this amount for restricting sugar production even after Pearl Harbor was attacked as a non-essential measure when Congress passed the appropriation within a month of that time. In a letter to Senator Harry Byrd, economy advocate, Secretary Wickard defended the cash outlay, in March 1942, as necessary to get production.

It cannot be stated too emphatically [he wrote] that failure to make this appropriation would have a serious effect on beet-sugar production in this country this year. . . . The immediate effect of the failure to appropriate would be to cause considerable confusion and uncertainty among beet growers today when planting is just getting under way and would unquestionably lead many growers to curtail, if not cease, planting beets.

The battle within the bloc over giving to each group of producers and processors a fair proportion of the market was equally bitter. When the 1937 law was under consideration, setting quotas for each area, a freely spending lobby descended on the capital and lodged in the city's finest hotels, feeding on problems like this: How much refined sugar should be allowed to enter the United States? With well-heeled refiners on the East coast glaring at each boatload refined outside the country, it was small wonder that any measure to be friendly with Puerto Ricans, Cubans, and others, by letting them sell us more refined sugar, was met with resistance of a death-struggle variety. The Sugar Act of 1937 treated the combine of Eastern refiners well— so well that President Roosevelt, in reluctantly signing the bill, took unusual occasion to slap at their monopolistic success and promise that it would someday end.

The problem before me raised by the enactment of the so-called sugar bill [the President wrote Congress] is that the bill, intended primarily to benefit the many thousands of farmers who produce beets and sugar cane and those who, at the place of production, refine the raw material into sugar, has been seriously impaired in its value by the inclusion of a provision intended to legalize a virtual monopoly in the hands of a small group of seaboard refiners.

I am approving the bill with what amounts to a gentlemen's agreement that the unholy alliance between the cane and beet growers, on the one hand, and the seaboard-refining monopoly, on the other, has been terminated by the growers. . . .

The end of monopoly is definitely in sight, and I sincerely trust that nothing will be done by the domestic growers of beets and cane to perpetuate it. The monopoly · costs the American housewife millions of dollars every year, and I am just as concerned for her as I am for the farmers themselves.

With the sugar bloc, as with everything else, the whole is no greater than its parts. It is most accurately described by looking into its component blocs. First, the organizations represented in Washington by Clarence J. Bourg: the Farmers and Manufacturers Beet Sugar Association and the American Sugar Cane League.

The latter of these, an extremely militant lobby of Louisiana cane interests, is probably the most effective of all and the least cognizant that such a thing as public interest exists. Representing, as he does, the highest-cost producers of all domestic areas, legislative favors are apt to be gratuities in terms of the national economy; but lobbyist Bourg keeps right on being indignant at any compromise forced on him.

Because no one is elected to Congress from Louisiana unless he will go blindly down the line for sugar cane, Bourg has his legislators so completely in hand that they sometimes perform jobs which amount to little more than errands for his organization. Within the American Sugar Cane League, Bourg is fourth vice-president and no errand boy himself. In spite of its Solid Southness, the league is collectively a Department of Agriculture fighter, as it has had imposed on its members many reforms in traditional planter economy, such as honest-weight chemical analysis of the commodity involved and written contracts for sale to refiners. David W. Pipes, Jr., a member of the league's Executive Committee, ran for Congress not long ago on the Republican ticket, in pure retaliation for the impudence of the Democrats in running former Secretary Wallace for Vice-President.

Bourg's additional role with the Farmers and Manufacturers Beet Sugar Association is a bit difficult to comprehend, in view of the historical competition between beet and cane sugar. Frequently he is asked which suit he is wearing on a given day. The explanation lies in the fact that the beet association's name is misleading, because it comprises only Michigan, Ohio, Indiana, and Wisconsin— only the Eastern part of the beet area. Michigan is also a high-cost producing area and has to hang on tight at the legislative table. Only by getting high prices can both of Bourg's set of constituents stay in business. By joining hands against Western beet people he has been quite successful to date, though persons who have watched him in action report that he still acts as if he were being persecuted.

But the Farmers and Manufacturers Association has another, even better, pipe line to Washington in the person of Price Administrator and ex-Senator Prentiss M. Brown, of Michigan. Brown's interest in the beets of that area is more than local pride; he is also vice-president of the Paulding Sugar Company, of Paulding, Ohio. The other vice-president of the company is A. A. Shoup, who also acts as executive secretary of the Farmers and Manufacturers Association.

Brown displayed concern for beet sugar all through his

terms in Congress, but it did not end there. Just after he had hammered through the Senate the Administration amendment to the Price Control Act which knocked out 110 per cent of parity, his interest increased. Along with Representative J. W. Robinson, of Utah, he paid an important visit to Secretary Wickard—about six weeks after Brown's defeat for re-election and a few days after Wickard had been named food administrator. The mission, according to the Detroit *Free Press*, was to formulate a definite program of sugar production that would permit farmers to expand their yields and assure them in advance that they would obtain a "fair price and one which also was fair to the consumer."

It was the lameduck senator's opinion that "the rubber situation has shown that this country must not be left dependent on imports for its supply of an essential product."

At the time it was generally assumed in Washington that Brown would take the place vacated by Henderson, but it was never noted that he had a financial interest in a sugar company. The labeling of Brown as being against the farm bloc and for the President's anti-inflation program becomes a bit shallow in view of the Wickard visit and a five-page letter about sugar written to Brown by Secretary Wallace on April 6, 1938.

Wallace was answering in detail Brown's request that he re-examine the sugar-price picture. The answer was almost a department white paper, reviewing the entire subject. Wallace wrote that the three protective devices in the Sugar Act of 1937 were then equivalent to a specific tariff duty of $2.65 per hundred pounds of sugar. The total public subsidy then being received by the domestic sugar industry, he stated, amounted to about $8.40 per ton of sugar beets—considerably greater than the entire amount received by growers for the sugar beets they produce. "It might be said," he added, "that in effect the public is providing sugar-beet processors with free raw material and a substantial price subsidy in addition."

This special treatment of the sugar people, Wallace wrote, is several times as great as that afforded other protected industries. The Secretary then pointed out an axiom of every beginning economics course which beet producers purposely avoid: "A decrease in imports from foreign countries unavoidably involves a decrease in the foreign markets for American exportable products, of which we have great surpluses."

Wallace then estimated that American consumers are obliged to pay more than $350,000,000 a year more for their sugar than they would have to pay if the industry were not pampered with high tariffs. "This is equivalent to a tax of approximately $2.70 per capita . . . and it represents an amount of purchasing power equal to more than 50 quarts of milk and 50 loaves of bread for each family in the United States."

His letter closed with the finding that sugar-beet growers would appreciably exceed parity, while producers of other crops were below parity. Brown apparently remembered some of Wallace's strictures about parity, but none of the tariff lesson sunk in.

Brown is not the only big shot in Washington who has kept financial connections with a sugar company. The fact that Marriner Eccles, chairman of the Board of Governors of the Federal Reserve System, is also chairman of the board of the Amalgamated Sugar Company, in Odgen, Utah, one of the four biggest Western sugar companies, has aroused unsavory comment now and then. Thus, when the general manager of Amalgamated hotly protested that while sugar was being rationed warehouses were bulging with it, Price Administrator Henderson replied with a scorching letter which was written up by capital newsmen along with the fact that it was Eccles' company involved.

The thirteen processors of beets from irrigated land west of the Mississippi have their own organization: the United States Beet Sugar Association. Each manufacturer member has several factories, located in various centers; together they process 85 per cent of all beet sugar in the country.

The association, whose headquarters are in Washington, is managed by Neil Kelly, who is listed as secretary-treasurer and who holds down a spacious suite of heavily carpeted offices on the tenth floor of the Tower Building, with the aid of two stenographers. The slender, middle-aged Kelly, whose large tortoise-shell glasses and prematurely graying hair make him easy to remember, is a former news reporter, an alumnus of the New York *Herald Tribune* and the old *World,* among others. After a turn as press agent for the association, he became keeper of its keys about the time Roosevelt entered the White House.

In spite of his newspaper background, Kelly works around the capital very qui⸌ ⸍ly, having begun to release stilted publicity blurbs only recently. An excerpt from one of them will show how the war cut down on real issues. In a story aimed at women's pages, plugging the idea of making watermelon pickles for the next winter's basement preserve shelf, the industry gave itself this pat on the back:

Just imagine what it would have been like if we weren't able to grow a great part of our own sugar right here in the form of sugar beets. . . . This year, according to the United States

Beet Sugar Association, our farmers expect to provide us with two million tons of sugar from this season's crop of sugar beets. That represents enough sugar to supply an eight-ounce weekly household ration to everybody in the country for a whole year!

The same type of straight-faced boasting was done in the state of Washington by one of the association's members. The good citizens of that state were exposed to a number of billboards beseeching them to buy home-state products. Only a few readers realized that in the signature on the advertisement, "U. - I. Sugar Company," the two letters stand for Utah and Idaho.

U. S. Beet Sugar is about the same as any other trade association except that it is more tightly knit—having 100-per-cent membership in a concentrated industry—and does more industry-wide bargaining on prices and production. The association has demanded big acreage quotas, just as have other groups within the sugar bloc; but only in the past year have those wishes been granted. All stops are out now in an effort to overcome the shortage of manpower in the hand-tilled fields and the large converting factories.

One aspect of the sugar-labor problem is the legislative ban on child labor which used to furnish, as the beet industry now admits, one of the ugliest chapters in labor history. A bill introduced in 1942 to lift the child-labor bans as a means of enlarging the manpower pool met stiff opposition from the U. S. Beet Sugar Association. "We don't want any more of that business" is its policy.

The association's position on continuing the cash-subsidy program for the first year after Pearl Harbor is this: Because of the Price Control Act's floor under farm-commodity prices, the Administration had the choice of boosting the retail ceiling, at a cost of $125,000,000 to consumers, or continuing the subsidy system along with its processing tax which is paid by the manufacturers. This tax, which amounts to more each year than the cash subsidy to growers (thus making the program self-liquidating in a sense), is not passed on to consumers, they say, but is absorbed by the processor.

It is difficult to believe, however, that the processors pay the tax from the goodness of their hearts. It must be added to the consumers' bill somewhere along the line. What the tax-subsidy system has accomplished is stabilization of the industry, which is no virtue when applied to an uneconomic industry.

On Capitol Hill the Western beet men have always had solid representation. Until he was defeated in 1940, Representative Fred Cummings, a big beet grower from Colorado, headed an unofficial House committee to look after beet sugar solely, while Wyoming's O'Mahoney was depended upon in the Upper Chamber. Harry B. Coffee, Nebraska rancher, took Cummings' place for two years, then, on being defeated for the Senate, threw the mantle to Representative Robinson, of Utah.

Beet farmers in the same area are organized into the National Beet Growers Association, with headquarters in Cheyenne, Wyoming. President of the growers is W. I. Sanford, long-time beet farmer from near Pueblo, Colorado. Although Sanford is green as president, he served many years as an officer of his local unit, which—like all others— negotiates prices to be paid the following year by processors. Personally he votes Republican and never fights with the manufacturers, as some grower leaders have done bitterly. He once said of his organization: "We fight the industrial East. I hate to say 'fight,' but there's a lack of understanding of our problems." Sanford succeeded a familiar face in Washington, Charles Kearney, who is now only a director of the association. Kearney was known as a politician of the first order who handled his congressmen like a master.

The association claims a membership of 25,000 growers in Kansas, Colorado, Wyoming, Montana, Nebraska, Nevada, California, Utah, and Idaho. The association has no initiation fee; it collects two cents on each ton of beets grown, of which the national organization gets one and one tenth cents. It varies by states, but the association has to compete with other farm groups for membership. For example, when a strike of beet laborers was threatened in Colorado in the late thirties, Jim Patton wooed members of the Beet Growers Association to the Farmers Union by exposing the fact that one of the high officers of the Growers was a substantial stockholder in the Great Western Sugar Beet Company.

A highly organized Eastern bloc is the United States Cane Refiners, with New York headquarters and the ability to throw shock troops into Washington on the double-quick. Regarded as the most powerful of the sugar groups, the cane refiners illustrate the admixture of rural and industrial forces in what is too conveniently called the farm bloc. Cane refining is big business. Its lifeblood is the stream of raw, unrefined sugar which comes in from island possessions and other territories. It was the cane refiners who fought from March to September of 1937 against limiting imports of *unrefined* sugar. Hence, although the refiners were on the side of free trade so far as importing raw sugar was concerned, they were striking at our neighbors' imperative needs for refining their own sugar in order to save heavy transportation costs of shipping the crude product.

The cane refiners' lobby is different from other sugar lobbies in two general ways: First, when the heat is on in Washington individual refiners send down lobbyists to augment association men. Second, the refiners have skillfully drafted organized labor to come to their rescue.

Although the total labor force of all refineries is only 14,000 men, any threat to the flow of imported *raw* sugar immediately raises a hue and cry among refinery labor. Quantitatively, of course, labor in the refineries is less than that of competing segments in the bloc. Service and women's clubs are also mobilized by the wily refiners. Once they got Mayor Fiorello La Guardia and the New York City Council to oppose a bill because it would cut into that port's business.

Spark plug of the refiners is Jack Dalton, formally their secretary and formerly administrator of the Department of Agriculture's Sugar Agency, the top regulatory job in the industry. Other alumni of that bureau have done about as well with the industry. It is conceded that Dalton was an able chief—and uses his talents still.

On the domestic front there are two other pressure sources to be mentioned: the United States Sugar Corporation, which distributes about 95 per cent of all Florida-grown sugar, and the American Molasses Company, whose subsidiary, Sucrest Corporation, in Brooklyn, is a refiner.

U. S. Sugar is represented in Washington by Josiah Ferris, dapper Jack-of-all-trades for them. The American Molasses Company is relatively unimportant in the sugar-bloc picture, except to note that three high government officials are or have been employed by it in some capacity. President of the firm is Charles W. Taussig, whose present job with the government is chairman of the Joint Anglo-American Caribbean Commission. Governor Tugwell, of

Puerto Rico, and Adolf A. Berle, Assistant Secretary of State, were at one time with Taussig's firm.

Island producers of sugar are capably represented in the capital and have an added advantage of a semblance of official backing by their various governments. The outstanding of these lobbyists works for the Hawaiian Sugar Planters Association, which is generally dominated by the famous Big Five planters. His name is Ernest Greene, a former planter and liberal thinker who sometimes shocks those with whom he has to work by admitting that his position is wrong—and pleading with his principals to change it. Greene moved to Washington when the Hawaiian Planters dropped Royal Mead, archlobbyist of the old school.

Cuban interests are represented by Dr. Oscar Diaz Albertini in the name of the Cuban Sugar Stabilization Institute, a semigovernmental affair. Though Albertini is known as a shrewd and wily operator, he is respected as fundamentally a "high-grade gent"—partly because he realizes that he is not under the American flag and is not too grasping. The doctor lives in comfort and maintains excellent relations with government officials.

Lobbyist for the Association of Sugar Producers of Puerto Rico is James A. Dickey, another alumnus of the Department of Agriculture. Dickey's job is recognized as a tough one, as the Puerto Rican economy is notoriously resistant to progress, but he executes it ruthlessly.

The Philippine Sugar Association is eminently represented by former Senator Harry B. Hawes, from Missouri. Hawes became interested in Philippine affairs as a leader of their fight for independence, victory in which meant that the important islands could no longer hide under Uncle

Sam's tariff skirts. The Independence Act provides that Filipinos may export to America up to 1,000,000 tons annually, about one sixth of our consumption.

These many crosscurrents, each with a Washington watchdog, make it easy to understand why recognition of any public interest by the sugar industry is a rare trait. And they explain why government officials have singled them out for especially rough treatment at times. Were it not for the balancing features of the sugar legislation administered by the Department of Agriculture, the sugar mastodons would probably have gobbled each other until, by this time, only a giant concern would be left in the field, surrounded by carcasses of poor beet diggers side by side with fat plantation owners. But balance has been attained at the expense of compromise—subsidies, artificial respiration for submarginal farmers, and hard feelings among nations. Also the compromise has left 130,000,000 consumers paying unnecessarily high prices for 6,000,000 tons of sugar a year.

The fruit-and-vegetable bloc is well represented in Washington by two over-all organizations, the Co-operative Fruit and Vegetable Association (producers and shippers, chiefly) and the National League of Wholesale Fresh Fruit and Vegetable Distributors (mainly distributors east of Chicago who receive commodities from producers and shippers). The first is outside of the Co-op Council; the second thrives on attacking co-ops.

The Co-operative Fruit and Vegetable Association was put together in the middle of 1940 under very unusual conditions. The meeting out of which it grew was called by the Atlantic Commission Company, corporate affiliate of the Great Atlantic & Pacific Tea Company which does the buying of such commodities for the giant chain store. The

Fruit and Vegetable Co-op, as it is referred to, was incorporated as a co-operative association in the state of Florida and signed a contract to sell fruit and vegetables to the Atlantic Commission Company for A & P.

This arrangement rankled other farm co-operatives. Under the heading of Unfair Trade Practices, the Co-op Council resolved as follows in 1942: "Since buyers and sellers have divergent interests, this council favors and urges legislation that will, in effect, limit procurement departments or subsidiaries of retail stores to purchase farm products for resale in such retail stores and not for resale through other outlets."

On February 28, 1942, the unique contract between A & P and the Co-operative was terminated and the association changed from a straight business arrangement to a trade association in character. Soon thereafter it pirated the Agricultural Marketing Administration's fruit-and-vegetable chief, Porter Taylor.

Known and liked across the land as a walking encyclopedia of fruit-and-vegetable lore, Taylor now has headquarters in a modernly furnished, small suite in Washington's Munsey Building, where he acts as executive secretary and general manager for the association. The white-haired, conservative-looking, friendly representative spends considerable time in the field with his constituents, however.

Member organizations include the International Apple Association, the United Fruit and Vegetable Association (a group of terminal markets west of Chicago which maintains a special wartime office in Washington), the National Apple Institute, the Florida Citrus Exchange, the Mutual Orange Growers of California (second to the Sunkist combine), and other commodity associations, such as those for potatoes and peaches.

Actually the Co-operative Fruit and Vegetable Association is not completely co-operative; it is admittedly a combination of co-operative setups and grower-shippers who
produce and market their own wares. Its membership drive
has been subordinated to getting solidly under way as a
new organization, but a campaign is in the mill. When it
comes it will take the form of canvassing each marketing
area to set up "commodity groups" to function within the
association as units. For example, members on Long Island
have already put on a high-pressure advertising campaign
on the usually unglamorous cauliflower produced in that
area. Radio and other media were thrown into the effort to
lure housewives toward cauliflower. One cent per crate
was deducted from each crate marketed in an effort to
move the biggest crop on record.

This type of activity will be no small "taters" for the association when it gets into high gear. In August of 1942
it set up a subsidiary, called Fruit and Vegetable Pro-
motions, Inc., which is strictly an advertising agency. One
of Taylor's two assistants, located in one room of his office,
has charge of this work already. He has ten years of professional promotional and ballyhoo experience behind him,
including six years as advertising agent for the suave
Florida Citrus Commission. Taylor developed his belief and
technique in intensive pushing of seasonal surpluses at the
Department of Agriculture, where he helped brain-trust
the surplus-food drives which became an adjunct of the
Food Stamp Plan.

In addition to functions mentioned, Taylor is busy watch-
ing legislative trends, labor-relations agencies, reciprocal-
trade treaties, and developments in standard grades and
labels on produce. As chief strategist for the association,
Taylor works among producers in thirty-eight states who

handle a potential of 225,000 carloads of seventy-two farm products annually.

The middlemen who handle these commodities for a commission, extracted between producer and retail store-keeper, chiefly those east of Chicago, have the oldest trade association in the business: the National League of Whole-sale Fresh Fruit and Vegetable Distributors. Going strong in its fifty-first year, the league has its large headquarters in Washington, where it has watched legislation and haggled with administrative agencies since 1920 to great advantage.

Secretary, and keeper of the Washington office, is Horace H. Herr, balding, heavy-browed, bespectacled former newspaperman who still looks like a country editor as he rolls an occasional cigarette between "tailor-mades." Herr became interested in agriculture while covering interna-tional assignments, including the Institute of Agriculture at Rome, and came to the league as director of information and research work for two years before taking over opera-tions.

As much of its members' business is concerned with technicalities like freight rates, demurrage, and trade prac-tices, league officials also spend much of their time in technicalities; but not all of it. They once told prospective members that "in every session of Congress, literally thou-sands of bills must be checked to find out which may affect the fresh fruit and vegetable industry." Each must be fol-lowed through its legislative life or death, of course; but "frequently"—a recent report adds—"it is desirable to see the authors of bills and discuss with them certain features. Such discussions often lead to the elimination of provisions which might be harmful."

Operating on a budget of about $28,000 a year, derived from dues of $50 a year from about six hundred members, the league holds full-dress annual conventions which result in printed proceedings running as high as three hundred pages in length. "The league doesn't do much resoluting," an official explains, but its proceedings are full of detailed reports to the membership from which the policies are quite clear.

One of the basic principles is opposition to co-ops and chain-store groups which have set up their own commission houses for buying fruits and vegetables. "A co-operative system is not a competitive system," the league asserts, in its clinging to an "independent" marketing system. Both targets of its opposition raise interesting questions.

First, if the league opposes retail chain stores buying their own produce, eliminating an independent wholesaler, why does its membership include about 100 "producer-shippers" who grow and wholesale their own fruits and vegetables? Second, if co-operatives destroy the American competitive system, why does the league's traffic consultant, J. R. Van Arnum, also work for the Co-operative Fruit and Vegetable Association, which is not only dedicated to co-operative marketing but is viewed with great suspicion by the league for having been created by the A & P chain system? Apparently it is more a matter of keeping what the league has than fighting to the death for a neatly classified American system of distribution.

Until 1935 the league was known as the National League of Commission Merchants of the United States. In its early days one of the main functions was to regulate conditions by which a commission man in one city could honor the account of that in another area without wiring his bank for formal credentials and credit rating. Thus, it is explained, membership required "a family tree and a bank roll." To protect this type of restriction the principle of local autonomy was established, and today five or more members in one market area, banded in a "Branch League," pass on membership qualifications. This system is given as the probable reason that no chain groups are members, even though their credit is not questioned.

On the subject of labor the league is quite definite. In 1942 Secretary Herr testified in favor of the Walter and Hobbs bills to bring union activities, particularly those of truckers, under the mercies of the courts. The league has also been active in trying to keep agricultural commodities away from social-security and wage-hour regulation. When the Barden bill to amend the Fair Labor Standards Act in favor of agricultural processors and distributors, but not workers, was thrown overboard by the house in 1940, Herr and his staff drafted overnight a proposal for a 48-hour work week for wholesale distributors' workers. Next day it was introduced by Louis Ludlow, of Indiana, but was defeated. The following day Representative Joseph E. Casey, of Massachusetts, offered an amendment sponsored by the Council of Wholesale Associations with which the league was co-operating. The Casey amendment would have exempted *all* wholesale activities from *all* hours regulations. The House adopted it but defeated the bill to which it was attached. Early in the 1941 session Casey reintroduced his amendment, and Scott Lucas, of Illinois, submitted it in the Senate. It expired with the 77th Congress.

The league is not concerned with farm prices as such, but is concerned about the share coming to its members after transportation, storage, and handling costs are paid out. Thus it opposed a provision in the 1942 Revenue Act which would have taxed freight 5 per cent, and, with the aid of other pressure groups, it saw the figure knocked down to 3 per cent.

The difference between 5 and 3 per cent on freight rates may seem small, but such a margin may be a major issue in commodity organization. It symbolizes the reason for having Washington representatives.

XIII

Country Cousins

Like many others, the farm movement has coattail riders, mavericks, unwanted children, and unclassified helpers. The three general farm organizations, the Co-op Council, and the commodity-pressure groups, including the Milk Producers' Federation, are reinforced from time to time by several miscellaneous forces. Some of them out-bloc the bloc, without the formality of being farmers. They are country cousins.

Two of the most difficult to classify are the National Association of Commissioners, Secretaries, and Directors of Agriculture, and the Association of Southern Commissioners of Agriculture. Both are composed of the top administrative officials for agriculture in states and are really councils rather than associations, as membership is limited to one person from each state.

The Association of Southern Commissioners is only one of three "auxiliary" groups within the National Association, but it is by far the most militant on the Washington front and is the only one with a full-time official in the capital. That man is C. C. Hanson, paid secretary of the organization, who operates from a bedroom-office suite in Washington's Raleigh Hotel on Pennsylvania Avenue. As "personal representative of the president" of the National Association of Commissioners, etc., of Agriculture, Hanson can act for both organizations, however.

President of the parent group is R. A. Trovatten, Minnesota's commissioner of agriculture; president of the Southern contingency is "Uncle Harry" D. Wilson, Louisiana's commissioner of agriculture for the past thirty-five years and head of the Southern Commissioners since their organization twenty-six years ago.

Functions of the two setups naturally overlap at times, but in general the Southern association, representing thirteen states of the Solid South, takes over problems peculiar to the South, such as the boll weevil, cotton grading and classification, cotton seed, and peanut matters. But now and then the Southerners will ask their well-oiled congressmen to back a program for something like corn, which would be initiated by the national body.

A feature of both organizations is that they are supported not by membership drives, but by taxes. Each state authorizes, by constitutional or legislative provision, its agricultural official to co-operate with the association. Most states also authorize contribution of funds. Those which do not go along for the ride.

Another interesting feature, pertaining particularly to the Southern auxiliary, is that the association claims to represent both producers and consumers. Secretary Hanson, known as "Colonel" Hanson because of a traditional honor bestowed to those who figuratively serve on the staff of the governor of Tennessee, explains that there has never been a quarrel between producers and consumers. He adds, however, that his organization represents producers principally. Incidentally, the colonel sometimes acts without pay as Washington representative for the National Cotton Council.

Reasons for the lobbying strength of the two associations require little elaboration. What senator or representative would fail to listen attentively to the highest agriculture official of his home state—to the man who works with rural voters every day that congressmen are away?

Although Hanson has reached the age when he cannot be one of the most active lobbyists, his is an organization which requires only a contact man to keep it on the march. With the aid of a long-distance telephone, to get signals from his bosses, Hanson fills the job well.

It was five years ago that the tall, white-thatched colonel added his soft Southern voice to that of the farm bloc. A train dispatcher and telegraph operator by early profession, Hanson wound up his railroad career as chief clerk to the traffic manager of a Southern railroad. Turning to King Cotton, Hanson entered a compress and warehouse business, sharing in the operation of two companies with sixty or seventy plants throughout the South. One of the firms was taken over by supercotton merchants Anderson, Clayton & Company (W. L. Clayton, Assistant Secretary of Commerce).

Hanson next took a 2,000-acre farm near Memphis, with two dairy herds, a creamery, and extensive crops. Upon the death of his wife the colonel liquidated the farm, retired briefly, then came to Washington for Uncle Harry Wilson to have something to do. While in Tennessee he was a member of the State Board of Education. Today his bespectacled, ruddy face, accentuated by an ultraconservative suit and hard, high collar, is familiar to Washington's farm crowd. Hanson is a member also of the National Grange, and he often finds his stand coinciding with that of the

Grange and Farm Bureau; but the coalition is off and on.

One time that it was *on* with the Grange but *off* with the Farm Bureau was during the unique farm conference held in and around Hanson's office on October 9 and 10, 1941. The reason for the extraordinary meeting was to study a "redefinition of" parity—sharply upward. Their goal is referred to gingerly as "true parity" among its friends. Claiming to represent 6,500,000 farm units, the following farm organizations answered the call:

National Grange.

National Association of Commissioners, etc., of Agriculture.

American Wool Growers Association.

American National Livestock Association.

Farmers Guild.

California Walnut Growers Association.

National Council of Farmer Cooperatives.

Central Livestock Co-operative Association of South St. Paul.

American Soy Bean Association.

American Pork Producers, Associated.

National Co-operative Milk Producers' Federation.

The session was presided over by Senator Elmer Thomas, of Oklahoma, leader of the superparity thinkers in and out of Congress. Results of the confab came out in the form of an amendment to be offered to the Agriculture Department appropriation bill. Chairmaned by Charles Holman, the drafting committee included: Fred Brenckman, of the Grange; Dr. E. W. Sheets, of the U. S. Livestock Association; Edward E. Kennedy, then vice-president of the Farmers Guild; Tom Linder, from Georgia, most militant of the Southern Commissioners, and E. E. Everson, Commissioner of Agriculture from South Dakota.

The amendment, as modified later by a coalition of dairy and livestock lobbyists, was offered soon thereafter by Senator Joseph C. O'Mahoney, of Wyoming, and pushed through the Senate. The move was spiked, however, when parliamentary vagaries kept it from being voted on in the House. Gist of the measure was to include in parity an index of the cost of hired farm labor, so as to gear it to the cost of production.

This was too much for even the 110-per-cent-parity warriors of the Farm Bureau, however, and its delegates withdrew from the meeting with a splash. They were unwilling to change the basic parity formula, for fear of inflation, they explained. It was this groundwork which was built on in the fall of 1942, when Hanson's group reconvened the assembly with the aid of Senator Thomas again.

On October 19 the commissioner crowd congregated as usual in the Raleigh, mainly for the purpose of attacking Leon Henderson and price ceilings imposed by him on the controversial basis of the Price Control Act amendments. An exclusive story next morning in the Washington *Times-Herald* listed representatives from the Grange and Farm Bureau as participating, but both groups withdrew as soon as it became apparent that Thomas and Hanson intended to offer formal resolutions. Privately their leaders confide that they do not recognize the commissioners as a bona fide farm organization and that they dislike sitting at the same table with a spokesman for Lewis' Dairy Farmers.

In addition to demanding a congressional probe of OPA, several speakers burst forth with a demand for Henderson's impeachment. The crowd, including several farm-state congressmen, applauded wildly when one Ralph W. Moore shouted: "Henderson is the dagger in the farmer's back. The greatest thing that could happen for the Allied war effort is the impeachment or resignation of Henderson, and a flat warning to his successor that his tactics will not be tolerated any longer."

Moore was listed erroneously as legislative counsel of the Grange, but denials from that organization led to disclosure that he actually represented only the Commissioner of Agriculture in Texas.

A few weeks later Henderson resigned, maybe by coincidence and maybe not; but Thomas and his followers kept thumping the tub. On December 18 the Oklahoma inflationist told reporters that the farm bloc would be in control of both houses of the 78th Congress and predicted that the Administration would be powerless to prevent enactment of a superparity formula. Adding that the farmers are convinced that the Administration is against them, Thomas announced that "all" farm organizations would meet in Washington early in January to agree on a farm-price program.

That they did, except that not quite all attended. The first week of the new year, executive bodies of the Grange, Farm Bureau, Co-op Council, and Milk Producers' Federation held special meetings of their own, then converged on the Raleigh for two days together. Congressmen, state commissioners, and stragglers were picked up on the way, like a snowball rolling downhill. The consensus of the powwow was released in a statement from the Big Four, but not until oratorical heights by old reliables such as Earl Smith, Ed O'Neal, and Milk Producer John Brandt had literally stampeded more cautious colleagues.

"We reaffirm the position of our respective organizations in offering our fullest co-operation to the government in carrying out sound means to prevent inflation" was the first sentence. Following it were demands for including all farm labor in the computation of parity, a threat of new legislation for an entirely new parity definition, opposition to the use of subsidies in place of a fair price in the market, a demand that the work week be extended to at least 54 hours with no overtime, a request for adequate farm equipment, and an abandonment of efforts to impose union conditions in the employment of farm labor.

Thirteen days later the House Agriculture Committee, a number of whose members had participated in the all-out meeting, unanimously approved a bill to revise the parity formula to include the costs of all farm labor.

A steady power behind the scenes, and the most versatile Washington farm pleader, is a quiet man named Dr. Earl W. Sheets. He not only plays both the general farm organization and commodity organization game, but typifies the new kind of Washington association man with his emphasis on research and public relations, while doing little actual cloakroom work. As representative of beef, wool, and hog producers, as well as the National Grange, Dr. Sheets quarterbacks many more blitzes than he has been given credit for.

Sheets's title of doctor denotes graduate study in agricultural subjects, after which he was a teacher and a government employee. Aside from being reared on a farm and devoting his life to agricultural science, Sheets has no claim to being a farmer. After teaching country school and completing his own education, he became head of West Virginia University's agricultural curriculum and married the youngest daughter of T. C. Atkeson, Grange historian and kingpin of early days. It was after the young scientist had moved to Washington to work for the Department of Agriculture that he convinced his father-in-law that the

Grange should have an office in the capital city. Atkeson took the job himself shortly thereafter, and Sheets moved up the civil-service ladder to become chief of Animal Husbandry in the department.

At this point the New Deal took over the department and things started popping. Immediately Sheets began having conflicts with his superior, brain-trusting Rexford Guy Tugwell. Sheets had been put in charge of building up the department's gigantic research center at near-by Beltsville, Maryland, and was suddenly drafted for the job of buying up millions of cattle that were slowly starving to death in the gruesome drought of the early thirties. As director of Agricultural Drought Relief, Sheets purchased about 15,-000,000 head of cattle and sheep and sent checks to the thousands of owners who could no longer find feed for the animals. About that time he fell out of sympathy with the New Deal, would no longer follow Tugwell, and resigned—to everyone's satisfaction. Today he looks back on those hectic days as a nightmare.

After withdrawing for a few years to Mississippi State University, where he resumed teaching, Sheets returned to Washington to practice animal husbandry in a new capacity —as representative of the cattle feeders, occasionally helping the state commissioners, directors, and secretaries of agriculture as well.

In addition he is secretary of the U. S. Livestock Association, making him Washington nursemaid to a claimed 87,000 to 90,000 cattlemen from nearly thirty states, centered in about sixteen corn-belt states. Members of the U. S. Livestock Association, who fatten their cattle primarily in feed lots, are frequently confused with those of the American National Livestock Association, who graze their stock on pasture. Because the American National has no Washington contact man, Sheets is sometimes actually spokesman for both kinds of beef producers.

That was not true early in 1941, however, when the recurrent fight over Argentine beef was up again. The secretary of the American National beef bloc favored allowing the Argentine Good Neighbors to send Uncle Sam some of their beef, reasoning coldly that to do so would pacify the Latin Americans. Senator O'Mahoney presented that school of thought, after much confusion, but was defeated by the U. S. Livestock position, championed by Senator Butler, of Nebraska. Typically, for farm-bloc operations, the occasion for opening Argentine-American wounds was not a momentous debate on the Good Neighbor policy, but a rider on the Navy's appropriation bill. The issue was whether the Navy should be allowed to buy beef where it could get it most cheaply. Upshot of the scrap was to let the sailors have Argentine beef and other foreign products only when in foreign stations or when American products are unobtainable.

Sheets's connection with the commissioners, directors and secretaries of agriculture is chiefly advisory. He furnishes statistics and charts to Colonel Hanson, secretary of the Southern auxiliary, for use in both organizations. For example, when Senator Elmer Thomas' superparity conference of July 1941 was being held in the Raleigh Hotel, Sheets furnished the commissioners, etc., who attended a 27-page document entitled *Fair Prices for Agricultural Commodities*. The burden of this treatise was that parity needs revision upward, that real parity with industry and labor had not then been approached, and that control of farm prices would be ruinous financially and from the standpoint of getting food grown.

Some of Sheets's other expressions of policy are of use in

appraising the man who speaks for the bulk of meat and wool producers and sometimes for the Grange. One who thinks that the AAA was a good emergency measure but should have been discontinued, Sheets reported to the farm-bloc meeting that "the new policy for agriculture which seems to be taking form is a philosophy of plenty instead of scarcity, which has been followed for a number of years. It has been a long, hard fight to change these established policies, but the results to be attained for agriculture and for all of the people are well worth the effort made."

A possible key to Sheets's complaints against price control, in the summer before passage of the Price Control Act, lies in his citation of three commodities on which Leon Henderson had fixed prices on the basis of an executive order: hides, combed yarn, and fats and oils. It was probably more than coincidence that Sheets then represented the producers of cattle hides, fats, and oils, and was speaking to friends of cotton yarn. In any event, he quoted approvingly an assertion by Senator Taft that "there is not even a respectable argument in behalf of Mr. Henderson's right to fix prices; that there is no statutory authority; that there is no constitutional authority and no authority in precedent."

One of Sheets's chief complaints to the parity parley dealt with the base period used by Administration economists. "The producers of livestock have contended with much merit that the five-year period, 1909 to 1914, was, from the standpoint of those who produced meat, milk, and wool, most unfortunate and unfair," he stated, proposing that the equitable period to use as a base is the five years *during* the World War.

Sheets admitted that farm prices at that time stood only

a little over 50 per cent of his proposed level, 1915 to 1919, and presented a table of figures comparing the conventional parity base period with the proposed one. This is the way five items, in which Sheets has an interest, look in his chart:

Commodity	Average Price		Per Cent of Parity by Regular Method
	1909–14	*1915–19*	*June 15, 1941*
Hogs, per 100 lbs.	$7.22	$11.93	96
Beef cattle, per 100 lbs.	5.21	7.93	127
Veal calves, per 100 lbs.	6.75	10.24	113
Lambs, per 100 lbs.	5.87	10.87	120
Wool, per lb.	.183	.394	153

Thus, with most farmers calling for parity, Sheets and others were stoking a farm-bloc meeting with the idea that parity should be about doubled—at the very time when the items in which Sheets was primarily interested were well above the parity formula in use.

Another of Sheets's points was put across to his sympathetic audience by showing the prices farmers would have gotten if their prices had kept pace with non-farm commodities and services. According to his data, which he borrowed from Senator Bankhead, the following increases over the October 1940 prices would be gained: cotton, from 9.35 cents a pound to 27.58; potatoes, from 52 cents a bushel to $1.51; eggs, from 23.7 a dozen to 59.5, and hogs, from $5.83 per 100 pounds to $16.03. The question of whether consumers would have paid those prices or revolted was not answered.

Another very graphic way of demonstrating the effect

of his proposed parity formula, likewise taken from Senator Bankhead, was used by Sheets. By comparing the 1940 average earnings of certain industrial workers with what they would have been if they had stayed in line with farm prices, he got something like this as an example: Electricians who earned $2,995 in 1940 would be pared down to $1,743.

Perhaps the keynote of the occasion was struck in Sheets's quotation from Senator Elmer Thomas: "Congress to my knowledge for ten years has been laboring and appropriating money to get the farmers parity prices, at least, upon their basic agricultural commodities. . . . The Congress has enacted legislation, it has passed appropriations, and the Treasury has been drained of some billions of dollars to get farm prices up. Now we have a chance to get farm prices up, we find an agency of the Government, presumed, or otherwise, driving the prices down."

A phase of Sheets's work which is not so well known is indicated by yet another title he holds, executive secretary of the American Fats and Oils Institute, one of the numerous outfits with no fixed headquarters or staff. The institute was set up in September of 1940, a few months after introduction of the so-called Fulmer bill, H. B. 4313, which Sheets had a hand in and which would have thrown up a tariff wall around American fats, oils, starches, and jute. Although the bill failed to pass on its debated merits, Senators Butler, Bankhead, and Eastland lost by only one vote an effort to tack it onto the 1942 Revenue Act.

The institute lasted only a year before the war made its program a moot one, but it will undoubtedly be revived in some form after the war when the mad scramble for protection begins again. Therefore a glimpse from a paper on fats and oils which Sheets read to a January 6, 1941, meeting of the institute at the Raleigh Hotel is illuminating. In general it was a mixed plea to preserve the American market for American producers and to produce greater yields of fats and oils to bring the annual consumption up to its proper dietary level.

"If the adult population consumed enough fats to supply maximum requirements, a potential market for another two billion pounds of fats and oils would be created," he said. Then, after declaring that the American farmer now realizes that his welfare necessitates "putting up the bars" to fats and oils from other lands, Sheets piously added: "Neither is the American farmer unmindful of the many sacrifices he has made and is making, which prove that he is a good neighbor and a patriot."

Sheets is one of the very few professional farm-bloc prodders who will concede that butter and margarine should be allowed to fight it out on the basis of merit before the jury of consumers. He has reasons other than scientific ones, if that is necessary, however. Of course, as representative of beef producers, who sell even a comparatively small amount of animal oil to margarine manufacturers, Sheets wants the market broadened. Also his connection with the slumbering institute is not one of charity. But the third motive proves beyond all else the fallacy of trying to tax margarine almost out of existence.

As an expert on animal husbandry, Sheets pioneered development of what is called a dual-purpose cow. Most cows are bred either for milk or for meat, but Sheets worked on a breed which would be moderately good for both purposes. Thus a dual-purpose cow might contribute to either margarine or butter, and her owner, if an earnest joiner of farm groups, might go loco deciding which lobby to support.

For an affirmative program, Executive Secretary Sheets

proposed that the institute indulge in research and education to bring about increased consumption of its product
and work to stabilize the market some way on the basis of
a new and higher parity.

Working in his one-room office below the Grange,
Sheets denies that he is a lobbyist on the grounds that he
only appears before committees and prepares official positions. He does seek to influence legislation, he adds—if that
is lobbying.

Sheets has a list of scientific honors, publications, and
titles as long as his arm, which is indicative of the way he
operates. In addition to the many organizational contacts
he maintains, he is a special assistant to National Grange
President Goss and travels often for him.

The well-grayed agriculturist, now in his late fifties, is
not overly academic in his presentation, however. A sense
of humor crops out readily, and he is a good fellow among
other farm-bloc leaders. When times were not so rushed
he enjoyed a week or so of deep-sea fishing in the Gulf,
but now he is busy with one or more of his organizations
nearly all the time. And because of his experience, whether
biased or not, it is likely that he will remain busy long after
the more aggressive high-pressure Washington lobbyists
have retired.

The latest entrant in the farm-organizing business is
neither a farmer, an economist, nor a salesman. He is the
long-time chieftain of the United Mine Workers, John L.
Lewis, the bushy-browed, gray-maned, slugging bad boy
of the labor movement. And he has been made about as
welcome as most other unionists who trespass the barnyard. Several farm leaders, including the one most directly
threatened by Lewis' bid, Holman, talk menacingly of

using a pitchfork on labor-union organizers who get too close. But with the blandest hypocrisy they will meet around the high-parity table with Lewis men.

There are two theories as to why Lewis stirred up such acrimony with his announcement that the heterogeneous District 50 of the Mine Workers would organize dairy farmers, and eventually others. First, those who feel that the Grange, the Farm Bureau, and the Milk Producers' Federation are not aggressive enough and have been too chummy with distributor interests think that established leaders are quaking from a well-earned scare from the most militant union leader.

Second, and most prevalent, is the opinion that farmers genuinely hate Lewis because he is too radical, or even too liberal, for them.

Be that as it may, the new drive has not been recognized as accomplishing much of its goal since forming ranks early in 1942. However, the Lewis platform and technique are worth examining from the standpoint of analyzing the farm bloc, even though they may be of more value to students of labor unionism than to students of farm organization.

Formed in 1936, District 50 set out to unionize workers of coal by-products. From the first, UMW officials justified taking in the United Dairy Farmers of Flint, Michigan, on the grounds that casein, a milk product, is mixed sometimes with coal by-products. Soon that nicety was dropped, and Lewis stated at a send-off press conference that both the Michigan Milk Producers' Association and the Dairy Farmers Union (New York, Pennsylvania, and Vermont) had asked him to do the same thing for them that he had done for miners.

Enemies of Lewis always sneer at his assertion that he

lifted not one stubby finger to recruit the dairy farmers. Actually the mixture of coal and milk originated in this way: The young editor for the CIO paper in Flint, Ralph Marlatt, contacted Lewis after other overtures had died in one way or another. Lewis agreed to see the cow milkers and soon thereafter issued them a charter in rambling District 50.

Because the United Dairy Farmers has never elected officers, the personnel chosen by Lewis to organize and staff it is important in detecting direction and potentialities. The two main officers between Lewis and the UDF are the two key officials of District 50, also never elected: its secretary, daughter Kathryn Lewis, and its president, John Kmetz, veteran mine-union official.

Marlatt was retained as director of organization and was soon joined by no less a farm-organization veteran than Edward E. Kennedy, former secretary of the National Farmers Union who came to Lewis as director of research for the UDF. Marlatt and. Kennedy have spent most of their time in the field so far, but when in Washington they sit at two of the six or eight desks scattered around one of the ornate, high-domed, paneled rooms of the UMW headquarters which Lewis bought from the University Club.

Marlatt and Kennedy make a good team for the job to be done, unless the former is too young and scholarly looking to reach maximum effectiveness in appealing directly to owners of dairy herds. That weak point is balanced, however, by his experience as publicity strategist for the growing CIO in the hot spot of Flint and by his youthful earnestness.

Kennedy, nearing fifty, is a soft but firm speaker, like Marlatt, but has in his head the complete background of the farm struggle. Frequently whipping out a pencil, Kennedy is always ready to prove statistically the soundness of his movement to get cost of production for farmers. With his shock of dry, wavy hair, Kennedy is a well-known character among farm leaders, though he is snubbed by some of them because of his past intimacy with Milo Reno, the late firebrand leader of the Farm Holiday movement which sought to improve desperate farm conditions by strikes and violence where necessary.

By cost of production, the UDF means getting a price to the farmer which will pay his out-of-pocket costs of operating, a fair return on his investment in land and improvements, and a sum which represents the value of the farmer's own services as a manager of the enterprise. The latter figure is calculated on the basis of average industrial wages. Applying this formula, the UDF figures it costs $4.10 per hundred pounds to produce milk; the average price reported by the Department of Agriculture on December 15 of last year was $3.01.

Although hired hands on dairy farms are not eligible for membership in the new union, it is UDF's position that cost of production must include good wages for them. Exclusion of farm labor from the new drive has caused Lewis enemies within organized labor to charge, however, that UDF is not a labor union, but a businessmen's protective association.

UDF's official organizing pamphlet treats the subject thus: "For over fifty years the American farmer and the American worker have been kept apart because of the false propaganda that the two groups had nothing in common. Today these Americans realize that it takes the effort of all Americans to protect the free institutions which have been won through such great sacrifice."

There is no initiation fee in the UDF, which was admittedly financed at the beginning from UMW coffers. Dues are 75 cents per month to the parent body, with most locals adding a 25-cent tariff for their own purposes. At this rate, officials claim a signed-up membership between 75,000 and 100,000 dairy farmers. Many of these were recruited by a UDF pamphlet which ends: "The dairy farmers will get through a national organization the things the politicians and milk trusts have been denying them for years. They will get their cost of production and a fair return on their investment. That is what they are entitled to under our American form of government."

One of the chief enemies of UDF in the field is the network of milk co-operatives which of course have their own investment to protect. The hatred is mutual. In a current piece of literature UDF said of producer co-ops that they "have policies and resources controlled and manipulated by the bureaucracy of officials to perpetuate their own power and salaries so that they are in effect only milk companies."

Achievement of their ultimate goal is envisioned by UDF officials as their representatives sitting around a big table with officials of the big dairy companies, drafting a contract to govern the sale of milk throughout many states. They see no reason why a giant corporation which makes many trade-name products should buy milk from hundreds or thousands of places under hundreds or thousands of different price arrangements.

That is not their only complaint about the corporations which have long dominated the dairy industry, however. In the August 15, 1942, issue of the *United Dairy Farmer*, Kennedy explained to his readers that the following per cent of net profit had been made on 1941 capital by the "Big Four" companies: National Dairy Products Corporation, 23.7; Borden, 13.2; Pet, 20.4; and Carnation, 25.4 per cent.

The UDF paper takes frequent shots at the Administration, the CIO, and the National Farmers Union, asserting that none of them is really in sympathy with milk farmers. The dislike is reciprocated.

Joseph Curran, president of the Greater New York CIO Council, denounced the Lewis move, and the Wisconsin state CIO executive board declared that it "had nothing in common with the principles of the CIO." National CIO officers, who are not only at odds with Lewis, but are sympathetic to the National Farmers Union in the farm field, privately attack, laugh at, and otherwise disparage the new baby.

Established farm groups have been more outspoken in their bitterness. Within a few days after birth of the new union a coalition of Northeastern farmers, calling itself Free Farmers, Incorporated, sprang up for the express purpose of beating Lewis off. "We do not need as a 'bargaining agent' a man with the record of John L. Lewis," it declared.

An even stronger clue to general farmer attitude toward Lewis came immediately thereafter at a House Judiciary subcommittee hearing, April 17, 1942, on legislation to bring labor unions more certainly within the Federal Anti-racketeering Act. Most of the parade of farm witnesses who testified in favor of the bills took a roundhouse swing at what they considered Lewis' ultimate aim to stop traffic in farm products whenever he so desired.

The United Dairy Farmers have an ally, though a small one, in the Farmers Guild, which Kennedy organized as a protest to the Farmers Union when the great split occurred. At the time Kennedy left the guild to go with the UDF he resigned as vice-president, but did not break all ties. He attended each 1942 state convention and, with Marlatt, addressed the national convention. There representatives of the alleged 10,000 to 15,000 guild members pledged a friendly attitude toward the UDF, both organizations believing in the cost-of-production technique, and recommended that individual members who are dairy farmers join both groups.

Those who have closely followed the career of Lewis know that he has come up with many a trump card and that he gets what he goes after, but they also know that what is primarily a one-man show cannot go on forever. Though the Dairy Farmer drive is well financed, though it has many regional offices of District 50 at its service, and though many dairy farmers are aggrieved, it is doubtful that the UDF is any stronger than Lewis' personality. Maybe the infant union will be grown before a test of that proposition is made; but until it is decided whether the rough-and-tough mine leader is washed up, is on the right track, or is just having a John Barrymore fling after leaving the stage as an idol, the UDF cannot be brushed off.

XIV

USDA

THE PHYSICAL CENTER OF GRAVITY of the farm bloc is the U. S. Department of Agriculture, though front-line shooting has been done for years on Capitol Hill, a mile away. The modern farmers' rural free delivery is well-sprinkled with USDA forms and bulletins on any of a thousand subjects. His graded meat is stamped "USDA." His crop and marketing reports come from USDA. Benefit payments come from USDA. When he and his neighbors want action they call on USDA. And the swivel chairs of the Washington bureaucrats he cusses are marked "USDA."

More than any other cabinet department, Agriculture is the protagonist, the pleader for its constituents. It teaches them to be self-sufficient, to use government credit, and to live inexpensively. Like the Department of Labor and the Department of Commerce, it grinds the ax *officially* for one part of the national economy—only more so. That is not to say that it should not do so; it is only to say that the farm bloc is not made of thin air. It is nurtured, consciously or unconsciously, twenty-four hours a day. It is a facet of the democratic way of lending a helping hand to one chunk of society.

For these reasons the farm bloc cannot be appraised

without knowing something about its nurturers, its friends, and its enemies within the department. And sometimes it is difficult to tell whether a given official has retained membership in the bloc or is working for the public.

Surprise reigned in agricultural circles in September of 1940 when Claude R. Wickard was appointed to succeed Henry Wallace as top man at the U. S. Department of Agriculture. Although Wickard had been Under Secretary for several months, the smart money was not on him, mostly because he had worked for about seven years under better-known officials in the department. Some thought it significant that Wickard hailed from Indiana, also the home state of Republican presidential candidate Wendell Willkie. If that dictated his appointment, however, it was futile strategy, for the Democrats lost Indiana that year. In any event, when Wickard was confirmed by the Senate, the USDA got a corn-hog farmer of great repute.

He was born in 1893 on a Camden, Indiana, farm which has been in the family since the 1840s. With the assistance of his father and a daughter just out of Purdue University, Wickard still operates the 380 acres on a general grain and livestock basis. Newspapermen who attend his press conferences occasionally hear him josh about some personal problem, such as his complaint last fall that the Haitian fly had destroyed part of his crop, but he had not yet been able to get the department to pay insurance on the loss. After one week-end visit at home the secretary devoted an entire speech to a homely narration of the new perspective he felt from the visit.

His operation of the family farm began while Wickard was still in high school and continued through his days at Purdue, from which he was graduated the year before the

World War started, when he took over complete management.

In addition to regular farming he became associated with the Farm Bureau and did other co-operative work, as well as part-time assignments with the Indiana Extension Service. He was named a Master Farmer by the Midwestern farm magazine, *Prairie Farmer*, in 1927—the same year that farmer O'Neal won his special award. Wickard received gold medals and other recognition for his use of soil-building conservation practices on his farm and for his success in increasing crop yields and hog production—a job which he was to be assigned to undo in large part as a Triple-A official. In July of 1933 he was an Indiana delegate to the National Corn-Hog Conference at Des Moines, Iowa. He was also a member of the National Corn-Hog Committee of Twenty-Five which was delegated by the conference to advise with the Secretary and his AAA on means for carrying out the wishes of producer representatives.

In 1932 the voters of three Indiana counties sent neighbor Wickard to the state Senate, but he resigned to go to work for AAA in 1933 as assistant chief of the corn-hog section. In 1935 he was made chief. Then, when the conservation program was started the next year, he became assistant director of the North Central Division of AAA. By jumping to the directorship of that division later in the same year, he was in charge not only of corn and hogs but of all AAA matters in his rich corn-belt home area.

At the age of fifty Wickard is a big, affable, handsome farm leader, well founded in scientific methods and progressive practices. As such, he is capable of sitting on top of USDA's multitude of old-line bureaus, including Agricultural Chemistry and Engineering, Animal Industry, Dairy Industry, Entomology and Plant Quarantine, Home

Economics, Plant Industry, and the Office of Experiment
Stations. Add to that list the Agricultural Conservation and
Adjustment Administration, which he learned from the
bottom up, and Wickard's strong departments are pretty
well taken care of.

The bureaus which indulge in looking over the next
horizon and applying imagination to farm problems are
usually a step ahead of their Secretary, however. Because
he trails, rather than directs and encourages pioneering,
Wickard has seen an exodus of that kind of personnel. He
is not an idea man and is slow to capitalize on the ideas
of his advisers, which accounts for the discontent or resignation among officials who had felt encouraged under the
farseeing Wallace to explore the next problem before it
appeared as a head-on collision.

Because Wallace's elevation to the Vice-Presidency co-
incided so closely with the coming of war, the issues of
agriculture were scrambled. Also, waging a food war required an especially tough administrator. Wickard neither
unscrambled the thinking nor displayed toughness. His top
assistants are more nearly "yes" men than "no" men. Com-
bined with the fact that Wickard is personally sensitive to
pressure and slow to cause friction with any group this
makes for circumlocution rather than circumvention. The
department which was once known for its perspective has
been almost reduced to the status of just another rambling
Washington bureau.

As director of AAA's North Central Division, according
to the department's own press release, Wickard "stressed
farmer administration of the AAA, and has been chiefly
responsible for developing the effective farmer-committee-
men setup which now exists in the corn belt."

The corn belt is not the only area in which farmer

committeemen run the AAA locally, nor is Wickard the only Farm Bureau man who has been responsible for developing the unusual administrative technique. The militant organization's private reason for perpetuating the system was brought out at hearings in February of 1942 before the Joint Committee on Nonessential Federal Expenditures, headed by Senator Harry Byrd, of Virginia, and bent at that time on castrating the Farm Security Administration. A few lines from the testimony reveal Farm Bureau President O'Neal's hand on the lofty ideal of dirt-farmer democracy.

SENATOR LA FOLLETTE. I am simply trying to find out if you would be satisfied to have the clients of the Farm Security Administration [which O'Neal was attacking] select the personnel which is to administer that program, just as the beneficiaries of the AAA program . . . select the persons who are administering those programs.

MR. O'NEAL. You have a different proposition, Senator, there, but I think they would do a better job than Baldwin is doing. [C. B. Baldwin, administrator of FSA.]

SENATOR MCKELLAR [Tennessee]. Now let me ask you a question. Is it not true that in these AAA setups only about 12 per cent of the members actually vote and that 12 per cent is constituted of the representatives of the government, that is, the committeemen and others belonging to their families . . . ?

MR. O'NEAL. Senator, I am not quite familiar with the figure, but I think it is a very much larger percentage than that. . . .

SENATOR MCKELLAR. The department has furnished the average to this committee, and it is 12 per cent. Your original county in Alabama is which?

MR. O'NEAL. Lauderdale.

SENATOR MCKELLAR. It is close to Tennessee, that is why it is so good. Let us say they have got five or ten committeemen there.

Mr. O'Neal. Yes.

Senator McKellar. And only 12 per cent of the people of the county function. Don't you and I know, as sensible men, that those committeemen do the voting and virtually no one is called in except those and their friends?

Mr. O'Neal. No, Senator. You don't know Lauderdale County.

Senator McKellar. It may be different in Lauderdale County, but it is that way in every other county that I know of.

Mr. O'Neal. I have got my Alabama Farm organization leader here. There are about 5,500 farmers, small landowning farmers, Negroes and whites, and, boy, do they vote!

Senator McKellar. They vote?

Mr. O'Neal. Yes.

Later the record was supplied with the percentage of eligible farmers voting in the 1940 elections of community committeemen. In part, this is what it revealed: Alabama, 6.03 per cent; average for the United States, 12.3 per cent.

The incident dramatized a strange twist which more often than not leaves the department attacked by the Farm Bureau Federation which it suckled so long by generally building up farm organizations and the Farm Bureau in particular. O'Neal has not only led his people away from the department, because of resentment at Washington bureaucracy and some differences over policy, but has also tried to bring the department out into the field where he still has much control. By urging decentralization of the department O'Neal may cash in on his organization's strong ties with the agencies which are already established in the field, the Extension Service and the AAA.

There are those who years ago would have declared war on the Farm Bureau, believing then that its basic philosophy had little in common with the department's aims other than crop restriction. Recently, even though the Farm Bureau has been the department's most caustic critic in Congress and at the crossroads, it has received very little return fire from the USDA fort. The dominant officials, including Wickard specifically, are enough like the Farm Bureau fundamentally to pass off its attacks instead of fighting back. The only resignations or firings during the anti-inflation war involved men personally opposed to the Farm Bureau. Those who were promoted treaded the straight and narrow AFBF path, except for endorsing subsidies as a means of averting punctures in price ceilings. The trend in personnel was no mere coincidence.

One of the strangest chapters in USDA's history is known as the purge of 1935 and happened while the AAA was groping around for a policy in its infancy.

The offices of the General Counsel and the Consumers Counsel of AAA were the hot spots of behind-the-scenes activity leading up to the purge. The former section, AAA's lawyers, was headed by Jerome Frank, later chairman of the Securities and Exchange Commission and now a Circuit Court of Appeals judge; the latter unit was the watchdog of consumer interests. Officials of both became intensely interested in revamping the distribution system for milk so as to eliminate inefficiencies.

At one period the solution was tried in the form of price fixing at the retail level. When Charles Holman and his milk producers balked, however, the department instituted Federal audit of distributors' and handlers' books in half a dozen cities instead. Before long, studies of the books in these areas began to show high profits by distributors. As a result of these disclosures, Secretary Wallace hied himself off to Madison, Wisconsin, and delivered a blast at the milk industry.

Holman immediately came to the defense of the distributors, whom he, as a representative of producers, presumably also tries to squeeze down to a lean profit, and the fight was on. Wallace, ordinarily a mild-mannered administrator, issued a statement in answer to Holman's group, in which he referred to them as "distributors masquerading in overalls."

That was in the fall of 1934. In the next several months Holman took the lead in maneuvering to "get" the officials whom he regarded as having designs on upsetting the status quo of the milk industry. In a strategy meeting at Philadelphia, attended by the strange alliance of milk producers and distributors, there was drawn up a list of heads to be chopped off. As someone quipped when Holman joined forces with the distributors, he was carrying milk on both shoulders.

Soon after, early in 1935, AAA Administrator Chester Davis sent curt termination of service notices to almost the exact list of persons in the two controversial sections of his agency as had appeared in Holman's hands after the Philadelphia meeting. Thereafter both AAA and Holman rolled quietly along their ways. The only steps of a fundamental nature which have been taken since then in milk distribution have been taken under legislation obtained or supported by Holman's Milk Producers' Federation or at the order of Economic Stabilizer James Byrnes, who is trying to cut costs which the department has watched motionlessly for years. The Consumers Counsel unit was not guillotined, however. It continued to be a burr under Holman's blanket, but only as an advisory agency without authority to act.

Asked by a senator in the spring of 1937 to explain his

attitude toward the Consumers Counsel, Holman was drawn into a bit of explanation of the 1935 purge. The occasion was an interlude in hearings before a Senate Agriculture Subcommittee.

Holman speaking: "To understand the situation, Mr. Chairman, our organization is now in its twenty-first year. That part of it which represents the fluid milk sheds . . . by a process of wear and tear, you might say attrition, and in some places fairly clever price movements, managed between 1916 and the beginning of the depression to increase the producer's share of the consumer's milk dollar on the average . . . from about 45 per cent up to about 55 per cent; that is, 55 cents out of the dollar."

Next he explained that the depression drove his federation to support the AAA and turned to a discussion of AAA personnel: "Now, we had a new administration and suddenly we found crowded into the Department of Agriculture a new type of person, people that it never occurred to us would be associated with agricultural problems. Many of them were from the endowed universities of the East. Many of them were city men. Many of them were very brilliant young fellows, and they approached this problem of milk agreements, having had absolutely no experience whatsoever, in most cases, with milk, and some of them would have had trouble in finding their way around a dairy farm . . ."

Next Holman complained that these alleged brain trusters delayed execution of marketing agreements. "We could not understand why it would be necessary with our own practical knowledge of how to draw these agreements, that the very first milk-marketing agreement was revised within the department twenty-eight times before we could get it moving up to the Secretary for his signature," he said. Along this same line, Holman added: ". . . we could not understand why, in many instances, the revisions which these technical experts in the department would make had a tendency to weaken the operation of our co-operatives."

The catch has been, of course, that the only way to meet the industry's definition of "experienced" is to be on the industry's side of the fight. Some unkind person, in retaliation, once asked where Holman gained the experience he is presumed to have in milk.

Holman then blandly denied to the senators that his group had been instrumental in getting its enemies removed. "Very frankly," he said, "we do not have that much influence with the Secretary or the Agricultural Adjustment Administration." He admitted, however, that in March of 1934 some of his people participated in a Washington conference which passed, among others, one resolution which began: "We demand the immediate removal of those persons in the Department of Agriculture and in the AAA who have so unequivocally demonstrated their inexperience, inability, inefficiency, and inaptitude in dealing with the fundamental problems facing our dairy farmers . . ."

In the face of that language, it is difficult to follow Holman's denial of having been instrumental in the purge. The sham of his position was clinched when he paid a compliment to Donald E. Montgomery, then consumers counsel. "Let me say at this time," Holman said graciously, "that since Mr. Montgomery has been made head of this work our relations have been very much more amicable than they were under the earlier administration. We find Mr. Montgomery approaching the problem more realistically."

Those who have followed milk regulation know that Montgomery's has been the only governmental voice against the march to increase milk prices. In fact, at the very time of these pious statements Holman was complaining to the AAA administrator about Montgomery's opposition in the District of Columbia hearings on milk prices.

Finally Holman candidly told the senators his idea of the kind of consumer representation which should be allowed —or, rather, should not be allowed. It is a historical statement.

"We ourselves frankly resented the establishment of a Consumers Counsel in a farmers' department," he explained. "We feel further that the Consumers Counsel should never be permitted to exercise any policy-making authority. If there is to be a Consumers Counsel in the Department of Agriculture, we have just as much right to have a Farmers Counsel over in the Department of Labor when the question comes up of the settlement of strikes and the wages for labor, which may involve a rise in the prices of farmers' products.

"In other words," he continued, "if there is to be such an agency, it should be purely fact finding. It should not be attached to the Department of Agriculture, or perhaps to any other department, and should not have the right to sit at the table in the judge's seat." Though they hate to admit it, consumer officials agree with this logical position.

The department has not only done nothing to alienate the veteran milk lobbyist; it has played directly into his hands, yet privately some of its top officials will express nothing but scorn for his tactics. Only one man spoke his mind on the milk bloc. That was Montgomery, whose thankless job included appearing in behalf of consumers at hearings on milk-marketing agreements. Montgomery also felt strongly that scarce supplies of food should be rationed before it became impossible for consumers to get their share. When Wickard became food administrator at the end of 1942, and set up a Food Distribution Administration, Montgomery felt convinced that no attention would be given to consumer problems and resigned. A few days later it was revealed that the department had decided to abandon its Food Stamp Plan. With this prop pulled from under the very lowest income group and the buck being passed from OPA to Agriculture on rationing, Montgomery's departure helped greatly in pointing up the real issue.

As he said in a press release at the time, his resignation marked "the end of the last, but one, of a half-dozen experiments made by the New Deal to set up offices to fight for the interests of consumers in the administration of government programs." Of his own unit, Montgomery accurately said: "It has been called 'Dangerous' by advertisers, 'Subversive' by Dies, 'Official conscience' by Henry Wallace (who started it), and a pain in the neck by administrators who didn't want to be bothered. . . . Few consumers . . . have been able to send paid spokesmen to Washington to look after their interests. That was why consumers counsels were set up in the first place. And that is why consumers counsels have been liquidated, one by one."

The original function of the department, service to farmers, is sometimes overlooked, but is a daily bulwark of the agency's work. The Extension Service is an outstanding example. In fiscal '41 county agents held 1,369,650 meetings in the 2,909 counties reporting, with a total attendance of 46,369,976. Also the service claimed that changes in practices had definitely resulted on 3,802,114 farms through agricultural-extension programs. Counting nearly 1,500,000 boys and girls in the 79,721 4-H Clubs which the Extension Service sponsors, it estimated that 4,791,433 farm families and nearly a million other families had been "influenced by some phase of extension program" that year.

Above the service bureaus of the department, however, has grown a huge superstructure that deals in subjects other than animal husbandry, agronomy, and soil chemistry. Its business is rehabilitating farmers who have been tossed about by the winds of misfortune, adjusting supply to demand, distributing surplus commodities, stabilizing the sugar industry, insuring crops against failure, etc. These are the action agencies. They constitute the political, philosophical, cultural, and economic battleground of the department. National differences of opinion and clashes of personalities occur in the action programs. That is one reason they get action.

The undercurrents of opinion which have caused one program to merge with or eliminate another have already been traced up to the 1942 clash over price control. What happened after that brought into sharp contrast the two schools of thought which had been growing in the department. Adherents of the Food Stamp Plan and Farm Security Administration, plus officials with consumer interests, had always wanted increased production, whether right or wrong. Also they favored rehabilitation of the down-and-outers. To do the wartime job of feeding the world they proposed to strengthen the hand of FSA by stepping up its supervised credit job so as to bring in the small fry who, with their families, had not worked at top speed in years.

Against this approach stood the dominant group of officials, with AAA as its backbone. Early in the war a coalition of the more conservative bureaus succeeded in setting up County War Boards in every county, with local AAA committee heads serving as Chairmen. Men from other agencies sit on the Committees, but AAA retained control.

When Wickard was appointed food administrator, in addition to remaining as secretary, he created two divisions: the Food Distribution Administration, to keep supplies rolling to American and foreign consumers alike, and the Food Production Administration, with the job of attaining history-breaking crop goals. Roy F. Hendrickson, former Associated Press reporter stationed at USDA, personnel director for the department and chief of the Agricultural Marketing Administration which ran the Stamp Plan, was made distribution administrator. For the tougher production job Wickard chose Herbert W. Parisius, former preacher, FSA regional director, assistant to the Secretary, and associate director of the department's special war unit which was abolished.

Parisius, following the school of thought which held that marginal producers—many of them FSA clients—should be helped out of the margin and into war production, soon came up with a proposed reorganization and laid his plan on Wickard's desk. What happened for a few days thereafter is confused, but it is certain that Parisius was stopped in his effort to build a field staff around FSA lines at the expense of AAA's status quo. Wickard balked and Parisius picked up his marbles and went home, tired of sitting around.

The Farmers Union protested that a sellout had been perpetrated, but others in the farm bloc applauded loudly. They were not only gloating over the defeat of a Farm Security partisan as such, but also had been saved from what might have been an interruption of their game. Their joy was confirmed within a few days when Wickard popped into the Parisius vacancy his old friend and Indiana neighbor, M. Clifford Townsend, former governor of the Hoosier State and Farm Bureau organizer there. Townsend had also been, for a short time, administrator of the Agricultural Conservation and Adjustment Administration, holding company for AAA.

The realignment amounted to something of a compromise. Townsend chose J. B. Hutson, president of the Commodity Credit Corporation, as his executive officer, and A. G. Black, governor of the Farm Credit Administration, as his associate director in charge of credit. FSA was not frozen out, but only carried along as another agency with a condescending pat on the head.

The farm bloc had been reassured so far as personnel was concerned, but was still smarting from rebuffs to its demands that the Administration cease using subsidies to get around price boosts. Then Wickard announced a subsidy for canners of important vegetables and a $100,000,000 program of incentive payments for farmers meeting war goals.

Farm Bureau, Grange, and Co-op Council elders worked overtime to head off further anti-inflation moves of this kind and gathered ranks for a showdown on those already announced. The Administration countered with the appointment of Judge Marvin Jones, on loan from the U. S. Court of Claims, as agricultural assistant to Economic Stabilizer Byrnes. As chairman of the House Agriculture Committee through most New Deal farm legislation, Jones had acquired the respect of all factions of the bloc; it was a crowning blow when he jumped on the side of subsidizing instead of inflating prices.

Wickard was still on his hot spot. The Congress in which his party had a numerical majority, the Farmers Union which had stood by him during the last battle, and the farm organizations which he had befriended so many times were all on his neck. And the consumers for whom he was trying to keep prices uninflated by use of public funds were clamoring for food. He could not win. At this moment, late in March of 1943, the President snatched his harried Secretary from the hot seat by dramatically recalling Chester Davis to Washington to run a new War Food Administration, housed in the department but reporting straight to the White House. The fact that Wickard remained as Secretary, though he had once been merely a bureau chief in the AAA while Davis was its administrator, hung a cloud over the genial Indianian which his friends resented, but they turned eagerly to their old pal Davis for strong leadership to get something done.

The fifty-five-year-old veteran of farm programs brought back with him an impressive record as farmers' friend and able administrator. After editing the Montana *Farmer* and serving as Commissioner of Agriculture in that state, he worked with Johnson and Peek in the McNary-Haugen fight from a vantage point in the headquarters of Earl Smith's Illinois Agriculture Association, Farm Bureau affiliate. Roosevelt leaned on him heavily to keep the AAA operating through congressional flare-ups and sent him to Europe where he studied foreign agriculture and came to back the reciprocal-trade program, after which he was elevated to the board of governors of the Federal Reserve System. On leave from that position, Davis represented agriculture on the old National Defense Advisory Commission until he left town with obvious but quiet disgust at lack of authority to convert to a wartime operation.

His return caused much reminiscence on agricultural policy, but only a few cynics, who were not even recorded in the press, wondered if he had come back to finish the 1935 purge of officials most friendly to consumers and sharecroppers.

Overwhelmingly the name of Chester Davis was a palliative to the farm-bloc headache, but, being only a palliative, it eased without curing. The potency of any bloc is present when a divided situation leaves each confused individual at the mercy of a coalition that can cut through distracted factions and steal the ball. There was still ample confusion, for the appointment of no one man will ever settle the issues of the farm bloc. They are as alive as the morning's market report, as fresh as the food on the dinner table, and as unpredictable as the weather on every farm in the country. Certainly a global war does not settle them; it only aggravates them.